ABBA EBAN

HERITAGE:
Civilization and the Jews

SUMMIT BOOKS
New York

PUBLISHED BY SUMMIT BOOKS, A DIVISION OF SIMON & SCHUSTER, INC.

SIMON & SCHUSTER BUILDING, 1230 AVENUE OF THE AMERICAS, NEW YORK, NEW YORK 10020.

SUMMIT BOOKS AND COLOPHON ARE TRADEMARKS OF SIMON & SCHUSTER, INC.

DESIGNED BY EVE METZ

PRODUCTION DIRECTED BY RICHARD L. WILLETT

MANUFACTURED IN THE UNITED STATES OF AMERICA

TYPESET BY DIX TYPE, SYRACUSE, NEW YORK

PRINTED AND BOUND BY R. R. DONNELLEY & SONS, CO., WILLARD, OHIO

10 9 8 7 6 5 4 3 2 1

LIBRARY OF CONGRESS CATALOGING IN PUBLICATION DATA

EBAN, ABBA SOLOMON, 1915–

   HERITAGE : CIVILIZATION AND THE JEWS.

   1. JEWS—HISTORY. I. TITLE.

DS117.E18 1984   909'.04924   84-2696

ISBN 0-671-44103-5

The author and Summit Books gratefully acknowledge the following for their permission to quote from the works listed below in order of appearance in the book.

James B. Pritchard, ed., *Ancient Near Eastern Texts: Relating to the Old Testament,* 3rd ed. with Supplement. Copyright © 1969 by Princeton University Press. Excerpts, pp. 372, 391.

Leon Poliakov, *The History of Anti-Semitism,* Vol. 1, reprinted by permission of the publisher, Vanguard Press, Inc. Copyright © 1965 by Leon Poliakov. English translation copyright © by Vanguard Press.

Isidore Twersky, ed., *A Maimonides Reader,* published by Behrman House, Inc., New York. Used with permission.

Jacob Marcus, ed., *The Jew in the Medieval World: A Source Book.* Copyrighted by and used through the courtesy of the Jewish Publication Society of America.

Giorgio Vasari, *Lives of the Artists,* translated by George Bull (Penguin Classics, Revised Edition, 1971), p. 345. Copyright © 1965 by George Bull. Reprinted by permission of Penguin Books, Ltd.

Chaim Weizmann, *Trial and Error: The Autobiography of Chaim Weizmann,* reprinted by permission of Harper & Row, Publishers, Inc., New York, and Hamish Hamilton, Limited, London.

Eugen Kogon, *The Theory and Practice of Hell,* translated by Heinz Norden. Reprinted by permission of Farrar, Straus & Giroux, Inc.

Jacob Glatstein *et al.,* eds., *Anthology of Holocaust Literature,* copyrighted by and used through the courtesy of the Jewish Publication Society of America.

Arthur Hertzberg, *Being Jewish in America: The Modern Experience,* Copyright © 1979 by Schocken Books, Inc. Reprinted by permission of Schocken Books, Inc.

ACKNOWLEDGMENTS

My FIRST TRIBUTE of gratitude goes out to Geoffrey Horn for his meticulous research and versatile erudition. He accompanied this project throughout and showed great skill in contributing to the convergence of my text with the television series "Civilization and the Jews." To Marc Siegel, the leader of the PBS–Channel 13 team, I owe many views and insights culled from him during our filming sessions and our conversations in many places and on many continents. I am similarly indebted to the academic consultants and scriptwriters who have worked on the mini-series and have thus influenced me in the selection of themes and structures for this book. At Summit Books, James H. Silberman gave this project an affectionate concern beyond the call of strict duty. Catherine Tatge and Dominique Lasseur were responsible for finding the wonderful photographs culled from collections around the world. I am also extremely grateful for the superb work of Eve Metz, James Daly, Richard L. Willett, and Kathy Hurley, which turned my manuscript into the book that is in your hands. Last but certainly not least, I owe Arthur H. Samuelson my deepest thanks for the precision of his editing and the candor of his advice.

ABBA EBAN

TO SUZY, ELI, AND GILA WITH LOVE

CONTENTS

The ancient civilization of Sumer, which flourished in the Near East when Jewish history begins, produced this primitive statue of man, c. 2150 B.C.E.

A CIVILIZATION is a distinctive form of culture maintained through several generations. It implies transmission. If it is not inherited it passes away. The word itself is linked with the idea of "city" life, as if rural existence were intrinsically primitive and incapable of creating values and monuments worthy of being bequeathed. We know that this distinction is not real and that civilized arts flourish outside city walls. The real distinction is between those organized manifestations of the mind that are exclusively human and those that merely follow the animal instincts. Man becomes civilized when his animal impulses are tamed, subdued, and transcended by his social nature. The primitive condition is then refined into solidarities of feeling and reaction that assume a degree of particularity.

It is in the general nature of civilizations to be born and die, says Oswald Spengler. Not quite to die, replies Arnold Toynbee; civilizations evolve from lower to higher forms into which they are absorbed and give up their identity. For all such theorists the Jewish story is a source of endless irritation. It refuses to fit the doctrinal mold and thus incurs a great deal of academic hostility. Jewishness is a notion that extends across the graveyards in which other civilizations are buried, expressing itself anew from generation to generation and refusing to follow a cycle that ends either in Spenglerian death or in Toynbeean sublimation. It is, in fact, a unique story utterly recalcitrant to comparative study or research. It has always had something to transmit and has thus preserved its continuity. Wherever Jews have traveled across continents and oceans and encountered other Jews in their path, an instant kinship has been ignited between them into which no stranger can totally enter. Jews have acted upon others and have been acted upon in their turn. Their ways of thought and speech and action have been drastically transformed but never beyond recognition in the specific terms of their history. There is

Foreword

always a thread that leads back to their beginnings and continues into the uncharted future. No one can say what the end will be or if it will ever come, or where exactly the thread will lead and what riches, if any, will be woven in its path.

All the Mediterranean and Mesopotamian and European and American cultures have had some encounter with the civilization of the Jews, and a mutual interaction has been at work. Some civilizations, such as those of China and India, have scarcely met the Jews in their wanderings, so that there is little mutual fertilization to report. Most of the encounters have been harsh and often tragic, but they have left a deep trace on all those whom historic chance or destiny has brought into contact or collision.

This book is about encounter; it is the history of meetings more often imposed than consciously sought but never sterile of consequence, for good or ill. It has been the general fortune of the Jews to be linked with one civilization to a dominant degree before passing on to the encounter with the next one. This makes the life of the historian less arduous than it might well have been if the story had been more dispersed. Survival in the past is no automatic guarantee of future survival, so that the existential question about a distinctive Jewish civilization poses itself forever anew. It is a story with no uneventful chapters. The spiritual and intellectual history of mankind is a huge country that no other people has traversed so broadly or for so long a time as the Jews. In telling the story we see a large horizon through a small but intensely penetrating eye.

The reign of the Egyptian Pharaoh Amenhotep III, in the fourteenth century B.C.E., marks the emergence of "solar monotheism"—a doctrine that strikingly parallels and may have profoundly influenced the development of Hebrew belief.

1. A People Is Born

THIS IS the story of a small people with a large place in the destiny of mankind. There are about 14 million Jews in the world, a small fraction of the human family. They have never had much power or space or size; yet we cannot recount the history of civilization without coming face to face with what the Jews have thought and felt and written and done.

The Jews trace their history back 4,000 years, to the time when their ancestor Abraham migrated into Canaan from the land between the two rivers the Tigris and the Euphrates. Generations later, their leader Moses took them out of Egypt, where they had gone for food and pasture, out of servitude into the wilderness of Sinai, where they experienced the transcendent vision of a single God set above nature—a vision that rebelled sharply against the confused and chaotic superstitions of the surrounding pagan world.

After a few centuries of settled national life in their own country, in the kingdoms of Judah and Israel, their land was conquered, the people exiled and dispersed. From this time onward, we find the Jews in every age and to a greater or lesser degree on every great continent, sometimes closed in upon their own life and legacy, sometimes pouring themselves into the oceans of other civilizations, always creating, suffering, resisting, and above all surviving in their own form and image. We might say of the Jews what a Greek historian said about the Greeks: This people was born to have no rest itself, and to give none to others.

Why do we tell this story? We tell it because of its constant drama, but also because

For the ancient Hebrews, these Red Sea waters marked the dividing line between bondage in Egypt and freedom in the Promised Land.

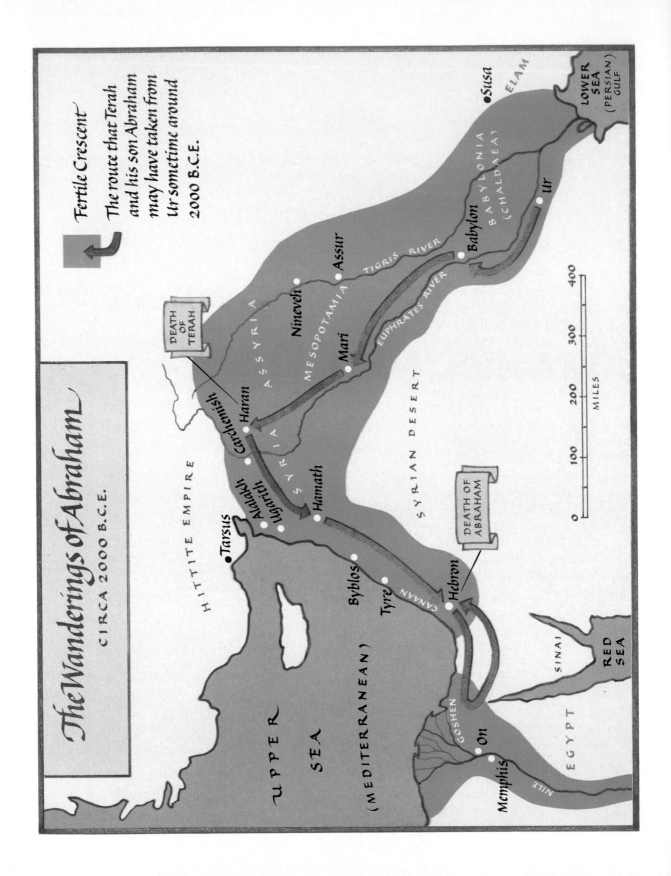

The Wanderings of Abraham

CIRCA 2000 B.C.E.

Fertile Crescent

The route that Terah and his son Abraham may have taken from Ur sometime around 2000 B.C.E.

DEATH OF TERAH

DEATH OF ABRAHAM

UPPER SEA (MEDITERRANEAN)

HITTITE EMPIRE

•Tarsus

Alalakh
Ugarith

Carchemish

Haran

SYRIA ASSYRIA

Nineveh

•Assur

MESOPOTAMIA

Mari

Hamath

TIGRIS RIVER

EUPHRATES RIVER

Babylon

BABYLONIA (CHALDAEA)

Ur

SYRIAN DESERT

Byblos

Tyre

CANAAN

Hebron

GOSHEN

On

Memphis

EGYPT

NILE

SINAI

RED SEA

•Susa

ELAM

LOWER SEA (PERSIAN) GULF

0   100   200   300   400

MILES

the whole of history has been powerfully agitated by the currents of the Jewish mind. And from that story the Jews take this lesson: There is salvation and significance for the Jew only when he stands straight and aims high within his own authentic frame of values.

What are those values, and what kind of people are the Jews who fashioned them? The answers lie in the history of every land and of every age.

THE ANCIENT WORLD

It was in a remote wilderness, deep in Sinai, that, according to ancient tradition, Moses received the Ten Commandments and the Law of Israel. But it is not only the memory of the Jewish people that lingers with persistent affection on the Biblical narrative about the Law revealed to Moses on the mountain. What emerged at Sinai was a universal legacy, a formative and revolutionary heritage whose originality can be grasped only in the context of what we know about the ancient world, and the beginnings of civilization on this planet.

Probably not more than 4 million people—less than one-thousandth of the world's present population—were alive in the year 10,000 B.C.E. In the land of what was to become the land of Israel, whose present population is

Civilization has no single birthplace or simple pattern of growth. This cave painting, created at Lascaux in southwestern France between 10,000 and 30,000 years ago, is among the earliest known expressions of the artistic and religious impulse. The cavern was sealed from human view for thousands of years until its discovery in 1940.

also about 4 million, fewer than 100,000 people were living when, according to the Biblical account, Abraham settled in Beersheba nearly 4,000 years ago.

We know what tools the prehistoric peoples made, what animals they hunted, and what grains and roots they ate; indeed, it is by our estimates of regional food resources that we can estimate the size of prehistoric populations. We may gain an inkling of how ancient man envisioned the natural world from cave paintings created 10,000 to 30,000 years ago. Such paintings have been found in the Dordogne region of southwestern France, in the Pyrenees, and in the Cantabrian Mountains of northwestern Spain. There are also painted rock slabs in Namibia (South-West Africa) dating from between 25,500 and 23,500 B.C.E. But we do not know with any certainty what our ancestors 12,000 years ago thought, felt, and believed; they left no written record. We can only conjecture, on the basis of the artifacts that they left and on a comparative study of a few peoples that have remained in their primitive state—

Strategically situated just west of the Euphrates, not far from the present Syrian-Iraqi border, Mari was a major center of Mesopotamian cultural development during the third millennium B.C.E. and remained prosperous until conquered by Babylonia during the reign of Hammurabi.

or had remained so until Christian missionaries and professional ethnologists discovered them.

How did our prehistoric precursors believe the world had come into being? In their view, what powers controlled the destiny of man —and what powers did man have to invoke or resist? Here we must proceed carefully. Religious phenomena are complex and volatile, so that it is not prudent to describe them in oversimplified terms. Even for much later periods, with their abundance of artifacts and inscriptions, great caution is in order. One scholar began his discussion of Sumerian worship with the assertion that "a systematic presentation of Mesopotamian religion cannot and should not be written." As the rabbinic saying goes, "The adornment of wisdom is humility."

What, then, can we say about the religious beliefs and practices of our ancient ancestors?

It appears that early man shared a body of myths involving creation, magical flight, the origins of fire, the bond between hunter and hunted, the ecstasy of the religious leader, and the magic of language—the power of the word. Accompanying this body of belief came a set of rituals that marked the great transitions from birth to death and from childhood to adulthood.

Ancient man did not believe that the world had come into existence casually, or that the events of his life occurred by chance. The world owed its existence to a "creator" or "creators," who fashioned or engendered heavens and earth from "the face of the waters." As widespread as the belief in creation out of primordial waters is the myth of the Great Flood, accounts of which appear not only in Genesis but also in Mesopotamian epic and religious texts and among extant primitive peoples such as the Amerindians, Australian aborigines, and indigenous peoples of South Asia and the Pacific islands.

Although written accounts of the Deluge date from a much later period, they are worth examining both as evidence of the universality of the story and as a reminder of how radically the Jews transformed the mythology of Mesopotamia. The earliest written flood story was excavated at Nippur, Sumer's most important religious center in the third millennium B.C.E., and first published in 1914. In this narrative, less than a third of which survives, the gods conspire to destroy the earth, sparing only the reverend King Ziusudra and his household. Ziusudra's mission parallels that of the Biblical Noah. Just as Noah makes burnt offerings to the Lord after the flood waters recede, so King Ziusudra sacrifices to the sun-god Utu, whose appearance signals the end of the week-long catastrophe.

A more famous Mesopotamian version of the flood story, embodied in the Epic of Gilgamesh, antedates Moses' arrival at Sinai by at least 500 years. In this account, Utnapishti the Far Distant, the Noah-figure, narrates his experiences to Gilgamesh, the legendary ruler of the Sumerian city-state Uruk. Discussions of the construction and dimensions of the Ark are similarly detailed in both the Genesis and Gilgamesh versions, and like Noah, Utnapishti preserves not only his own household but also specimens of the animal kingdom:

Yea, of the species of all living creatures, all that I had did I load aboard her. I made enter the vessel all my family and kindred; beasts wild and domestic and all of the craftsmen I made enter the vessel.

Like Noah's vessel, Utnapishti's comes to rest on a mountain, but named Nisir rather than Ararat. Again like Noah, Utnapishti sends out both a raven and a dove to see whether the flood waters have fully abated.

And yet we should not let these similarities in the Genesis and Gilgamesh stories obscure the significant differences between them. They show how markedly the Israelites were to diverge from the older Mesopotamian world view. In the Gilgamesh Epic the Deluge is the product of a quarrel among the gods, whereas in Genesis the Lord's decision to inundate the earth stems directly from the wickedness of man and corruption of the flesh:

And the Lord said, I will destroy man whom I have created from the face of the earth, both man, and beast, and the creeping thing, and the fowls of the air; for it repenteth me that I have made them.

(Genesis 6:7)

In the ancient world, no palace or temple was without its images of the gods. The tallest of the figures shown here, from the Abu Temple at Tell Asmar, measures only 30 inches (76 cm)—small enough to serve as a household idol.

The outcome of the Genesis account is eternal and universal. Gratified by Noah's pious offerings, God promises that He will never again destroy the world that He created:

And the Lord smelled a sweet savour; and the Lord said in his heart, I will not again curse the ground any more for man's sake; for the imagination of man's heart is evil from his youth; neither will I again smite any more every thing living, as I have done.

While the earth remaineth, seedtime and harvest, and cold and heat, and summer and winter, and day and night shall not cease.
(Genesis 8:21–22)

FROM VILLAGE TO EMPIRE

The notion that manlike creatures inhabited the earth 5 million, one million, or even 10,000 years ago would have shocked the most sophisticated seventeenth-century scholar. Until the 1800s the Bible was virtually the sole source of information on world history before the Pharaohs. Though the Bible itself gives no absolute dates, Biblical commentators could and did deduce a chronology of ancient times from the succession of generations in Genesis.

Like so many developments in the modern world, the revolution in Biblical archaeology, which continues to this day, can be traced to the advent of Napoleon. It was in July 1799 during Napoleon's Egyptian campaign that a French engineer, Boussard, working near the town of Rosetta (in Arabic, Rashid) at the mouth of the western branch of the Nile, found a black basalt slab bearing inscriptions in Egyptian and Greek. Napoleon himself thought the find so important that he ordered copies of the inscriptions to be distributed to European scholars. When British forces dislodged the French from Egypt in 1801 (and Napoleon, having abandoned his troops, returned to France), the slab, known today as the Rosetta Stone, was removed to the British Museum, where it remains. The first steps toward deciphering the stone's Egyptian hieroglyphics, or picture writings, were taken by Thomas Young (1773–1829), an English physicist and physician. However, it was a French Egyptologist and classical scholar, Jean François Champollion (1790–1832), who by 1822 had unlocked the secrets both of the hieroglyphic inscriptions and the popular Egyptian writings that accompanied them. With that discovery, Champollion also unlocked thousands of years of Egyptian history, much of which overlaps the Biblical period. The task of decoding Old Persian inscriptions had begun even before the Rosetta Stone was discovered, and by the mid-nineteenth century the work of unraveling the most ancient written languages of Mesopotamia was well under way. There is thus a fairly full picture of the two civilizations, Egypt and Sumer, that flourished in the Near East when Jewish history begins.

In Egypt, by the fifth millennium B.C.E., people were cultivating wheat and barley, herding cattle, building houses, making pottery, weaving baskets, and burying their dead in shallow oval graves, along with food and drink, eating and drinking vessels, tools for grinding cosmetics, and other implements that the deceased might need in the life to come. In India, recent evidence suggests domestication of sheep and cattle and cultivation of rice during this same period, if not earlier. And in Mesopotamia (which in ancient Greek meant "between the rivers"), in the fertile alluvial plains of the Tigris and Euphrates, wheat and barley were grown as early as the seventh millennium B.C.E. Here ancient man made the technological, social, and cultural transition from village to empire between 6,000 and 4,300 years ago.

Although we cannot say with any certainty that "history begins at Sumer," we are on

The Rosetta Stone, a black basalt slab inscribed in 196 B.C.E. and discovered by a French engineer nearly 2,000 years later, held the key to the mysteries of Egyptian hieroglyphics and, therefore, to Egyptian history during the Biblical period.

The development of cuneiform (literally, "wedge-shaped") writing to replace pictographs in Mesopotamia was the essential precondition for the growth of commerce and city life.

firm ground in claiming that Jewish history begins there. It was out of this Sumer, with its rich tradition of culture and civility, that the first Hebrews came, beginning with Abraham and his family.

It is clear that an agricultural revolution swept across Mesopotamia well before Abraham's time. Together with the agricultural metamorphosis came a revolution in settlement patterns. The villages that sprang up throughout Mesopotamia after 5000 B.C.E. were succeeded around the middle of the fourth millennium B.C.E. by temple communities, managed by priests and devoted to serving the god of a particular locality. In the temple, on a pedestal, stood an image of the god, usually in human form. Individual households might have their own cheap rep-

licas of the image. Although these images were fashioned in temple workshops by human hands, the ancients believed that they could be brought to life by special rituals designed to open their eyes and mouth. The temple god was dressed, like a king, in gold-plated garments, and on ceremonial occasions was carried, as in a royal procession, through the temple courtyard or the streets of the city. The king's bond with the rituals of idol worship was equally intimate: he had the privilege of eating the meal that had been offered to the image by the priests.

The gods might be beneficent or vengeful, constant or capricious, but one thing was certain: They were always hungry. From a later, incomplete Akkadian text from Uruk (Erech in the Bible), we learn just how large was the appetite of the many deities in that city:

The daily total, throughout the year, for the four meals per day: twenty-one first-class, fat, clean rams which have been fed barley for two years; two large bulls; one milk-fed bullock; eight lambs; thirty *marratu*-birds; thirty [other] birds; three cranes which have been fed [a certain kind of] grain; five ducks which have been fed [a certain type of] flour; two ducks of a lesser quality than those just mentioned; four wild boars; three ostrich eggs; three duck eggs.

The Sumerian idea that a god might welcome some sacrifices and reject others was not lost on the ancient Hebrews, though the Bible presents this concept in a characteristically monotheistic and ethical guise:

And in process of time it came to pass, that Cain brought of the fruit of the ground an offering unto the Lord.

And Abel, he also brought of the firstlings of his flock and of the fat thereof. And the Lord had respect unto Abel and to his offering:

But unto Cain and to his offering He had not respect.

(Genesis 4:3–5)

The development of Mesopotamian city-states around 3000 B.C.E. marks the emergence of Sumerian civilization. At the head of the Sumerian city-state's political and religious hierarchy stood the king and the chief priest. Whereas the cult center or temple community served a single local deity, the city-state typically had several gods. It may have taken other communities' idols in conquest. And as in the case of Uruk, there were several temples. This same period witnessed the introduction of cuneiform writing, which offered greater flexibility in record keeping and administration. As the Near East entered the Early Bronze Age, the use of metal weapons became widespread. Advances in the arts of war and civil organization thus went hand in hand with the rise of kingship as a Sumerian institution.

How did the Sumerians look at the world? Central to their view of the universe were the sky-god An; Enlil, god of the atmosphere; and Enki, variously identified as the god of "foundations" and of the "primordial waters." Over time, however, the mixture of cosmic and local deities grew exceedingly complex. Names of gods changed, and new gods were added to the pantheon as the Sumerians came into contact with other peoples. Mesopotamian god-lists can include up to 3,000 names, but this may mean only that learned scribes preserved the memory of hundreds of deities that no longer had any claim to popular worship. With such a superabundance of gods, many of them, like the city-states they inhabited, were at war with one another. Ancient man feared the failure to placate the gods he knew. He also feared offending the gods he had never heard of. Moreover, the gods and goddesses had their

Malleable, durable, and lustrous, gold might have been the first metal worked by man. The gold dagger shown here was found at Ur and dates from the third millennium B.C.E.

own requirements and taboos. How could anyone obey them all, or even know—until the offended deity took vengeance—that a transgression had been committed?

The sin which I have done, indeed I do not know.
The forbidden thing which I have eaten, indeed I
* do not know;*
The prohibited place on which I have set foot,
* indeed I do not know.*

The result, in this late stage of Sumerian spiritual development, is a feeling of helplessness and desolation:

The god whom I know or do not know has
* oppressed me;*
The goddess whom I know or do not know has
* placed suffering upon me.*
Although I am constantly looking for help, no one
* takes me by the hand;*
When I weep they do not come to my side.

Undoubtedly, the ceaseless warring first of city-states, then of royal alliances, and finally of empires in the ancient Near East was a prime source of human suffering. Wars were waged for booty, tribute, slaves, raw materials, control of trade routes, and imperial ambition. As a Sumerian proverb puts it;

You go and carry off the enemy's land;
The enemy comes and carries off your land.

Taking the long view, however, we can see that war, like trade, was also a powerful vehicle of cultural contact. When one Near Eastern state conquered another, it tended to absorb rather than eradicate the vanquished state's culture, including, of course, the images it worshiped.

In a century of conquerors, no name looms larger than that of Sargon of Akkad. Unlike the Sumerians, the Akkadians were of Semitic origin, and Sargon (in Akkadian, Sharrum-Kin) was likewise a Semite. Probably after 2350 B.C.E., Sargon became king of Kish, an Akkadian city-state situated be-

Complex rituals of sacrifice, purification, and prayer developed around the increasingly long list of gods to whom the peoples of Mesopotamia paid homage. Serving the gods required special implements and vessels, such as this ritual bowl, and a priestly caste that knew how to use them.

tween the Tigris and Euphrates rivers. From his power base in Kish, Sargon the Great made war on Sumer, defeating the king of Uruk, whose own empire embraced virtually all Sumeria. As the monarch of a united Sumer and Akkad, Sargon then turned his imperial attentions to the Elamites in the east and the Eblaites in the west, launching military campaigns that, according to ancient texts, gave him control over the Near East all the way from the Mediterranean to the Persian Gulf. An inscription boasts that "Sargon, king of Kish, was victorious in 34 campaigns and dismantled [all] the cities, as far as the shore of the sea." Sargon and his successors also opened trade routes with Dilmun (probably present-day Bahrain) and with the peoples of the Indus Valley, who by that time had developed one of the world's most advanced civilizations.

The Akkadian dynasty founded by Sargon crumbled through a combination of palace intrigues and external pressures. But after the collapse of Akkad about 2180 B.C.E., the Sumerian city-states regained much of their power. Prominent among these was Ur, whose dynasty reached its cultural zenith in the reign of Ur-Nammu (c. 2100 B.C.E.), called by one writer the "first Moses." At least 300 years before the Babylonian king Hammurabi promulgated his famous law code, Ur-Nammu propounded decrees of which fragments have come down to us.

About a century after Ur-Nammu, Ur also fell. And it is at this point, about 2000 B.C.E., with the fall of Ur and the advent of Abraham, that the history of the Jewish people begins.

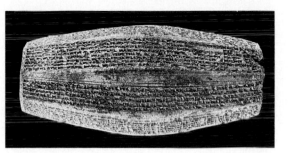

This prism, which was inscribed in cuneiform characters, was found at Khorsabad, the Assyrian capital in the time of Sargon II.

THE AGE OF THE PATRIARCHS

For some centuries, until about the year 2000 B.C.E., a group of nomads known as the Amurru (Martu), or Amorites, had been pressing on the settled cultures of Mesopotamia and Palestine. Then the city of Ur, the great center of Mesopotamian culture, fell, and the Amorites—a term meaning "westerners"—flooded the southern Mesopotamian plain. They adopted the culture of Sumer and Akkad, and the Akkadian language, which was the vehicle of international commerce in that day. It is among these diverse clans of "westerners" that the ancestors of Israel are to be found.

The Third Dynasty of Ur died slowly and painfully. As the Amorite threat intensified, farmers abandoned their lands for the temporary safety of cities. Food production declined, and by 2000 B.C.E. the price of grain was sixty times above normal. Ur and its satellite cities literally starved to death. Besieged from without, decaying from within, Ur's satellites collapsed one by one. Finally, Ur too was overrun, and its king made captive.

What had brought on this calamity? To this question the Sumerians offered a characteristically fatalist reply. Empires would fall, kings would be toppled, no dynasty could last forever. And the will of the gods was irreversible.

A bull's head from Ur (third century B.C.E.). The central role in which the bull was cast in Near Eastern mythology underlies the "golden calf" episode in Exodus 32, in which the Israelites, led by Aaron, make an idol in Moses' absence.

A lyrelike instrument from Ur, c. 2450 B.C.E. Probably invented in Babylonia, the lyre may already have reached Egypt by this time.

Here, as with the Deluge story, we can sense how radically the Hebrews would diverge from the prevailing Near Eastern worldview. For the people of Israel, recalling the disaster that engulfed the cities of the plain, the answer lay first of all in God's words to Abraham:

Because the cry of Sodom and Gomorrah is great, and because their sin is very grievous . . .

(Genesis 18:20)

The Israelite belief in collective and personal responsibility opened the door to repentance and communal salvation, as in the Book of Jonah:

So the people of Nineveh believed God, and proclaimed a fast, and put on sackcloth, from the greatest of them even to the least of them. . . .

And God saw their works, that they turned from their evil way; and God repented of the evil, that He had said He would do unto them; and He did it not.

(Jonah 3:5, 10)

As the rabbis of the Roman period would say many centuries later, "We have been taught that deeds make atonement for a man, and that repentance and good deeds are a shield against punishment."

Amurru is the word for "west" in Akkadian. It was also the Akkadian name for the unlikely land of Canaan—the land to which, from the city of Haran, Abraham and his

Sargon the Great, the Semitic monarch of Sumer and Akkad, ruled the Near East all the way from the Mediterranean to the Persian Gulf.

family came, pursuing, according to the Bible, a promise:

Get thee out of thy country, and from thy kindred, and from thy father's house, unto a land that I will show thee:

And I will make of thee a great nation, and I will bless thee, and make thy name great; and thou shalt be a blessing:

And I will bless them that bless thee, and curse him that curseth thee; and in thee shall all families of the earth be blessed.

(Genesis 12:1-3)

After this migration, which must have occurred after the Dynasty of Ur fell to the Amorites, Abraham moved his household southward to Shechem; thereafter, when famine afflicted Canaan, down to Egypt; and finally eastward across Sinai to Beersheba in the Negev. These traditional "wanderings" of Abraham are consistent not only with the life of a seminomadic pastoralist but also with what we know of the Amorite dispersion throughout the Fertile Crescent during the period. Equally interesting is the evident fluidity of cultural contact. If, as seems likely, Abraham kept to the main trade routes along the Euphrates most of the way from Ur to Haran, he would have passed through or near the great centers of Sumer and Akkad. There he would have encountered the diverse cultures of Syria and Palestine and the magnificence of ancient Egypt, where, by

A battalion of Egyptian soldiers as depicted during the Twelfth Dynasty (c. 2000–1800 B.C.E.), when the Middle Kingdom was in full flower.

Babylonian legend tells of the defeat of Akkad by barbarians called Guti during the reign of Naram-Sin ("king of the four quarters of the world"), the successor of Sargon the Great.

1900 B.C.E., the Middle Kingdom was in full flower. This dynasty marks the classical age of Egyptian literature. It is also an era in which the jeweler's art reaches its zenith. Egypt's earliest pyramid, the Step Pyramid of Zoser, is already more than 700 years old, but with a resurgence of the Egyptian monarchy—the Pharaohs—a new epoch of pyramid building is under way. Each pyramid is a royal tomb, a monument in death to the Pharaoh who in life was worshiped as the incorporation of the deities of Upper and Lower Egypt:

According to the evidence of the Egyptian Execration Texts—so called because they list the enemies of Egypt along with various curses and maledictions—there appears to have been a resurgence of city life in Canaan

during the twentieth and nineteenth centuries B.C.E., the period of Amorite absorption. Beginning in the time of Abraham, we can see the movement of Amorite tribes from seminomadic pastoralism to a more settled agriculture and commerce, and from patriarchal rule to urban monarchies, not only in Canaan but in Mesopotamia. But not all the Amorites followed this pattern. Some Amorite tribes were slow to give up their seminomadic ways. And their number seems to have included Abraham and his descendants, the Patriarchs of Israel.

Once you have a nomadic existence, then the differences that mark you and distinguish you from settled civilizations are not merely those of economic necessity. Differentiation follows you in almost everything. If you are nomads, subjected to the fatalities and vicissitudes of climate and natural disasters, if you fight your way through deserts to live, you develop a certain solidarity, a social organization that might seem very harsh in modern terms.

For the Hebrews there was another effect. Whatever the spirit could create could only be in terms of words. Nomads cannot build monuments in cities. They cannot paint or sculpt, or leave durable things or monuments behind. And so the creative expression of the Jews had to be portable—it had to be an expression that was not dependent on place. The only thing that is portable among the major creative forms are the beliefs and ideas that you carry with you. And nobody can prevent you from carrying them. They can prevent you from taking your sculptures and your buildings, but not your words, your literature or—your religion.

Both Christian and Muslim tradition admit Abraham as their spiritual ancestor. To the Jews, he is the first and unique patriarch, the model of Hebrew excellence.

Christians and Muslims tend to emphasize the archetypal Abraham as a man of faith and

Five hundred years before the time of Moses, the Babylonian king Hammurabi promulgated his famous law code. At the head of the diorite slab on which his 282 laws are engraved, Hammurabi stands before the sun-god Shamash—a scene emphasizing that these laws were of divine origin.

monotheistic commitment. Preserved in Islamic tradition is the rabbinic tale that Abraham was the son of an idol maker and that, left to sell the idols in his father's absence, Abraham smashed them instead. In Hebrew tradition, of course, Abraham is equally a man of faith—indeed, of a faith so profound that he was willing to sacrifice his son Isaac when God appeared to require it. But the Biblical Abraham was also a man of the covenant, through whom God was said to have forged a special link with the people of Israel. This link and covenant were later ratified in the immortal words that Moses heard as he stood on the rugged mountain top in Sinai.

It now is thought that the ancient Hebrews conceived this covenant as a kind of treaty in which God, as sovereign, promised His subjects land and protection in exchange for their homage and allegiance. The idea of the patriarchal covenant is illustrated in the Biblical account of a "vision" that came to Abraham in the Plain of Mamre, near Hebron, at a time when Abraham—or Abram, as the Bible calls him at this point—was still childless:

The word of the Lord came unto Abram in a vision, saying, Fear not, Abram: I am thy shield, and thy exceeding great reward. . . .

And He brought him forth abroad, and said, Look now toward heaven, and tell the stars, if thou be able to number them: and He said unto him, So shall thy seed be.

And he believed in the Lord; and He counted it to him for righteousness. . . .

In the same day the Lord made a covenant with Abram, saying, Unto thy seed have I given this land, from the river of Egypt unto the great river, the river Euphrates.

(Genesis 15:1, 5–6, 18)

After Abraham's death, the Bible tells us, this covenant was renewed with his son Isaac:

And the Lord appeared unto him, and said, Go not down into Egypt; dwell in the land which I shall tell thee of:

Sojourn in this land, and I will be with thee, and will bless thee; for unto thee, and unto thy seed, I will give all these countries, and I will perform the oath which I sware unto Abraham thy father;

And I will make thy seed to multiply as the stars of heaven, and will give unto thy seed all these countries, and in thy seed shall all the nations of the earth be blessed;

Because that Abraham obeyed my voice, and kept my charge, my commandments, my statutes, and my laws.

(Genesis 26:2–5)

And again with Isaac's son Jacob, in the magnificent dream-vision that has inspired artists from the third-century fresco painters

at Dura-Europos through Raphael, Ribera, Rembrandt, Murillo, Blake and Chagall:

And Jacob went out from Beersheba, and went toward Haran.

And he lighted upon a certain place, and tarried there all night, because the sun was set; and he took of the stones of that place, and put them for his pillows, and lay down in that place to sleep.

And he dreamed, and behold a ladder set up on the earth, and the top of it reached to heaven: and behold the angels of God ascending and descending on it.

And, behold the Lord stood above it, and said, I am the Lord God of Abraham thy father, and the God of Isaac: the land whereon thou liest, to thee will I give it, and to thy seed;

And thy seed shall be as the dust of the earth, and thou shalt spread abroad to the west, and to the east, and to the north, and to the south: and in thee and in thy seed shall all the families of the earth be blessed.

(Genesis 28:10–14)

Abraham had broken with the idolatrous element in paganism. But his God was not unique or omnipresent or fully transcendent. He was the deity of Abraham's family—of Abraham, Isaac, and Jacob—not of other families, still less of all mankind.

The conception of God as a tribal deity, though with universal powers, still governs the Bible's portrayal of the renewal of the covenant at Sinai:

And Moses went up unto God, and the Lord called unto him out of the mountain, saying, Thus shalt thou say to the house of Jacob, and tell the children of Israel;

The great Step Pyramid of Saqqara, near Cairo, was built as a funerary monument to Zoser, who ruled Egypt as Pharaoh nearly 5,000 years ago.

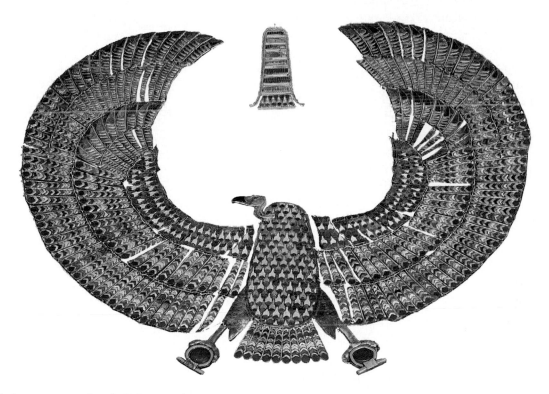

Ye have seen what I did unto the Egyptians, and how I bare you on eagles' wings, and brought you unto Myself.

Now, therefore, if ye will obey My voice indeed, and keep My covenant, then ye shall be a peculiar treasure unto Me above all people: for all the earth is mine:

And ye shall be unto Me a kingdom of priests, and an holy nation. These are the words which thou shalt speak unto the children of Israel.

(Exodus 19:3–6)

The Mesopotamians, as we have seen, had cosmic gods and local gods of varying attributes. In the revelation to Moses from the Burning Bush, however, it is clear that the Hebrews of Biblical times had come to conceive their tribal deity and the cosmic deity as one and the same: they had risen above parochialism into a sense of human destiny.

From the tomb of the Egyptian boy-king Tutankhamen (fl. c. 1355 B.C.E.) a necklace showing the goddess Nekhabit in the form of a vulture.

And Moses said unto God, Behold, when I come unto the children of Israel, and shall say unto them, The God of your fathers hath sent me unto you; and they shall say to me, What is His name? what shall I say unto them?

And God said unto Moses, I AM THAT I AM; and He said, Thus shalt thou say unto the children of Israel, I AM hath sent me unto you.

(Exodus 3:13–14)

The task of understanding the origins of the Jewish people would be much easier if all the Hebrews dwelling in Canaan after Abraham's time had moved down to Egypt in the days of Joseph. But to maintain this is to ignore the complexities of Genesis and Exodus and to gloss over the formidable difficulty of tallying the Biblical account with the scant mentions of the Hebrews in sources other than the Bible. Scholars are by no means unanimous on the question of whether the Hebrews (*ivrim*) of the Bible, the Habiru (Hapiru, Apiru) mentioned in cuneiform documents, and the '*prw* described in Egyptian hieroglyphic inscriptions are the same people. A further complication—but one that does not necessarily exclude the identity of the Hebrews and the Habiru—is that the term Habiru in Egypt seems to have meant a social class rather than an ethnic group. The Habiru were stateless persons who appear, at various dates and in various places during the second millennium B.C.E., as pastoralists, city dwellers, laborers, slaves, brigands, warriors, mercenaries, even—like Joseph—as high officials in the service of foreign monarchs. It is likely that although some Hebrews took part in the entry from Canaan to Egypt, as did Jacob and his sons, others remained in Canaan; that while Moses led some of the Hebrews out of Egypt, not all the children of Israel chose to leave, and not all of those who left with Moses were Hebrews; and that when the Israelites reentered the Promised Land, they allied themselves with the descendants of their nonnomadic kinsmen.

The ancient histories of Israel and Egypt became fully intertwined over a time span extending roughly from 1800 to 1550 B.C.E. This epoch encompassed what generations of Egyptians would consider an era of national humiliation. For it was during this period that an Asiatic people, including at least some Semitic elements, first exacted tribute from the Pharaohs and then ruled Egypt directly. These were the Hyksos, and at its height (about 1650–1550 B.C.E.) their empire embraced not only Upper and Lower Egypt but also Palestine and Syria. The Hyksos period saw the introduction of the horse to Egypt, and the conquest by the Hyksos may be attributable to their prowess as charioteers and to their skill at designing and building fortifications.

In Roman times, some 1,600 years after the Hyksos dynasty had collapsed, the Jewish historian Flavius Josephus (b. Joseph ben Mattathias, A.D. 37–100?), citing the Egyptian authority Manetho (third century B.C.E.), claimed that the Hyksos were patriarchal Jews and equated the expulsion of the Hyksos from Egypt with the Exodus. This is plainly impossible if we accept the likely dates of about 1550 B.C.E. for the expulsion of the Hyksos and the late thirteenth and early twelfth centuries B.C.E. for the Exodus and the Israelite conquest of Canaan. Few modern scholars would go so far as to assert that the Hebrews and the Hyksos were the same people. But it may well be that the dynasty of the Hyksos, some of whom were Semites, provided an opportunity for the ancient Hebrews and other Semitic groups to settle peaceably in Goshen and even to rise in the ranks of Egyptian officialdom. Conversely, the expulsion of the Hyksos may have marked the end of Hebrew power and influence in Egypt and the beginning of the descent into bondage.

Under the dynasties of the New Kingdom (c. 1550–1075 B.C.E.), Egypt sought to extend its sphere of influence into what had been the Hyksos empire, and during the first two or three centuries of the New Kingdom, Hebrews who had earlier remained in Canaan may have been brought to Egypt as slaves.

Among the dynasts of the New Kingdom we encounter one of the most controversial figures in Egyptian history, the Pharaoh Amenhotep (Amenophis) IV, or, as he styled himself, Akhenaten. It is not for any great foreign exploit that Akhenaten's name was revered—or, more frequently, execrated—but for a ruthless political, social, and religious reform that established a new capital,

Like so much of the Hebrew Bible, the dream vision of Jacob's ladder has inspired artists from the fresco painters of Dura-Europos to the creators of our own day. This radiant portrayal is by the Italian Renaissance master Raphael.

Akhetaten (Tell al-Amarna), renounced conventionality in manners and morals, reduced the power of the priesthood, and sought to eradicate worship of most of the traditional gods of Egypt. Akhenaten and his queen, Nefertiti, reigned about the middle of the fourteenth century B.C.E.—a hundred years before the time of Moses—so the nature of Akhenaten's religious thought, and specifically the question of whether Akhenaten was a monotheist, is of great interest for an understanding of Moses' environment.

Like Mesopotamia, Egypt had developed a highly complex system of gods. In addition to revering state and local deities, the Egyptians also worshipped gods in the form of animals—cows and bulls, monkeys and crocodiles, vultures and serpents. Pharaoh was deified, and so was the life-giving Nile.

Hail to thee, O Nile, that issues from the earth and comes to keep Egypt alive! . . .

When he rises, then the land is in jubilation, then every belly is in joy. . . .

The bringer of food, rich in provisions, creator of all good, lord of majesty, sweet of fragrance. What is in him is satisfaction. He who brings grass into being for the cattle and thus gives sacrifice to every god, whether he be in the underworld, heaven, or earth . . . He who takes in possession the Two Lands, fills the magazines, makes the granaries wide, and gives things to the poor.

A special place both in Egyptian theology and in popular worship was reserved for Osiris, god of vegetation and king of the dead, and as such central to Egyptian

Scenes from the life of Moses by the fifteenth-century Florentine painter Sandro Botticelli.

The baby Moses plucked from the bulrushes and given to the Pharaoh's daughter, as shown in this fresco in a third-century Syrian synagogue.

Moses and the Burning Bush, a stone mosaic at San Vitale in Ravenna, Italy. The San Vitale mosaics date from the sixth century C.E.

The <u>Moses</u> of Donatello, a pioneer of sculptural realism in the Italian Renaissance.

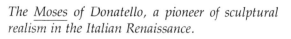

The expulsion of the Hyksos may have marked the end of Hebrew power in Egypt and the beginning of the descent into bondage. Here, a Semite humbles himself in an Egyptian tomb painting.

Jewish history, of course, his chief importance resides in the likelihood that he is the tyrannical Pharaoh in whose reign the Exodus occurred. For the rebellion of Moses against his Egyptian environment took place in Rameses II's reign.

Moses was born and bred into Egyptian life and tradition. Yet he was of Hebrew ancestry, and the persecution of his kinsmen moved him to ardent and creative anger. Out of his indignation there would emerge events and new understandings, unique for his time . . . and valid for all generations. . . .

In the Bible, the revolt of the Hebrews begins with an isolated act of indignation—and compassion.

And it came to pass in those days, when Moses was grown, that he went out unto his brethren, and looked on their burdens: and he spied an Egyptian smiting an Hebrew, one of his brethren.

And he looked this way and that way, and when he saw that there was no man, he slew the Egyptian, and hid him in the sand.

(Exodus 2:11–12)

But this act of righteous indignation, supposedly executed in secret, does not remain secret very long. Moses has been observed, and when report of his action reaches Pharaoh, Moses is forced to flee. In exile in the land of the Midianites, in the wilderness of Sinai, Moses marries Zipporah, the daughter of a Midianite priest. It is in Sinai, at Horeb, that Moses first hears the voice of God, coming from a bush that burns "with fire" but that the fire does not consume:

Now therefore, behold, the cry of the children of Israel is come unto me: and I have also seen the oppression wherewith the Egyptians oppress them.

Come now therefore, and I will send thee unto Pharaoh, that thou mayest bring forth my people the children of Israel out of Egypt.

(Exodus 3:9–10)

thought concerning fertility, death, and the rhythms of creation. During the many centuries when Thebes was capital of Egypt, a local deity, Amon, rose to supreme national importance, especially when linked in worship to Re, the sun-god who each night descended to the nether world and was reborn the following morning.

It is around this time, probably in the year 1290 B.C.E., that the long reign of Rameses II begins. Like his imperial-minded predecessors, Rameses II campaigned in Syria and Palestine. After a prolonged war of doubtful outcome, he concluded a treaty with the Hittites, the rulers of Syria at that time. This Pharaoh, who had numerous wives and was reputedly the father of more than a hundred children, won renown as a builder of monuments, at least partly through the use of Habiru slave labor. From the standpoint of

Domesticated horses first appeared in Babylonia around Abraham's time and were introduced into Egypt by the Hyksos a few hundred years later.

In speaking of God, Moses was capable of an unprecedented exercise in abstraction. He could envisage a God above nature, a God immune from human passion and natural vicissitudes.

Uniting the Israelites in the worship of a single God, Moses managed, without physical authority or sanction at his command, to organize the straggling seminomad tribes for concerted revolt and to lead them out of their Egyptian birthplace in an Exodus from slavery to freedom.

The struggle of the Exodus was not only a liberation from servitude. It was the crucial event in Israel's self-conception.

But it was more than that. For the Exodus would become a metaphor for all human history in the struggle for freedom.

The Biblical narrative here departs from the traditional way of writing history in ancient times. Most ancient history is dominated by self-glorification. In the Egyptian inscriptions that have come down to us, the Pharaohs nearly always appear as glorious conquerors. When an Egyptian monarch meets with disaster in a foreign land, the scribes keep silent—or else they fabricate victory. This is not the way of the Bible.

After their departure from Egypt, the children of Israel are described frankly as experiencing fear, hunger, thirst, doubt, and dissension. The honor of victory, the Bible tells us, belongs not to Moses nor to his followers but to the Lord:

Then sang Moses and the children of Israel this song unto the Lord, and spake, saying, I will sing unto the Lord, for He hath triumphed gloriously: the horse and his rider hath He thrown into the sea.

(Exodus 15:1)

Sustaining the Hebrews during their first three arduous months in the wilderness were the Lord's protection and Israel's faith—the two basic foundations of God's covenant with Abraham, soon to be reestablished with the Israelites at Sinai. When they looked back upon the Exodus, the Israelites understood that God had brought them out of Egypt not merely to ease their misery and end their oppression but to offer them the true gifts of human freedom and human responsibility—through law.

The God of Moses is a Divine Power who is no longer indifferent to humanity. All previous and contemporary religions saw human destiny as subject to the laws of nature. In the Sinai, human destiny would be separated from the cycle of nature. Human destiny would break loose from the fatalistic, hopeless chain of recurrence. Progress, not repetition, would become the law of life, and humans would bear a responsibility for human destiny.

What was born in Sinai was a concept as revolutionary as the wheel, an idea as influential as the plow—the idea of hope and progress and the stubborn belief that human life can be improved. That was the eternal meaning of the words given to Moses on the mountain:

I am the Lord thy God, which have brought thee out of the land of Egypt, out of the house of bondage.

Thou shalt have no other gods before me.

Thou shalt not make unto thee any graven image . . .

Thou shalt not take the name of the Lord thy God in vain . . .

Remember the Sabbath day, to keep it holy . . .

Honor thy father and thy mother . . .

Thou shalt not murder.

Thou shalt not commit adultery.

Thou shalt not steal.

Thou shalt not bear false witness against thy neighbor.

Thou shalt not covet thy neighbor's house, thou shalt not covet thy neighbor's wife . . . not any thing that is thy neighbor's.

(Exodus 20:2–17)

It is difficult for us now to grasp the revolutionary nature of the Ten Commandments and the Law of Moses. Ideas that were adventurous yesterday become routine today, and one forgets how rebellious they were in their own historical context.

The concept of One God was quite irrational in terms of contemporary civilizations which were based on the pluralism of the forces of nature.

"Thou shalt not make unto thee any graven image"—this was an assault on the most treasured convention of the Mesopotamian and Egyptian civilizations.

The Sabbath day involved an element of compassion through rest from labor which cannot be found in any contemporary literature of the ancient world.

Thus, much in the Decalogue, in the Ten Commandments, was new—without precedent—revolutionary. And overriding these commandments was a concept of the ability of human beings to choose between good and evil, to break free from hopeless and repetitive disaster, to fulfill the divine purpose through their own acts. Humans were to be responsible for their future. It was a threatening idea, and still to be tested.

Many Israelites were afraid of the challenges that lay ahead of them. Their faith wavered, and they yearned to return to bondage in Egypt rather than face the perils of an unknown future in a hostile land:

And all the children of Israel murmured against Moses and against Aaron: and the whole congregation said unto them, Would

The funeral mask of Tutankhamen, one of the many Egyptian treasures restored to the world when the Pharaoh's tomb was discovered in 1922.

God that we had died in the land of Egypt! or would God we had died in this wilderness!

And wherefore hath the Lord brought us unto this land, to fall by the sword, that our wives and our children should be a prey? were it not better for us to return into Egypt?

(Numbers 14:2–3)

The Bible tells us that God answered these conspiracies with a curse and a promise:

And the Lord spake unto Moses and unto Aaron, saying, How long shall I bear with this evil congregation, which murmur against Me? I have heard the murmurings of the children of Israel, which they murmur against Me.

Say unto them, As truly as I live, saith the Lord, as ye have spoken in Mine ears, so will I do to you:

Your carcasses shall fall in this wilderness; and all that were numbered of you, according to your whole number, from twenty years old and upward, which have murmured against me . . .

But your little ones, which ye said should be a prey, them will I bring in, and they shall know the land which ye have despised.
(Numbers 14:26–29, 31)

From this place they would go forward, turning once again toward the land of Canaan and a new future.

In what were they so different from their contemporaries?

Their greatest discovery and intuition was the idea of a single God. A God responsive to injustice. A God above nature—not a personification of the awesome powers of nature.

The age of patriarchal innocence ends with the descendants of Abraham setting out across the Sinai to their promised home.

Somehow a new force had entered history. Israel had become an organic unity, a people. Not just any people but—in their own eyes —God's people.

As the successors of that wilderness generation turned their faces toward Canaan, Israel had achieved a new identity.

From this point onward the Bible describes Israel as a nation apart with little reference to other cultures. Historians do not doubt that the "Israel" that came into Canaan was strongly impregnated with Sumerian and Egyptian ideas, but it is very difficult to trace the origins of those ideas.

Other than the Jews, few nations have a continuous record of their lives extending

Are these the mountains the Bible calls Sinai? After centuries of controversy, still no one knows. But for Jewish history—for the history of Western civilization—the exact location of the Biblical Sinai is far less important than the revolutionary ideas that were born there.

over thousands of years. There are, of course, the Egyptians and the Chinese. But each of their national histories unfolds within the very compact framework of a single land. Jewish history, on the other hand, weaves in and out of other civilizations and epochs, rather like the thread in a complex tapestry that sometimes gets lost from view but always reappears in its own texture, color, and identity.

One of the difficulties in recounting Jewish history is the absence of any independent record. There is nothing surprising about the original obscurity of the Jews. Why should the Egyptians and Mesopotamians have taken any notice of them? By the time the ancient Israelites appear in history, Egypt has many centuries of stable national life behind it. The Egyptians had built their pyramids in testimony to their intuition for grandeur; their painting, their statues, their hieroglyphics, reveal a lofty artistic imagination. Similarly, the peoples dwelling between the Tigris and the Euphrates have long left their primitive epochs behind by the time the

Hebrews appear. Their city-states were alive with varied commerce and sophisticated culture. They built great temples in devotion to the gods of sun and sky and air. They invented irrigation canals carrying water beyond the immediate proximity of the rivers. They invented cuneiform writings, much more flexible and mobile than hieroglyphics.

The kings and emperors of the Babylonian and Egyptian empires did leave inscriptions behind, but they were much more concerned with praising themselves than recording the obscure deeds of others. And yet we find this little Hebrew people in an arid, inhospitable piece of land struggling for a foothold between the two great empires of the south and east, maintaining themselves in the shadow of one or the other but ultimately surviving and outshining both. Today the pyramids reach into the sky, but they tell of things long past. The city-states between the Tigris and the Euphrates have crumbled into the dust. But the ideas and words of this little people in that unlikely piece of land have a louder echo and a stronger impact today than when they were first proclaimed.

The Jews would bequeath no great cities, monuments, irrigation systems, works of art. But they did have a special way of thinking about God, mankind, and nature. And so they bequeathed to posterity a double gift: a moral law within a unique vision of history, and a body of splendid and passionate writing, revered and studied across the centuries by more people than have ever come under the spell of any other literature.

"And the Egyptians made the children of Israel to serve with rigour: and they made their lives bitter with hard bondage . . ." (Exodus 1:13–14). Semitic captives are shown in this ancient Egyptian painting.

Miriam, sister of Moses and prophetess of Israel, is shown, tambourine in hand, celebrating the crossing of the Red Sea and the victory over the Egyptians, in this colorful miniature from the fourteenth-century Spanish Golden Haggadah.

2. The Power of the Word

T HE HEBREWS entered history suddenly, without much storm or drama. Indeed, history barely noticed that the Jews had entered it at all. Why should the powerful, sophisticated empires in the rich, green valleys of the Nile and the Euphrates be impressed by those ragged, wandering tribes? They had no cities, no temples, no buildings, no armies. All that they had were ideas expressed in words.

All subsequent history bears witness to the unconquerable power of those words. A few thousand Hebrew words uttered in Israel a few thousand years ago have been sending sharp impulses of thought and feeling into mankind ever since. We cannot imagine the history of civilizations, of religion, of philosophy, literature, drama, science, art, without acknowledging the potency of those words.

The words preserved the people in their separate identity. Israelites insisted on settling in the land of Canaan, which illustrated their peculiar talent for looking for trouble. It was an unhappy, infertile land with a few green watering places. But it was in the middle of every route across which the powerful empires would send their armies in time of war. To insist on living there was no prescription for greatness, or even for stability. Even the smallest Canaanite city-states seemed to have a more developed material culture than the Jews. But the Jews did have a startling revolutionary idea, the idea of a single God presiding over the course of nature and the fate of mankind, with Himself independent of them both.

We can understand how revolutionary this idea was if we compare it with the Egyptian, Mesopotamian, and Canaanite environment. The monuments of those cultures include gods with human heads and animal bodies, bulls with wings, birds with four legs. To equate divinity with beasts is to degrade

Flanked by the plateau of Moab to the east and the hills of Judea to the west, the Dead Sea region has played a key role in the history of the Holy Land —as the presumed site of Sodom and Gomorrah, as the home of the Essene sect, and as the juridical boundary of ancient Israel.

With the head of a man, the wings of a bird, and the torso of a bull, this Assyrian sculpture from Khorsabad typifies the gods of the ancient world.

round and back to a starting point in darkness and chaos.

So the Jews from Abraham and Moses onward through the life of their settled kingdom carried a transcendent vision of great nobility of which they were the only custodians. If they would preserve the idea, the idea would preserve them. In future generations they would fight and suffer, their kingdom would be divided, both parts of it conquered, the temples destroyed, the people dispersed and deported. But through every vicissitude an irreducible core would endure. And from the endurance of a separate people in covenant with a single God would come a moral, spiritual, ethical legacy for all mankind. The walls and the temples would crumble, but the words would resound forever.

A broken portrait of the Mesopotamian goddess Ninsun, legendary mother of Gilgamesh.

mankind below the human level. Clearly, those civilizations, with all their outward sophistication and refinement, were plunged in a deep confusion of spirit. Magical and orgiastic rites flowed naturally from such an unharmonious vision of nature.

The Jewish vision of God was totally out of tune with the ideas of the pagan world. One God, invisible, supreme, without life or death, without passion or lust. From this there came an idea of unity and order. Man had a power of choice: Progress, not repetition, was the law of life. Man was not the helpless victim of a natural cycle. His life was not simply tied to a wheel going round and

THE CONQUEST OF CANAAN

The Bible conveys the unmistakable impression that the Exodus from Egypt was a mass movement. Barely more than a year after leaving the land of the Pharaohs, the Israelites are said to have numbered more than 600,000 men of fighting age—that is, at least twenty years old. With such an army, what had the Israelites to fear from any Egyptian garrisons in Sinai or from the Canaanite city-states that lay ahead of them? And yet the spies sent to search out Canaan trembled at the thought of the battles awaiting them:

And they brought up an evil report of the land which they had searched unto the children of Israel, saying, The land, through which we have gone to search it, is a land that eateth up the inhabitants thereof; and all the people that we saw in it are men of a great stature.

And there we saw the giants, the sons of Anak, which come of the giants: and we were in our own sight as grasshoppers, and so we were in their sight.

And all the congregation lifted up their voice, and cried, and the people wept that night.
(Numbers 13:32–14:1)

Female as well as male deities filled the ancient pantheon. This temple, built at Dandara, in Egypt, about 2,000 years ago, was one of many honoring Hathor, goddess of love and gaiety.

Even if we assume that the "Anakim" really were giants, or that the children of Israel had been utterly demoralized by their years of bondage, the Biblical census is difficult to reconcile with other elements of the historical record. According to that tradition Israel's fighting force at the time of the Exodus would have been almost as large as the mass influx of refugees that brought more than 680,000 Jewish immigrants to the new State of Israel between May 1948 and December 1951. The modern "Mass Immigration," of course, was not limited to men. If the census that, according to the Bible, God commanded Moses to make had likewise included women and children, along with the Levites, whose sons were not numbered among the warriors but were appointed instead to minister to the tabernacle, the total Hebrew population would have exceeded 2 million! This is a staggering figure, especially in view of the estimate by modern-day demographers that Egypt's entire population

during the second millennium B.C.E. cannot have been more than 3 million.

It is scarcely conceivable that a mass movement on a scale consistent with the Biblical account could have escaped the notice of other ancient observers. Nevertheless, we must face the fact that the only mention during the thirteenth century B.C.E. of the children of Israel in a non-Biblical text describes not an endless march of refugees from Egypt but an alleged military victory over the Israelites by the successor to Rameses II, the Pharaoh Merneptah.

Israel lies desolate; its seed is no more. . . .
All the lands in their entirety are at peace,
Everyone who was a nomad has been curbed by
   King Merneptah.

Considerations such as these have led critical scholars to conclude that the number of Israelites who left Egypt was closer to 25,000 than to 2.5 million.

The smaller figure is also in keeping with the route they followed. Of all the places the children of Israel traversed in the Sinai, only Kadesh-Barnea, on the border with Canaan, has been positively identified. At this oasis, situated about forty-six miles south of Beersheba, the Israelites camped after receiving the Law at Mount Sinai (Horeb). In this region died Moses' sister Miriam and brother Aaron, and it is here that, according to the Bible, Moses committed his act of disobedience: In a moment of anger he struck a rock in order to draw water from it—for which God forbade him to enter the Promised Land. Here also the spies dispatched to search out Canaan gave their fainthearted and fearful report. A mass migration of Israelites might have advanced out of Goshen, crossed the Red Sea—which some scholars

---

One artifact from the Hittite civilization whose power extended from Anatolia through Asia Minor into Syria and Babylon: a stone bas-relief.

locate at Suez or at the Great Bitter Lake (Al-Buhayrah al-Murrah al-Kubra), dividing Sinai from Egypt proper. Other commentators, citing "Red Sea" as an ancient mistranslation of "Sea of Reeds," identify it as a Mediterranean marshland in the northern Sinai.

From the sea-crossing the Israelites headed eastward to Kadesh-Barnea, which lay astride the "King's Way," an important caravan route through the desert. It is evident that the route followed by the Israelites was very circuitous. A small army of Israelites would have been anxious to avoid Egyptian strongholds, and there is new evidence, uncovered during the 1970s, that a large Egyptian community flourished in the Gaza Strip in the time of Rameses II. The argument that the Exodus involved tens (rather than hundreds) of thousands of Israelites also helps explain why other cultures found it so

---

The practice of erecting sacred stones, as (according to the Bible) Jacob did, was not confined to the ancient Hebrews. These pillars were unearthed at Hazor, a town in the Upper Galilee that served as an important Canaanite commercial center.

easy to overlook them amid the dramatic up-heavals in the Mediterranean region at this time.

Between 2000 and 1000 B.C.E.—roughly, from the time of Abraham to the reign of David—the earth's population nearly doubled, from about 27 million to 50 million. Of this increase, Asia and Europe accounted for a disproportionate share, with the bulk of European population growth concentrated in the Mediterranean region.

The centers of civilization that had emerged by 2000 B.C.E. remained in the forefront of human development, but each of these underwent significant changes that were paralleled in newer urban centers.

By the time of the Exodus, the Hittites—whose Indo-European forebears had first settled in Anatolia during the third millennium B.C.E.—had long been a major power in the Near East. Highly regarded as metalworkers, the Hittites may have been the first to use iron, although for ornamental purposes rather than for tools or weaponry. They were also innovators in the field of law, and some scholars believe that the Biblical covenants are modeled on Hittite treaties. Over the centuries the Hittites extended their control through Asia Minor and into Syria. In the sixteenth century B.C.E., during the reign of the Hittite King Mursilis I, Babylon was sacked and the Hammurabi dynasty toppled. Unable to consolidate their hold over Mesopotamia and blocked along the Mediterranean by Egypt's imperial ambitions, the Hitties vanished from history about 1200 B.C.E., their cities burned by invaders whom Egyptian records call the Sea Peoples. Not only did the Sea Peoples obliterate the empire of the Hittites, but they also launched debilitating attacks on Egypt during the reigns of the Pharaohs Merneptah (c. 1220) and Rameses III (c. 1180), captured Cyprus, and occupied Canaan's southern Mediterranean flank at a time when the Israelites were

infiltrating the hill country. Indeed, by distracting and weakening Egypt during this period, the Sea Peoples unwittingly aided the Hebrew conquest of Canaan, many of whose city-states were vassals to the Pharaohs.

Historians differ on the question whether, amid the convulsions of the Mediterranean world, the Israelite takeover in Canaan was partial, gradual, and steady, or total, bloody, and swift. At one point the Bible plainly conveys the latter impression:

So Joshua took the whole land, according to all that the Lord said unto Moses; and Joshua gave it for an inheritance unto Israel according to their divisions by their tribes. And the land rested from war.

(Joshua 11:23)

The Bible goes on to list no fewer than thirty-one kings whom Joshua and the children of Israel are said to have conquered. Among those mentioned is the "king of Hazor," a listing supported by archaeological excavations conducted during 1955–58 and 1968 under the direction of Yigael Yadin. At Hazor, about nine miles north of the Sea of Galilee, Yadin and his colleagues found the remnants of a Late Bronze Age city that had been destroyed in the late thirteenth century B.C.E.—that is, in the probable time of Joshua.

But this cannot be the whole story, for subsequent Biblical passages acknowledge that the conquest was not complete:

Now Joshua was old and stricken in years; and the Lord said unto him, Thou art old and stricken in years, and there remaineth yet very much land to be possessed.

(Joshua 13:1)

The modern view is that the Israelite conquest of Canaan did not take place entirely within the lifetime of Joshua but was a continuous process, extending over some 200

Another remnant of the great ancient civilization of the Hittites. This artifact is a libation vessel and dates from about 1800 B.C.E.

years—the period of the Judges—and involving both peaceful settlement and military conflict.

Thus, twelfth-century Canaan presents a patchwork pattern. Along the Mediterranean coast are the Phoenicians (whom the Bible calls Sidonians) in the north and the Philistines in the south. Inland, to the north, east, and south of Canaan, are other Biblical tribes and peoples—Aramites, Ammonites, Moabites. In the interior, on both sides of the Jordan River, are the children of Israel, arrayed in a league of twelve tribes and dwelling alongside Canaanite city-states (including Megiddo, Beth-shean, and Jebus, later the site of Jerusalem) that the Israelites are not yet powerful enough to capture. By tradition, all twelve tribes descended from the sons and grandsons of Jacob, were together enslaved in Egypt and entered the Promised Land as one body. Modern scholars believe that the separate tribes penetrated Canaan at

The Ark of the Covenant had been lost for more than a millennium when this third-century carving was made. But the essential idea of the covenant has never been lost: a mutually binding relationship between God and humankind.

various times in various places and that some of the tribes were already settled as a confederacy in Canaan when Joshua led the remaining tribes across the Jordan.

According to the Bible, the Israelite invaders carried with them the Ark of the Covenant, an acacia-wood box measuring about 4 feet long, 2½ feet wide, and 2½ feet high. Covered with gold both inside and out, the Ark was "defended" by two golden cherubim, poised at either end with wings outstretched. When the Israelites encamped, the Ark was lodged within a richly decorated tabernacle that was itself protected by a tent of ram and goat skins and guarded by Levites. When the Israelites marched, the Ark marched with them, supported on two wooden staves that slipped through four gold rings attached to its feet, two on each side. After Joshua settled at Shiloh, the Ark resided there, too, but even then it was often carried into battle. On one such occasion, near Eben-Ezer, the Ark fell into the clutches of the Philistines, but to them, the Bible tells us, it brought only evil; when they installed it in their temple at Ashdod, their chief god Dagon toppled from his pedestal and was shattered. Eventually, David brought the

Ark to Jerusalem, where it was later housed in Solomon's Temple, within the Holy of Holies, the most sacred of all Jewish shrines. But the Bible makes scant mention of the Ark thereafter, and by the time of the prophets it seems to have been lost. Thus, we know neither the ultimate fate of the Ark nor the exact nature of its contents. However the early Israelites conceived the Ark of the Covenant when they settled in Canaan, what was contained in that sacred chest was an essential idea, a covenant, the agreement that defined the responsibilities of human beings and their relationship with God. It was a mutual relationship. If they would fulfill His commandments, He would protect and sustain them. This voluntary moral obligation, freely accepted, was the only factor that gave the tribes of Israel any unity at all.

They would have need of unity if they were to survive. They were surrounded on every side by skilled warriors and by kings of undisputed authority. Against that constant danger, the tribes of Israel presented a picture of total disarray. They had developed as a people without any permanent central authority. The only authority they recognized was the superhuman authority of the God who had given them the choice between good and evil. The handicap arising from the lack of permanent central authority was compounded by their talent for free expression, dissension, and complaint—a talent they had brilliantly developed during the years of their wandering in the wilderness. Moreover, the early Israelites in Canaan often expressed that talent in intertribal animosities of the kind that can arise only between people who are close to each other in their views. There is no argument like a family argument.

There they were, settled in Canaan, a people among peoples, very prone to quarreling among themselves, threatened on every side, striving to preserve their ideas and ideals, tenacious in the presentation of their separateness. For the whole of this period of some 200 years, the Israelites recoiled from any attempt to establish a unified central state. In time of crisis a leader—called a *shofet*, or judge—would arise, a leader inspired, as the Bible tells us, by "the spirit of the Lord." He would champion the cause of all the tribes or lead them into battle. But the judge was in no sense a king. His authority rested exclusively on his personal qualities. We could say "his or her" personal qualities, for one of the first of these charismatic leaders was a woman, Deborah, the wife of Lapidoth. We are told that it was Deborah who summoned Barak—the name means "lightning" in Hebrew—to lead an army of the northern tribes against the Canaanite King Jabin. In this battle, which took place sometime in the twelfth century B.C.E. and marked

Base of one of the many obelisks erected by order of Thutmose III, Pharaoh in the fifteenth century B.C.E. The dominant figure in Egypt during the first half of his reign was not Thutmose himself but his mother-in-law, Hatshepsut, who ruled as queen for about two decades. Women generally enjoyed higher status for a longer period of time in Egypt than elsewhere in the Biblical world.

The ancient Israelites, having been seminomads, herders, and slaves, knew of agriculture only what they could learn from those who had settled the land before them. Inevitably, these lessons included worship of a fertility goddess—a practice as intrinsic to ancient agriculture in the Fertile Crescent as the use of plow and seed.

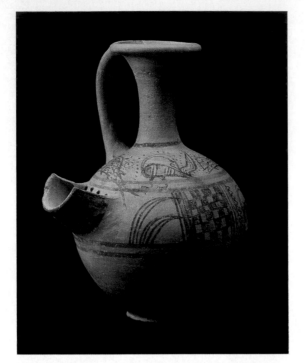

The Philistines were among the Sea Peoples, who, during the twelfth century B.C.E., invaded Egypt and settled along Israel's Mediterranean shore. Although the Israelites disparaged and despised them, the Philistines were not barbarians but skilled craftsmen, as this decorated vessel shows.

the decline of Canaanite military power, Jabin's army held the advantage in both manpower and weaponry. But along the muddy banks of the swollen Kishon and in the wooded hills of Galilee, the Canaanites' iron chariots proved useless, and the children of Israel turned their tactical superiority into a triumph.

We are not sure of Deborah's tribal affiliation. More important, in any case, is the Bible's portrayal of her as a *national* leader, providing both spiritual and military authority in a time of national crisis.

How unusual was it for a woman to assume national leadership? Rule by a woman was rare but not unprecedented in the an-

cient world. In particular, during the early fifteenth century B.C.E.—at a time when we may assume that Hebrews were in Egypt—Hatshepsut, the widow of Thutmose II, ruled as Pharaoh during the childhood of her successor, Thutmose III. Generally speaking, women enjoyed a higher status for a longer period of time in Egypt than elsewhere in the Biblical world, exercising full rights of inheritance as early as the middle of the third millennium B.C.E. Among the Sumerians and the Hittites, on the other hand, it appears that the status of women actually declined, a development that some commentators attribute to the increasing involvement of men in pastoral pursuits that had formerly been the province of women. There was a concomitant rise in the power of male deities, displacing fertility goddesses in worship.

Deborah was not the only Israelite woman to hold a position of power during the Biblical period. Moses' sister Miriam was a prophetess, as was Huldah, who prophesied in the Kingdom of Judah in the seventh century B.C.E., during the reign of Josiah. Yet it is unquestionably true that women held subordinate status in public and religious life. No females served in the priesthood, though they were permitted to take part along with men in Temple services. The monarchy, established about 1020 B.C.E., passed directly from father to son. In Roman times, rabbinic authorities would associate women of power —for example, King Ahab's queen Jezebel (d. 841 B.C.E.) and daughter Athaliah (d. 836 B.C.E.)—with immorality and disorder. As late as the twelfth century C.E., we find Maimonides counseling against the appointment of women to communal office.

In domestic life the situation was more complex. The Book of Proverbs, traditionally credited to Solomon but not actually compiled until at least two centuries after his death, concludes with a famous poem in praise of the "virtuous housewife":

This portrait of David, with crown and lyre, echoes the traditional depiction of the Israelite monarch in illuminated Hebrew manuscripts.

David Presenting the Head of Goliath to King Saul, by Rembrandt. In the figure of David, the vigorous young warrior, blooms the springtime of Israel, a hero in whom Europeans 2,500 years later would see their own hopes renewed.

The anointing of David by Samuel, depicted in the frescoes of Dura-Europos. The term Messiah, so pivotal in later Jewish and Christian history, is from the Hebrew word _maschiach_, which means the "anointed one."

Who can find a virtuous woman? for her price is far above rubies.

(Proverbs 31:10)

Elsewhere, however, the Bible is much more explicit about the value of a woman:

When a man explicitly vows to the Lord the equivalent for a human being, the following scale shall apply: If it is a male from twenty to sixty years of age, the equivalent is fifty shekels of silver by the sanctuary weight; if it is a female, the equivalent is thirty shekels.

(Leviticus 27:2–4)

Much is said in the Book of Proverbs concerning the womanly adornments of wisdom, kindness, piety, and devotion. But let us confine ourselves, for the purposes of social history, to the list of chores and responsibilities the poem attributes to the mistress of what is obviously, for Biblical times, a well-to-do household:

She seeketh wool, and flax, and worketh
  willingly with her hands . . .
She riseth also while it is yet night, and
  giveth meat to her household, and a
  portion to her maidens.
She considereth a field, and buyeth it; with
  the fruit of her hands she planteth a
  vineyard . . .
She perceiveth that her merchandise is
  good; her candle goeth not out by night.
She layeth her hands to the spindle, and her
  hands hold the distaff . . .
She maketh herself coverings of tapestry;
  her clothing is silk and purple . . .
She maketh fine linen, and selleth it; and
  delivereth girdles unto the merchant . . .
She looketh well to the ways of her
  household, and eateth not the bread of
  idleness.

(Proverbs 31:13–27)

Cook, seamstress, businesswoman, artful consumer—her special province is household management, and the praises of her husband and children are her special reward:

Her children arise up, and call her blessed; her husband also, and he praiseth her.

(Proverbs 31:28)

She not only occupied a place of honor in the household; she also shared equally in the moral responsibilities of Judaism. The covenant of Israel was equally binding on men and women though their religious obligations differed; and the penalties for moral and spiritual transgressions—notably adultery, idolatry, and apostasy—were equally severe.

Yet women also suffered from a burden of inequality under Jewish law, a burden that represents, in part, the Jewish inheritance from most other civilizations of the Biblical world. According to the Bible, a man was almost completely free to divorce his wife and dismiss her from his household, but a woman was not permitted to divorce her husband and send him away. (In Sumer a husband wanting to divorce his wife had only to say "You are not my wife," pay her half a mina of silver, and order her to leave.) To pay a debt, a man could sell his daughter, but not his son, into bondage. In custom, too, women held a subordinate role. Neither boys nor girls went to school during the Biblical period, for the Israelites had no formal schooling; much Jewish learning was passed down orally, but what literacy there was, was almost certainly confined to men. In Roman times and for centuries thereafter, learned Jewish women were rare. The rabbis were in general agreement that a woman was not required to study Torah, and a few learned men were openly hostile to the idea. "Whoever teaches his daughter Torah," said one rabbi, "teaches her lasciviousness." A legacy such as this, extending back even before Sinai, makes the achievement of Deborah—the lone woman among the Judges—all the more remarkable.

The deeds recounted in the Book of Judges, spanning the two centuries from the death of Joshua to the election of Saul, are a beguiling blend of history and legend, philosophy and folktale. Among the Judges are some of the Bible's most heroic and most tragic figures. There is Gideon, born to the tribe of Manasseh, leading a force of only 300 men, equipped with trumpets, pitchers, and torches, in a successful nocturnal assault on the camel-riding Bedouin marauders called Midianites. There is Jephthah, driven from bastardy to banditry, who before making war on the Ammonites pledges to sacrifice to the Lord, should he be the victor, "whatsoever cometh forth of the doors of my house to meet me." Jephthah then has to sacrifice his only child—his daughter, who comes out to greet him "with timbrels and with dances." And of course there is Samson, son of the tribe of Dan, who couples earthy appetites with superhuman strength. His triumphs— which include slaying a lion barehanded, slaughtering 1,000 Philistines with the jawbone of an ass, and after his betrayal by Delilah, pulling down the pillars of a Philistine temple, thereby entombing himself and 3,000 worshipers of Dagon—have been retold and reinterpreted time and time again throughout the history of Western art and literature.

Amid these tall tales and martial exploits, a distinctive vision of history emerges. After a period of piety and tranquility, the children of Israel begin to follow false gods. The Lord punishes their transgressions by sending foreign warriors to oppress them. When the Israelites repent and call upon the Lord for deliverance, He sends a hero—the *shofet*—to their rescue. The oppressor is overthrown, and peace is restored to the land. This lasts until the cycle of apostasy, oppression, repentance, and deliverance repeats itself. Underlying this vision of history we see the uncertainties of life in Canaan during the twelfth and eleventh centuries B.C.E. as waves of migration from west, north, and east send new peoples into Palestine while the Israelite tribes, in league together, strug-

A magnificent silk rug crafted in central Persia around 1850 matches the opulence of the meeting between Solomon and the Queen of Sheba. Along the top and sides the weaver has arrayed the symbols of the twelve tribes of Israel.

gle to take command of the lands they were allotted in Joshua's time.

The league survived for nearly 200 years. In all this period, Israel made no move to create a unified central state. As for monarchy, the prevailing rule in Canaan, the very idea seems to have been anathema to the Israelites. The Lord alone reigns over all His

The building of Solomon's Temple, as envisioned by an eighteenth-century Dutch engraver. For this great enterprise, Solomon imported masons and architects from Tyre, who drew upon Phoenician and Canaanite models for their inspiration.

A sacrificial altar found at Megiddo, an ancient Canaanite and Israelite city-state that, in two of its many incarnations, was destroyed by the Hyksos and fortified by Solomon.

people and saves them through His charismatic representatives.

It is also evident from the Biblical narrative that the Israelites were not immune to cultural influence from their neighbors. A seminomadic people that had no agriculture, no architecture, and no political system had little choice but to adopt and modify the institutions of others. During the settlement period and after, the idols that lured the children of Israel were the gods of Canaan. Equally widespread—and one of the greatest

temptations to which the Israelites succumbed—was worship of Asherah, the goddess of fertility. Canaanite cults were so pervasive that only ethnic animosities and territorial rivalries between Canaanites and Israelites may have preserved the children of Israel in their historical uniqueness. Another factor was the revulsion of charismatic Israelite leaders from Canaanite cults. Because the Israelites never wholly conquered Canaan but remained eternally at sword's point with their fellow Semites, there remained a cultural distance between them and the other peoples of Canaan. A total victory, and universal peace in the land, might have caused them to become more fully absorbed by the Canaanite civilization, as were the Philistines.

THE KINGDOM OF ISRAEL

During the reigns of David and Solomon, from about 1,000 to 922 B.C.E., the United Kingdom of Israel was the most powerful and prosperous state in the eastern Mediterranean. Within the limit of a century, Israel not only transformed itself from a tribal to a monarchal society but also came to exercise sovereignty from the Euphrates river in Syria to the Brook of Egypt (Wadi el-Arish) in northern Sinai. The kingdoms of Aram-Cobah and Aram-Damascus in the north and of Ammon, Moab, and Edom to the east and south, all conquered by David, paid tribute to the Israelite monarchy and in some cases had Israelite governors. Israel's sphere of influence encompassed the coastal domain of the Philistines, whose city-states became vassals to the Israelite monarch. With the Phoenicians, David established and Solomon expanded an important commercial alliance. Nevertheless, this period of Israelite hegemony did not outlast Solomon. The United Kingdom was shattered by his death. The next two centuries witnessed the decline of the divided kingdoms of Israel and Judah. It was during this latter period of disunity and disorder that the prophets preserved and refined the authentic voice of Judaism.

The events that inspired the Israelites to transform their tribal league into a hereditary monarchy were the Philistines' capture of the Ark of the Covenant at Eben-Ezer and their destruction of Shiloh. Biblical antagonism to-

ward the Philistines survives in the term's modern meaning: a "philistine" is a person ignorant of, or smugly hostile to, culture. The fact is, however, that outside the fields of theology and ethics, the cultural accomplishments of the Philistines were markedly superior to those of the Israelites. Though not very numerous, the Philistines were well organized in a federation of five city-states, the Pentapolis. They had mastered the use of iron, not only for chariots, shields, and swords but also for heavy-duty tools such as the iron-tipped plow. This technology they jealously guarded.

High-prowed Philistine ships plied Mediterranean waters, and camel caravans provided the commercial links between Philistia and Mesopotamia.

Thus the Philistines—whom the Bible disparages as "uncircumcised"—posed an economic as well as a military threat to the

This carved ivory cherub decorated King Ahab's palace at Samaria in the ninth century B.C.E. Note the wings, face, and animal torso, evidence of the incorporation of Near Eastern polytheistic motifs.

This sculpture, showing Semitic features, probably dates from the second millennium B.C.E.

Eclectic in religion, inventive in weaponry, and efficient in administration, the Assyrians, by the seventh century B.C.E., had established the greatest empire the Near East had yet known.

Israelite tribes, who by 1020 B.C.E. were in sad disarray. The tribe of Dan had been pushed off its lands, the holdings of Judah were threatened, and the Negev was under Philistine control. There were no longer any tribal judges, but only the aging Samuel, who followed an annual circuit from Ramah to Gilgal, Beth-el, Mizpeh, and back to Ramah, across the lands of Ephraim and Benjamin in central Israel. Samuel made his two sons judges at Beersheba—an attempt at hereditary theocracy; but, as the Bible tells us, his sons were corrupt, and the remaining tribal leaders sought to impress upon Samuel the need for political reform:

Then all the elders of Israel gathered themselves together, and came to Samuel unto Ramah,

And said unto him, Behold, thou art old, and thy sons walk not in thy ways: now make us a king to judge us like all the nations.

(I Samuel 8:4–5)

Samuel resists their demand, sternly and presciently warning them:

This will be the manner of the king that shall reign over you: He will take your sons, and appoint them for himself; for his chariots, and to be his horsemen . . .

And he will take your daughters to be confectionaries, and to be cooks, and to be bakers.

And he will take your fields, and your vineyards, and your oliveyards, even the best of them, and give them to his servants.

And he will take the tenth of your seed, and of your vineyards, and give to his officers, and to his servants.

And he will take your menservants, and your maidservants, and your goodliest young men, and your asses, and put them to his work.

He will take the tenth of your sheep: and ye shall be his servants.

And ye shall cry out in that day because of the king which ye shall have chosen; and the Lord will not hear you in that day.

(I Samuel 8:11–18)

There are many traditions in the Bible about the means by which Saul the son of Kish became king of Israel. There is no reason to doubt that he was, as the Bible tells us, tall, handsome, courageous, modest, but emotionally volatile. Samuel did not fade from view during the early years of Saul's kingship; instead, he remained to convey to Saul what the Lord required the king to do. Samuel's break with Saul and his revocation of that kingship came as a result of Saul's failure to carry out the command to destroy the Amalekites utterly, slaying "both man and woman, infant and suckling, ox and sheep, camel and ass" (I Samuel 15:3). Samuel's fury at Saul's willingness to spare Agag, king of the Amalekites, and the best of their livestock, can be seen, of course, as the appropriate consequence of Saul's departure from the word of God. But it can also be considered as evidence of a monarch seeking to expand his powers at the expense of the old order. Be that as it may, Samuel's rejection of Saul forms one of the most tragic moments in the history of ancient Israel.

And Samuel came no more to see Saul until the day of his death; nevertheless Samuel mourned for Saul: and the Lord repented that He had made Saul king over Israel.

(I Samuel 15:35)

The subsequent history of Saul's reign, which lasted no more than twenty years, recounts his descent into melancholy and terror, along with his love and later his jealousy of a young shepherd, minstrel, and soldier—David, the son of Jesse of Bethlehem.

We know so much of David's life from the Bible that it sometimes seems as if there were not just one David but many: the warrior who topples the Philistine giant Goliath with a slingshot, the singer whose music has the power to ease Saul's fits of depression, the best friend of Saul's son Jonathan and husband of Saul's daughter Michal, the fugitive and rebel who flees Saul's anger to ally himself temporarily with the enemies of Israel, the anointed king who unifies the Israelites and establishes his new capital at Jerusalem, thenceforward to be honored as the City of David. Thus blooms the springtime of Israel, personified by the monarch in whom the artists of the Renaissance would portray the rebirth of Europe's own hopes and to whom modern Hebrew writers would likewise turn for inspiration.

Such a breathless and incomplete summary of David's accomplishments and influence barely hints at his centrality to Jewish history and Jewish thought. Though no claims of divinity attached to David, the be-

lief developed, probably within his own lifetime, that he enjoyed God's special blessing and that his dynasty would forever endure:

Now therefore so shalt thou say unto My servant David, Thus saith the Lord of hosts, I took thee from the sheepcote, from following the sheep, to be ruler over My people, over Israel. . . .

And when thy days be fulfilled, and thou shalt sleep with thy fathers, I will set up thy seed after thee . . .

And thine house and thy kingdom shall be established for ever before thee: thy throne shall be established for ever.

According to all these words, and according to all this vision, so did Nathan speak unto David.

(II Samuel 7:8, 12, 16–17)

Centuries later, after the division of the kingdom and the downfall of David's empire, this prophecy evolved into the belief that, in time, the House of David and the glory of Jerusalem would be reestablished:

In that day will I raise up the tabernacle of David that is fallen, and close up the breaches thereof; and I will raise up his ruins, and I will build it as in the days of old.

(Amos 9:11)

This view of Davidic rule as a golden age for Israel would undergo a further transformation as the Hebrew prophets envisioned a future monarch—an anointed one, or *maschiach*, the Hebrew word for Messiah—whom God would send to rescue Israel from adversity and bring peace and justice to the world.

Thus, the seeds of messianism lay in the reign of David. But the Israelites did not regard the Davidic period as an unapproachable ideal; rather, they saw it as a pattern for an even greater glory to come. By the first century C.E. the idea was widespread among the Jews of Palestine that the Messiah, the redeemer of Israel, would be a direct descendant of David. This was, of course, one of the claims made for Jesus of Nazareth by the early Christians, who sought to link Jesus with David both figuratively and genealogically. David also held a place of honor in Christian Europe as the supreme example of a poet, warrior, and king: Charlemagne, we are told, wanted his courtiers to call him the "new David." European Christians continued to exalt David even as they turned with increasing fury against the Jews of their own era. We can, if we like, imagine two groups of worshipers, Jewish and Christian, tragically divided, gathering separately to hear or sing this same Psalm of David:

The Lord is my shepherd, I shall not want.
　He maketh me to lie down in green pastures; He leadeth me beside the still waters.
　He restoreth my soul; He leadeth me in the paths of righteousness for His name's sake.
　Yea, though I walk through the valley of the shadow of death, I will fear no evil: for Thou art with me; Thy rod and Thy staff they comfort me.
　Thou preparest a table before me in the presence of mine enemies; Thou anointest my head with oil; my cup runneth over.
　Surely goodness and mercy shall follow me all the days of my life: and I will dwell in the house of the Lord for ever.

(Psalm 23)

Many of the Psalms could not have been written by David. But there is something unique about a tradition that expresses admiration for a national hero by awarding him the authorship of poetry some of which was written nearly a thousand years after his death. There is no question, however, about David's historical role. In Jerusalem—*his* city —he established the central authority of the monarchy and brought the twelve quarrelsome tribes into a new unity under a strong government. With that unity, Israel entered the mainstream of civilization for the first time. The Israelites were no longer living on the fringes of other people's civilizations. They were dwelling in cities; they had their own government; and they controlled a vital link in the chain of commerce in the Middle East, a section of the Via Maris.

Israel's transformation from confederacy to monarchy, from enclave to empire, brought with it a series of administrative reforms modeled on Egyptian and Canaanite practice. David commanded his own professional army, as well as an elite corps of personal guards; also at the service of the state was an army of foreign mercenaries. The two chief priests, Zadok and Abiathar, were members of David's "cabinet," and the Ark of the Covenant was housed in an official government shrine. David's most significant administrative reform was the transfer of the capital from Hebron—where he had reigned as king of Judah in the shadow of Philistine power— to Jerusalem. For David the city had obvious territorial and political advantages. It was centrally located and unencumbered by tribal claims. This meant that in establishing his royal court at Jerusalem, David could not be charged with favoring one tribe over another, but it also meant that there was no established tribal elite to check the growth of monarchal power. In Jerusalem, David maintained a household of some 2,000 people— including family, attendants, bureaucrats, soldiers, Levites, and priests—whose primary loyalty was to him and, through him, to God.

The vicinity of Jerusalem had been settled for at least 2,000 years prior to David's arrival. The earliest known urban settlements, probably from the late fourth millennium B.C.E., were on the eastern flank of a ridge (known as Zion) extending southward from what we now call the Temple Mount and overlooking the Valley of Kidron to the east, the Vale of Hinnom to the south, and the

Tyropoeon Valley to the west. By the eleventh century B.C.E., Jerusalem (then called Jebus) was the home of a people known to the Bible as the Jebusites. This rather obscure group may have migrated from Anatolia and northern Syria after the breakup of the Hittite empire. It is from them that David wrested Jerusalem sometime between 1000 and 990 B.C.E. David built a magnificent palace, for which not only the building materials but also the workmen, and, presumably, the design, came from Tyre (Sur), the chief city of the Phoenicians (II Samuel 5:11).

Side by side with this worldly growth there was also the continuation of a profoundly spiritual culture. No matter how powerful David had become, he was not exempt from that higher authority symbolized by the Ark of the Covenant, which he had brought to Jerusalem. For king and commoner alike there was that nagging differentiation between good and evil, between right and wrong, which had been placed upon the children of Israel ever since Moses received the Law in Sinai. At a time when it was not uncommon among other peoples for criticism to be punished by death, the prophets of Israel exercised their right to call even the nation's king to account for moral transgressions.

This is the right upheld in the otherwise sordid story of David and Bathsheba. Walking one evening on the roof of his palace, the king spies the beautiful Bathsheba bathing herself while her husband, Uriah the Hittite, is off fighting against the Ammonites on David's behalf. The king orders Bathsheba brought to his palace, impregnates her, and then arranges to have Uriah sent to the "forefront of the hottest battle," where his comrades are to leave him to die at the hands of the enemy (II Samuel 11:15).

This successful strategy for augmenting one's harem, increasing one's heirs, and eliminating a source of scandal and disgruntlement would not have come as a shock to any of the monarchs of David's time. But what would have astounded them was the sternness with which Nathan, the court prophet, rebuked David for violating the laws of Israel, and the meekness with which the great king accepted the prophet's judgment:

And David said unto Nathan, I have sinned against the Lord.

(II Samuel 12:13)

Nathan was among the first to challenge the institution of the monarchy. In Jewish tradition, the king was not divine: he could not place himself above the law. The law had been given to Israel by a Supreme King and had to be obeyed by all. The prophet saw himself as a divine messenger speaking the truth of the Lord, as if in a blast from heaven.

This was a time when the truth that had been revealed to the early Israelites was under challenge. The Israelites had now become a nation among the nations. They were involved in international commerce. Merchants and traders from other lands traveled among them and practiced their religions. By now the Jews were in touch with other cultures. As in many future ages, their legacy, their central belief, had to be strengthened; it had to be protected against the foreign influences by which the Jews were surrounded. The prophet's anger was directed against any erosion of the prescribed behavior that gave the Jews their identity. But the prophet raised his voice against specific transgressions, sins, and derelictions. He was not yet concerned with general principles of morality.

Although David laid plans for a Temple in Jerusalem, the honor of building it fell to his successor, Solomon, his second son by Bathsheba, whom he had married. The first, adulterously conceived, had died in infancy. If we accept the traditional date of 960 B.C.E. for the inauguration of Solomon's reign, then, according to the Biblical record, construction of the Temple took from about 957 to 950 B.C.E. Essential to this enterprise was Solomon's continuation of David's alliance with Tyre, for just as Phoenician materials and technology were employed in the construction of David's palace, so King Hiram of Tyre supplied—for a price—the builders, the masons, the famed "cedars of Lebanon," and other commodities for the Temple.

To what extent should these architectural borrowings be taken as evidence of a deeper bond between the religions of the Canaanites and Phoenicians and the religion of Israel? The differences in religious *belief* should be plain enough by this point, and there were also significant divergences in religious *practice:* Israel was strictly and explicitly forbidden to worship its deity in the form of an image, and human sacrifice, cult prostitution, and orgiastic fertility rites were likewise excluded. But we should not blind ourselves to the ways in which ancient Israelite worship more closely resembles Canaanite practice than it does the Jewish religion since Roman times.

The most obvious borrowing—and the most striking divergence from later Jewish practice—is the sacrificial rite, highly developed at least since Sumerian times. The Temple sacrifice was the center of state religion in the age of Solomon and remained so as long as the Temple stood in Jerusalem. It was carried out with pomp and solemnity. At the center of the Temple ceremony stood the awe-inspiring figure of the high priest, majestic in bearing and ornately garbed. The glitter and opulence of the Temple and priesthood contrast drastically with the world of the Jews who would huddle, so many centuries later, in the wooden synagogues of Poland or the little brownstone *shuls* of New York's Lower East Side.

Solomon's Temple was the crowning glory of a building program that rivaled those of the Pharaohs. In Jerusalem, Solomon, like David before him, erected a royal palace. At Hazor, which lay along the Via Maris, he transformed a small unfortified Israelite settlement into a royal city by constructing a casemate wall and a gate with guardrooms, flanked by two towers. At Megiddo, some twenty-two miles southeast of Haifa, he established a similarly fortified administrative center on the site of a Canaanite city probably captured by David. At Gezer, given to Solomon by Egypt as a dowry for Pharaoh's daughter, the fortifications were virtually identical to those at Megiddo; this Solomonic stronghold not only commanded the approaches to Jerusalem but also solidified Solomon's hold over an important trade route from Egypt to Mesopotamia.

THE AGE OF THE PROPHETS

Solomon seemed to have given Israel a Golden Age of peace and prosperity. His ships, built and manned in large part by the Phoenicians, sailed to Arabia, East Africa, and India from Ezion-Geber on the Gulf of Elath, bringing back gold and ivory, sandalwood and precious stones, even peacocks and monkeys for the royal court. In particular, the spice trade with Arabia flourished, and when the Queen of Sheba came overland from southern Arabia to Jerusalem "with camels that bare spices, and very much gold, and precious stones" (I Kings 10:2), she may have been seeking not only Solomon's wisdom but some kind of commercial agreement. Solomon also traded in horses and chariots and undoubtedly had a share in copper production, although archaeologists have so far been unable to confirm precisely where it was mined and smelted. Dynastic marriages—with Ammonite, Edomite, Hittite, Moabite, and Phoenician princesses, as well as with Pharaoh's daughter—were de-

For Renaissance Europe, King Solomon seemed the very model of a wise and judicious monarch. This illuminated fifteenth-century Italian manuscript shows the king framed by his Temple.

A stone carving of an eagle-headed genie from the palace of Ashurnasirpal II, who extended the boundaries of the Assyrian empire to the Mediterranean and extracted tribute from the Phoenicians.

signed to add both to the glory of the court and to the stability of the kingdom.

And yet, in hindsight, we can recognize that Israel and the monarchy were grossly overextended. Israel could not produce enough wheat and oil to pay for Solomon's lavish imports. When Solomon, short of cash, ceded certain border towns to the Phoenicians, King Hiram, dissatisfied with the pledge, sent less gold to Israel's treasury than Solomon had expected. To finance his building projects and support his splendid royal household, Solomon then imposed onerous taxes on his subjects. The levy was not merely monetary: tens of thousands of Israelites were also pressed into compulsory service as burden bearers, stonecutters, and lumberjacks. The result was a growing gulf between rich and poor, and since the levies fell unequally on north and south, tensions increased between Judah and Israel. When Solomon died, sometime between 930 and 922 B.C.E., the Davidic line retained power in the Kingdom of Judah, which included the tribal lands of Judah and Benjamin; but the ten northern tribes seceded, establishing the independent Kingdom of Israel.

It is clear that there were histories written of the two kingdoms. The Bible makes sufficient references to two histories to demonstrate that such existed. But there was also a spiritual history of the people that was being fashioned. This was made by gathering oral history and some written records that referred to the times before the settling of Canaan.

There is an important reference in the Bible to the finding of a book "of the law" in the Temple of Jerusalem, during the reign of King Josiah of Judah. It seems to have been an event that made an extraordinary impression on the people and was followed by a religious revival in Judah. What it shows, almost beyond doubt, is that there was written material relating to a covenant with the Lord that was associated with a series of covenant laws. In all likelihood the book that was found was some form of the Exodus narrative.

Neither of the two kingdoms, weakened as they were by domestic quarrels and corruption, could long withstand the power of the Assyrian war machine. In the eighteenth century B.C.E., during the reign of Hammurabi, an early Assyrian empire in northern Mesopotamia had been swallowed up by Babylon. But Assyria's capital, Assur (Ashur), now identified with the Iraqi town of Qal 'at Sherqat, on the Tigris River, never lost its separate identity, whether during the period of Babylonian rule or during the unsettled centuries that followed. By the thirteenth century B.C.E., Assyria again emerged as a major power, annexing Babylon. After 1200 B.C.E., however, Assyria bogged down in a

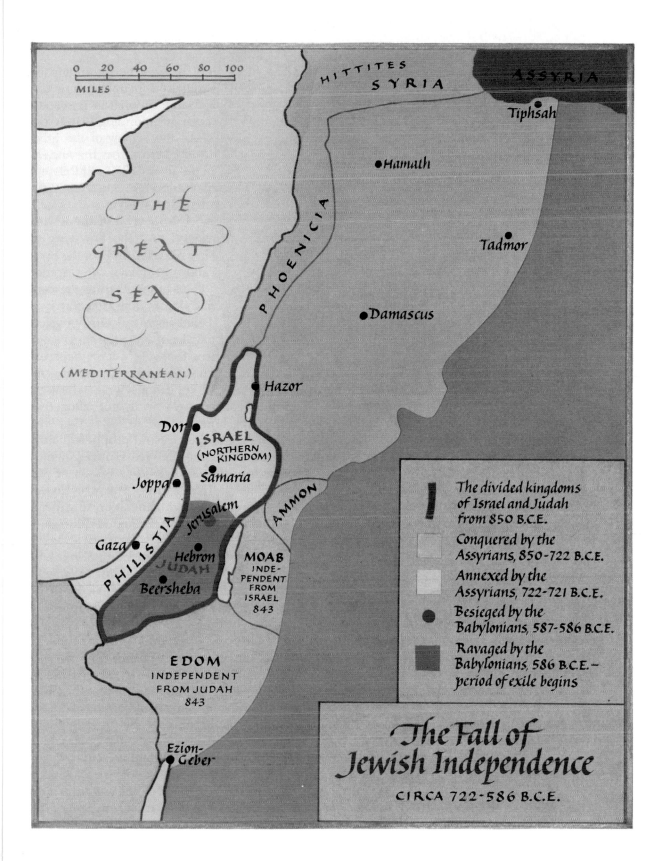

0 20 40 60 80 100
MILES

HITTITES SYRIA ASSYRIA

Tiphsah

THE GREAT SEA

(MEDITERRANEAN)

PHOENICIA

Hamath

Tadmor

Damascus

Hazor

Dor

ISRAEL (NORTHERN KINGDOM)

Joppa

Samaria

AMMON

Jerusalem

Gaza

PHILISTIA

Hebron

JUDAH

MOAB INDE-PENDENT FROM ISRAEL 843

Beersheba

EDOM
INDEPENDENT FROM JUDAH 843

Ezion-Geber

The divided kingdoms of Israel and Judah from 850 B.C.E.

Conquered by the Assyrians, 850-722 B.C.E.

Annexed by the Assyrians, 722-721 B.C.E.

Besieged by the Babylonians, 587-586 B.C.E.

Ravaged by the Babylonians, 586 B.C.E.— period of exile begins

The Fall of Jewish Independence

CIRCA 722-586 B.C.E.

And Isaiah's contemporary, Micah:

What doth the Lord require of thee, but to do justly, and to love mercy, and to walk humbly with thy God?

(Micah 6:8)

From then on, the most vehement reproaches of the prophets would concern social corruption. Micah did not hesitate to call down terrible punishment on his own people:

Hear this, I pray you, ye heads of the house of Jacob, and princes of the house of Israel, that abhor judgment, and pervert all equity. . . .

Therefore shall Zion for your sake be plowed as a field; and Jerusalem shall become heaps.

(Micah 3:9, 12)

The Assyrian invaders completely obliterated the Kingdom of Israel. Its people, henceforth to be known as the "ten lost tribes," were deported and dispersed. No book of the Bible bewails their fate, as the Book of Lamentations would mourn the subsequent destruction of the Kingdom of Judah. Smaller than the northern kingdom, less vulnerable to foreign influence, stabilized to some extent by the Davidic dynasty and the legacy of the Temple, Judah and its capital, Jerusalem, survived. During the reign of King Josiah, it even flourished for more than a century after Samaria fell.

After Josiah's death in 609 B.C.E., however, conditions in Judah deteriorated rapidly. Three years earlier, with shocking suddenness, an alliance of Babylonians, Medes, and Scythians toppled Nineveh, dealing a death blow to the Assyrian empire. Into the ensuing power vacuum rushed the armies of Babylon and Egypt, with Syria and Palestine caught in between. After Nebuchadnezzar II (Nebuchadrezzar) assumed the throne of Babylon in 604 B.C.E., the king of Judah,

Jehoiakim (r. 609–598), began paying him tribute. But when Babylon suffered a setback in its continuing war with Egypt, Jehoiakim withheld payment. Nebuchadnezzar's retaliation was brutal. Jerusalem, besieged, fell to Babylon in 597.

The end was not long in coming. Judah's new king, Zedekiah, like Jehoiakim before him, responded to a brief resurgence of Egyptian strength by renouncing ties with Babylon. This time, Nebuchadnezzar moved to stamp out Judah's resistance once and for all. On the ninth day of the month of Av in 586 B.C.E., after a year and a half of siege, the armies of Nebuchadnezzar stormed Jerusalem, looted the city, and burned its Temple and palaces. Many of Judah's leaders were executed, and much of the surviving population of Jerusalem was exiled to Babylon.

In the midst of these tumultuous and tragic times lived the prophet Jeremiah. Born about 645 B.C.E. in a village near Jerusalem, Jeremiah was the son of a priestly family who might have traced their descent to Abiathar, the priest appointed by David but later banished by Solomon for taking a rival's part in a dynastic quarrel. Jeremiah repeatedly warned Jehoiakim and Zedekiah not to turn against Babylon, but his warnings went unheeded. His prophecies brought him personal suffering, ridicule, even danger and imprisonment, yet he could not lay down the prophetic burden:

O Lord, thou hast deceived me, and I was deceived; thou art stronger than I, and hast prevailed: I am in derision daily, every one mocketh me.

For since I spake, I cried out, I cried violence and spoil; because the word of the Lord was made a reproach unto me, and a derision, daily.

(Jeremiah 20:7–8)

His anguish is profound, his sorrow limitless:

Cursed be the day wherein I was born. . . .

Wherefore came I forth out of the womb to see labor and sorrow, that my days should be consumed with shame?

(Jeremiah 20:14, 18)

Through all his sufferings, Jeremiah sometimes found rare joy in his calling:

Thy words were found, and I did eat them; and Thy word was unto me the joy and rejoicing of mine heart: for I am called by Thy name, O Lord God of hosts.

(Jeremiah 15:16)

As the corruption of the Israelites and the folly of Judah evoked from the prophets words of anger and warning, so the devastation of Zion and the exile to Babylon brought forth words of comfort, healing, and hope. These are the words of a prophet, whose message of reassurance is found in the Book of Isaiah:

I the Lord have called thee in righteousness, and will hold thine hand, and will keep thee, and give thee for a covenant of the people, for a light of the Gentiles;

To open the blind eyes, to bring out the prisoners from the prison, and them that sit in darkness out of the prison house.

(Isaiah 42:6–7)

Here now is the beginning of prophetic universalism. No longer did the prophets speak only to the children of Israel. Their preachments would now be directed to all the peoples of the earth, teaching a universal morality. And the nations, said Isaiah, would finally learn to live in peace with each other.

The Biblical texts are held to be the actual words of the prophets—three major and twelve minor—that were transmitted orally at first and later put down in writing, handed along by transmitters who considered it their sacred duty to preserve the prophecies exactly as they received them.

The temples of Judah would be burned down to the ground. The people would be deported and dispersed. But through every vicissitude an irreducible core would endure. And from the endurance of a separate people in covenant with a single God, there would come a moral and esthetic legacy for all mankind. The walls and the temples would crumble, but the words would resound forever.

CONCLUSION

In the heart of Jerusalem, it is hard to remember how many nations and kingdoms rose and fell in that city. It is by nature an area of transit. Whenever the land of the Nile and the land of the Euphrates were in conflict, the smaller states and kingdoms in the middle would be crushed by their invasions, most of the smaller nations leaving no trace behind.

This Babylonian cylinder made of clay was inscribed soon after the armies of Nebuchadnezzar had crushed Jerusalem in 586 B.C.E.

What the Jews left behind was not only the record of their kings but the ideas of their prophets. The prophetic message of the Jews is unique. In the history of mankind, there is nothing quite comparable to Hebrew prophetic literature. It is marked by originality of insight, by a great nobility of vision, and by poetic splendor of language.

By far the most revolutionary of all the prophetic ideas is the messianic idea: A day will come when human conflict and anguish will be transcended by divine grace into an era of perfect peace and harmony. We might ask if there was anything original about this idea? Did not other civilizations like those of Greece and Rome envision a golden age of peace and harmony? They did, but they all put their golden age in the past, at the beginning of history, so that all subsequent human destiny unfolds in constant descent. Perfection was in the past. Now things were what they were. This gave rise to a profoundly melancholy and pessimistic view of human destiny. Nothing could ever be quite the same as it had been. The result was nostalgia, a sense of Paradise Lost.

The Hebrews were the first and only people that saw its golden age not at the beginning of history but in the future, at the end of time, so that history unfolds forward and upward in constant ascent toward ultimate perfection.

Progress in history is a uniquely Jewish idea. It might be called the greatest contribution of the Jewish mind to other civilizations. A Roman emperor and philosopher, Marcus Aurelius (121–180 C.E.), reflecting the conventional view, spoke of human life as something tied to a wheel that goes round and round and round, back to its starting point in darkness and chaos. Human destiny is thus rather like the cycle of nature. There is birth, growth, decay, and death. Everything in the end is as it was at the beginning. The intellectual and emotional consequence is determinism. Nothing can change; nothing, therefore, is very much worthwhile.

The Hebrew messianic idea, on the other hand, is alive with a sense of hope and purpose. It is worthwhile to strive for human perfection, for social progress, for compassion, for justice, for freedom, for the protection of the poor, for universal peace. It is extraordinary that a people with such a tragic experience should have achieved such a buoyant and optimistic vision of human destiny. And the ultimate expression of that vision comes in the words of the prophet of Jerusalem who preached in Jerusalem, Isaiah, the son of Amoz:

Nation shall not lift up sword against nation, neither shall they learn war any more.

(Isaiah 2:4)

In this portrait by Rembrandt, Jeremiah mourns both for the devastation of Zion and for the "burning fire" of prophecy that will not let him rest.

These ancient pillars of Persepolis are the bleak remnants of what was once the lavish ceremonial capital of the Persian empire. The city was looted and burned by Alexander the Great in 330 B.C.E.

3. The Uses of Adversity

T HE DATE is 586 before the Christian Era. The Temple of Solomon is burned to the ground. The Land of Judah is ravaged. Thousands of its people are carried off into Babylonian exile by the armies of Nebuchadnezzar. The Jewish memory would never lose the anguish of that hour. And from year to year, from generation to generation, on the ninth day of Av, the descendants of the Jewish exiles would recite the lamentation for the departed glory of their kingdom

By all logic, the Jews should now have sunk into oblivion. But history does not always follow the voice of logic, and the Jews did not disappear, although for the next five centuries they roamed far and wide over the earth. They had learned what no other people had ever learned before—how to maintain their faith and identity away from home. They were autonomous, mobile, unfettered by territorial roots. For this very reason, exile now set the Jewish mind and spirit freer than ever before to make contact with other civilizations. Temple sacrifices could be made only in Jerusalem, but synagogues could be built anywhere, and prayer was not restricted to any single place. Exile was also a liberation in the purely religious sense.

Thus the Jewish era of universal contact begins. We shall trace the evolution of those contacts with Babylonian and Persian monarchs, with the Greeks from Alexander of Macedon and with Rome until the capture of Jerusalem by Titus and the great dramas of resistance and revolt at Masada and in the wilderness, where Bar Kokhba led his Jewish rebels in a final assertion of defiance. At the heart of this era stands the return to Jerusalem under Cyrus, the florescence of prophecy, and the rise of the Maccabees during the primacy of Greece. The interaction of Hebrew and Hellenic thought would have

The Arch of Titus was built by the emperor in Rome in 81 C.E. to commemorate the suppression of Jewish resistance in Jerusalem.

The Persians were formidable warriors, as this glazed-brick frieze from the royal city of Susa suggests. Formerly the capital of Elam, Susa (in present-day Iran) was conquered by Cyrus the Great of Persia during the sixth century B.C.E.

vast intellectual and spiritual consequences in the history of culture and faith.

After the Bar Kokhba revolt, Judea subsides into mournful silence. Jewish history, while looking back longingly to the land in which it dawned, is for the most part enacted far away, southward to the desert, eastward to the waters of the Euphrates—and westward across the Mediterranean.

OF EMPIRES AND EXILES

The history of the Near East and the Mediterranean during the three centuries after Nebuchadnezzar's destruction of Jerusalem portrays a succession of conquerors and their empires, each of which included Palestine

under its dominion. At its height under Nebuchadnezzar in the early sixth century B.C.E., the Babylonian (or Chaldean) empire extended in a great arc across Palestine, Syria, and Upper and Lower Mesopotamia, from the Mediterranean to the Persian Gulf. To the south lay the barely habitable Arabian desert; to the north and east, embracing most of Anatolia and Persia, stretched the empire of the Medes. The Persians came under Median rule about 625 B.C.E., at the beginning of the reign of Cyaxares; he had occupied the Median throne for some thirteen years when Nineveh—and with it the Assyrian empire—fell to his Babylonian allies.

Medes continued to rule Persia until the middle of the sixth century B.C.E., when the Persians rebelled under the leadership of Cyrus the Great (c. 600–530 B.C.E.). Aided by dissidents within the Median army, Cyrus overthrew the Median dynasts and began to carve out his own empire. He would reign as King of Persia from about 550 and as King of Babylon from 539. Within fifty years, the empire of Persia far exceeded the combined territories of Babylonia and Media. Cyrus's son Cambyses (r. 530–522 B.C.E.) conquered Egypt, and Cambyses's successor, Darius (r. 522–486 B.C.E.), extended the empire eastward as far as India, though his designs on Greece were thwarted in 490 at the Battle of Marathon, about twenty-two miles (35 km) northeast of Athens. Ten years later, the army of Xerxes (r. 486–465 B.C.E.) succeeded in occupying Athens, but a Greek counterattack resulted in a rout of the Persians on both land and sea. The Greek playwright Aeschylus (525–456 B.C.E.) recorded this epic encounter in *The Persians*, performed in 472.

At its peak, the Persian empire encompassed the lands we today call Turkey, Syria, Lebanon, Israel, Egypt, Iraq, and Iran, as well as much or most of Libya, Pakistan, and Afghanistan. Such a vast empire, extending all the way from the Aegean to the Hindu

Kush, posed a formidable administrative challenge; for example, Sardis, the empire's westernmost administrative center, was about 1,500 miles (2,414 km) overland from Susa, the imperial capital east of the Tigris. The Persian administrative system divided the empire into provinces (satrapies), each of which was governed by a civil official (the satrap) who served at the pleasure of the Persian king. The satrap headed his province's civil administration, commanded royal troops in his province in time of war, and collected taxes, which he then remitted to the king. Darius imposed a unified law code, built new roads, and established a postal system. Also characteristic of Persian imperial rule was the imposition of royal weights and measures, uniform gold coinage, and for official purposes a single language, Aramaic.

This Semitic tongue, closely related to Hebrew, is the language used in parts of the Bible and of certain Jewish prayers. It was the spoken tongue of the Jews of Palestine and Babylonia during the early centuries of the Common Era. Imperial standards of law, weight, value, and administrative procedure did not preclude great local diversity in language, custom, and belief. In this respect, Darius's most fitting monument was his ceremonial capital, Persepolis, whose decorative friezes carefully depict each tributary nation in a favorable light. Persepolis stood for a century and a half as testament to the Persian ideal of harmonious rule—until it was sacked and burned in 330 B.C.E., reputedly during a drunken revel, by the most extraordinary of all ancient empire builders, Alexander the Great. (In 1972 the Shah of Iran, Mohammed Pahlevi, partly recreated the ancient grandeur of Persepolis for a pompous commemorative ceremony, which made of him an international laughingstock. Some observers believe that his decline began with this occasion.)

The Persian empire, founded by Cyrus in

538 B.C.E., lasted for 200 years, and by the time it met its end at the hands of Alexander of Macedon, it had established principles of imperial government which would be reflected in the ensuing eras of Greek, Roman, and Byzantine rule. Previous empires had been held together by military government and owed no consideration at all to subject peoples or to their religious sentiments. The very success of the conquerors was held to be proof that their gods were superior to others. The Persian empire was the first that at-

With more color and grandeur than historical accuracy, this Iranian painting from the Safawid period (1502–1736) depicts the defeat of the Persian king Darius III by Alexander the Great.

PERICLES

PYTHAGORAS

HOMER

EURIPIDES

A gallery of ancient Greeks whose achievements left an indelible mark on Western culture: Homer, the epic poet presumed to be the author of the Iliad and Odyssey; Pericles (d. 429 B.C.E.), a great Athenian statesman and friend to architecture and the arts; Pythagoras (fl. sixth century B.C.E.), a philosopher and mathematician; the playwright

PLATO

SOCRATES

ARISTOTLE

Euripides (fl. fifth century B.C.E); Plato (427?–347 B.C.E.), master of the philosophical dialogue; his teacher Socrates (470? 399 B.C.E.), a tireless truth-seeker and questioner of received opinion; and Aristotle (384–322 B.C.E.), foremost of the Greek philosophers, a student of Plato's, and the tutor of Alexander the Great.

tempted to acknowledge the diversity and autonomy of conquered peoples. While the overall supremacy of the kings was paramount, the division of the empire into satrapies allowed some diversity in the treatment of subject nations. In comparison with Babylonian and Assyrian authority, Persian authority was wielded with a lenient hand, and the Jews were beneficiaries. The Persian kings were even more distinctive in their religious tolerance. Cyrus did not carry the Babylonian god Marduk into humiliating captivity to Susa or Persepolis. He actually became a worshiper of Marduk and claimed to be the divinely appointed heir of the Babylonian kings. His son Cambyses, having conquered Egypt, called himself the son of the Egyptian sun-god and founded a new dynasty of Pharaohs. This deference to the deities of other nations helps to explain why Cyrus enabled the Jews to return to Judah and to renew their religious experience, a notable contrast to their position under the intolerance of the Babylonians and Assyrians.

But Cyrus was not typical of all Persian rulers. By the time of Darius's accession in 522 B.C.E., Persia had already reverted to the imperial tradition of intolerance. When the last Jewish king, Zerubbabel, was dethroned and killed, the Davidian dynasty disappeared from history, leaving an impoverished and weak Judean community behind. It was a far cry from the "sacred nation" chosen by God to reveal the divine message to the world, as envisaged by Ezekiel and the Second Isaiah. Most of the exiles preferred the comforts of Egypt and Mesopotamia to the arid poverty of the Holy Land. In other parts of the Persian realm the Jews apprehensively watched the downfall of the Persians and the victory of Alexander.

Alexander was born in 356 B.C.E. in Macedonia, a kingdom that lay on Greece's northern frontier. Although Athens had successfully stopped the Persian advance, it never succeeded in achieving its own imperial ambitions, and for much of the fifth and fourth centuries B.C.E., the Greek city-states warred among themselves, while Persia remained on the doorstep. This stalemate was broken by Alexander's father, Philip II of Macedon (382–336 B.C.E.), a brilliant statesman and military leader who added light and heavy cavalry to his army, equipped his infantrymen with pikes twice as long as those wielded by the Greeks, and enhanced his navy with single-banked vessels that made up in speed what they lacked in size. Swiftly and surely, Philip enlarged and consolidated his kingdom and established Macedonian dominance over Greece.

Philip was assassinated while preparing to lead a Macedonian and Greek assault on Persia, but Alexander soon proved marvelously capable of executing his father's program. Having taken for himself the kingships of Egypt, Persia, and Babylon, he then led his troops northward to the Caspian Sea and eastward into Central Asia. Crossing the Hindu Kush, he reached the Indus River by 326 B.C.E. and then proceeded, beyond the boundaries of the Persian empire, toward the Ganges. It was in the Punjab, between the two major river systems of north India, that Alexander's troops mutinied and forced him to turn back toward Babylon, where he died three years later.

As extraordinary as is this external history of Alexander's imperial conquest, the internal history of these same centuries—the history of thought and belief, of literature, philosophy, and religion—is just as remarkable. The Persian prophet Zoroaster (Zarathushtra) might well have been a contemporary of Cyrus the Great. The Chinese philosopher Lao-tse also lived during this period. When he died, probably in 531 B.C.E., another Chinese philosopher, Confucius (Kung Fu-tse), was about twenty years old. When Confucius was living the life

of an itinerant teacher, his somewhat older contemporary, born to the nobility as Prince Siddhartha but known to posterity as Gautama Buddha—*the* Buddha, or "Enlightened One"—was seeking wisdom as a mendicant in northern India. If we accept the traditional dates for the deaths of Buddha and Confucius—483 and 479 B.C.E., respectively—we find that the last decades of their lives overlap the Persian Wars and the cultural ascendancy of Athens. Here, in the fifth century B.C.E., the Athenian polity attained the influence and immortality it never achieved through force of arms. This century alone saw the consecration of the Parthenon, the political leadership of Pericles, and the births of the playwrights Sophocles, Euripides, and Aristophanes, the historians Herodotus and Thucydides, the physician Hippocrates, and the philosophers Socrates and Plato. It is fascinating to reflect that Confucius, Buddha, Zoroaster, the Greek poets and philosophers, and the later Hebrew prophets lived in the same century without knowing of one another's existence.

The prophet Ezekiel, whose vision of the valley of the dry bones is portrayed in the frescoes of Dura-Europos, ancient city of Syria, offered hope to the Babylonian exiles of the resurrection of Israel and the restoration of the Temple.

Nowhere is the role of conquest as a vehicle of cultural transmission more evident than in the career of Alexander the Great. For this fourth-century conqueror, although born in Pella, was also a child of Athens: his tutor, Aristotle (384–322 B.C.E.), had studied for twenty years at Plato's academy in Athens and after eight years at Pella would return to Athens when Alexander launched his Persian campaign. Alexander, it is apparent, was well aware of his cultural mission. As heir to the Persian empire, he adopted the Persian provincial system, appointing Persians as well as Macedonians as his satraps. He himself married a Persian woman, thus ensuring a cross-fertilization of Persian and Hellenic cultures. During the course of his conquests he founded dozens of "Alexandrias," the most important one in Egypt. He consciously planted the seeds of Hellenism throughout the lands he conquered.

Less dramatically but with equally lasting effect, Confucianism and the doctrines of Lao-tse (Taoism) spread throughout China. From its home in India, Buddhism spread quickly to Ceylon and Burma, and reached China in the first or second century C.E. As for Zoroastrianism, the conquests first of Cyrus the Great and his Achaemenid successors and later of Alexander enhanced the influence of its doctrines—especially its belief in the struggle between the forces of light and the forces of darkness—in the development of Greek, Jewish, and early Christian thought.

By the time of the Babylonian exile, the basic elements of Jewish belief and Jewish law were firmly established. Now the challenge was to adapt the practices and institutions of Judaism to the radically changed circumstances of the Jewish people. How could a religion built around Jerusalem and the sacrificial cult withstand the loss of its holy Temple, its sacred Ark of the Covenant, and the City of David, which had been not just the political capital of the Kingdom of Judah but the spiritual center of Judaism itself?

The Psalms of the Hebrew Bible testify to the painful sense of loss and estrangement that these exiles felt:

By the rivers of Babylon, there we sat down, yea, we wept, when we remembered Zion.

We hanged our harps upon the willows in the midst thereof.

For there they that carried us away captive required of us a song; and they that wasted us required of us mirth, saying, Sing us one of the songs of Zion.

How shall we sing the Lord's song in a strange land?

If I forget thee, O Jerusalem, let my right hand forget her cunning.

If I do not remember thee, let my tongue cleave to the roof of my mouth; if I prefer not Jerusalem above my chief joy.

(Psalm 137:1–6)

The exiles' theological dilemma can be simply put: Since the Babylonians overpowered the Jews, did that mean the gods of Babylon were more powerful than the God of Abraham and his seed? No, the prophets answered, God alone had taken vengeance on Israel and Judah through His chosen instruments, Assyria and Babylon:

The Lord was as an enemy: He hath swallowed up Israel, He hath swallowed up all her palaces, He hath destroyed His strongholds, and hath increased in the daughter of Judah mourning and lamentation.

(Lamentations 2:5)

But why had God chosen to destroy the two kingdoms and to send His chosen people into captivity? Here the prophets saw the same cycle of apostasy, oppression, repentance, and deliverance that had earlier been enacted in the period of the Judges. Such was the message of Ezekiel, a priest deported to Babylon after Nebuchadnezzar's first siege of Jerusalem in 597 B.C.E. His theme was simple: Judah would be punished for its corruption—and ultimately redeemed as a reward for its repentance. This same prophecy of consolation and hope was preached by "Second Isaiah," the author of the book of Isaiah chapters 40–66:

Comfort ye, comfort ye, My people, saith your God.

Speak ye comfortably to Jerusalem, and cry unto her, that her warfare is accomplished, that her iniquity is pardoned: for she hath received of the Lord's hand double for all her sins.

(Isaiah 40:1–2)

These visions offered hope for the future,

but the Jews also needed to know how they should conduct themselves while in exile. For guidance they could turn to the words of Jeremiah, who, while in Jerusalem, had counseled two kings of Judah not to seek to throw off the Babylonian yoke, and who advised the first wave of Nebuchadnezzar's deportees to make for themselves a new life in Babylon: Jeremiah favored a pragmatic form of assimilation and even intermarriage. The aim was to survive until the distant day of redemption and not to imperil survival by useless resistance.

And seek the peace of the city whither I have caused you to be carried away captives, and pray unto the Lord for it: for in the peace thereof shall ye have peace.

(Jeremiah 29:7)

Economically, if not spiritually, those Jews who were brought to Babylon or who fled in 586 B.C.E. to Egypt—perhaps joining an established community there—were better off than their kinsmen who stayed in Judea. The Book of Lamentations offers a grim portrait of life in Zion after the fall:

Our inheritance has been turned over to strangers, our homes to aliens.
We have become orphans, fatherless; our mothers are like widows. . . .
Our skin is hot as an oven with the burning heat of famine. . . .
For this our heart has become sick, for these things our eyes have grown dim.
For Mount Zion which lies desolate; jackals prowl over it.

(Lamentations 5:2–3, 10, 17–18)

It was a different story for the Jews in the Babylonian diaspora. Although they came as captives, they were not slaves, and they played an increasingly important part in the empire's expansive economy. Many continued to farm, working their own lands as they had in Judah, but a growing number of exiles were attracted to the cities, and especially to the capital. They became bankers, merchants, contractors, landowners, rent collectors—indeed, one scholar has remarked that "there hardly was any important vocation, including public office, in which Jews and other non-Chaldeans were not represented." Some Jews appear to have taken Babylonian names—a sign of cultural and commercial assimilation—and Babylonian month-names were also adopted. As for the city of Babylon itself, the ancients considered it one of the wonders of the world, whose magnificence Nebuchadnezzar had further glorified through an ambitious building program. German excavations during the first two decades of the twentieth century uncovered two palaces erected by Nebuchadnezzar, as well as a thick-walled building containing rows of vaulted rooms that may have been the site of Babylon's fabled Hanging Gardens. The portrayal of Nebuchadnezzar as a tyrant and madman in later Jewish writings—for example, in the Book of Daniel—departs significantly from earlier Jewish tradition and appears to reflect more the experience of Seleucid and Roman oppression than any balanced sense of Nebuchadnezzar as a historic figure. But Jewish assimilationism in Babylon was neither total nor universal. Many Babylonian Jews zealously followed those religious laws that could be maintained independently of the Temple cult—strict observance of the Sabbath, of circumcision, and of ritual cleanness. They built no new temples, but they took care to preserve the words of the Prophets and the sacred writings that had been brought from Judah.

If the Jews of Babylon did not offer God their sacrifices, what then could they offer? Their solution to this dilemma was revolutionary: they would offer their words and music, their prayers and hymns. There was no such thing as a prayerbook at this time. The earliest known Jewish prayerbook (sid-

dur) dates from the ninth century C.E., more than 1,300 years later—and these first prayers may have been known (and sung or recited) by heart, or they may have been impromptu recitations or meditations. Perhaps families prayed together, or individual Jews gathered to pray in the homes of priests. Meetings of elders, or of the community at large, may also have included the chanting of psalms, hymns, and poems. In these prayer gatherings may lie the origins of the synagogue (the word is Greek for "assembly"), the prototype for the Christian and Muslim houses of worship, the church, and the mosque. The Jews in Babylon were creating for themselves the institutions and practices that would enable them to survive the longer dispersion that followed the destruction of Jerusalem's Second Temple by Rome.

"JUDAIZERS" AND "HELLENIZERS"

As the prophets had foreseen, Jews did return to Jerusalem, and the Temple was rebuilt. As in the days of the Judges, a leader arose to redeem the children of Israel—although in this case the leader was not a Jew, nor (so far as we know) did he take any particular interest in Jewish affairs. This redeemer, whom the Book of Isaiah calls God's "anointed," was none other than Cyrus the Great, whose conquest of Babylon in 539 B.C.E. inaugurated Persia's imperial epoch. Ruled by the Babylonians for about three-quarters of a century, the Jews of Palestine and Mesopotamia would now be governed by Persia for more than 200 years.

The Bible unambiguously portrays Cyrus as a righteous ruler, a "shepherd of Yahweh" —chosen by God to accomplish His will. Restoration of old cities and of ancient forms of worship—or, more generally, toleration of

This Etruscan mask, dating from the sixth century B.C.E., is from the Temple of Apollo.

diversity within the imperial fold—was the cornerstone of Cyrus's policy. It was in keeping with such a policy that in 538 B.C.E. he issued his decree allowing the Jews to return to Jerusalem and rebuild their Temple. (This decree is often compared with the Balfour Declaration of modern history, in which Britain, then the world's mightiest empire, promised to help Jews build their national home in Palestine.)

Cyrus's proclamation not only encouraged Jews remaining in Babylon to provide funds for the venture; it also pledged the return of the sacred vessels that Nebuchadnezzar had removed from the Temple and placed in the temples of the gods of Babylon. The Book of Ezra recounts an even more generous pledge:

Moreover I make a decree what ye shall do to the elders of these Jews for the building of this house of God: that of the king's goods, even of the tribute beyond the river, forth-

with expenses be given unto these men, that they be not hindered.

(Ezra 6:8)

Thus Persia not only would pay for the reconstruction of the Temple; it would even supply animals and other goods for the sacrifices to be made there.

Led by Sheshbazzar, a prince of Judah, a small group of Jews returned to the City of David in 537 B.C.E. That only a minority of the Babylonian Jews chose to make this journey should not surprise us: By this time the Jews were well established in Babylon, with their own distinctive commercial, political, and religious institutions, and had little reason to fear their new Persian rulers. Babylon for the Jews was the America of ancient times.

Jerusalem was a ruin, probably even more

The Warrior's Farewell, an ancient fresco from Lucca, a Tuscan site founded by the Ligurians and taken over by the Romans. War and conquest, the guiding principles of Roman political life, are the dominant themes of Roman art.

of a ruin than Nebuchadnezzar's troops had left it five decades earlier. Bad weather and crop failures left the pioneers without adequate food and clothing; chronic mismanagement of agricultural lands, whose owners had been deported to Babylon by Nebuchadnezzar, might also have contributed to the poor harvests.

The small Jewish community in Jerusalem languished for about eighteen years, until in 520 B.C.E., under the vitalizing spiritual leadership of the prophets Haggai and Zechariah, work on the Temple began anew. The Second Temple was completed in 515 B.C.E., seventy-one years after the first one was destroyed. Although it resembled Solomon's Temple in size and ground plan, it was far less ornate. This diminished magnificence reflected the diminished power of Israel itself. In Solomon's day, the Temple was a visible religious expression of a united kingdom at the height of its commercial and political power. Less elaborate, more austere, the Second Temple befitted a Judah that was no longer an independent kingdom but the subdistrict of a Persian province, within a satrapy of empire.

Palestine had suffered a loss in population as well as in power. The Biblical account indicates that by David's time there lived in Judah some 500,000 men of sword-bearing age, and in Israel perhaps twice that number; the total population of the Jewish Kingdom, including women, children, and others ineligible for military service, would thus have exceeded 5 million, a figure credible only if all the lands that paid tribute to David are counted. A modern estimate, based on demographic considerations, is that by 800 B.C.E. the children of Israel numbered about 300,000. By the middle of the fifth century B.C.E. there were probably no more than 70,000 Jews in Judah.

We have little knowledge of Palestinian history between the completion of the Second Temple and the year 450 B.C.E., but events in the latter half of the fifth century suggest that this was a time of political and spiritual stagnation and of a growing military threat. Hearing reports of Judah's danger and disarray, a Jew named Nehemiah, who in Susa had attained the influential office of royal cupbearer to Artaxerxes I, asked for and received permission to depart for Jerusalem. Artaxerxes, preoccupied with repelling Greek encroachments on the Aegean front and suppressing a Greek-abetted revolt in Egypt, must have been only too happy to allow this prominent Jew of undoubted loyalty to the Persian crown the opportunity to restore stability to Palestine and thereby shore up Persia's western flank.

Sometime between 445 and 440 B.C.E., Nehemiah arrived in Judah, at that time ruled by provincial authorities in Samaria, to the north. Only three days after he reached Jerusalem, Nehemiah made a surreptitious nocturnal inspection, finding the city's fortifications in desperate disrepair. He called the returning exiles to help him in rebuilding them. In only fifty-two days, according to the Bible, the reconstruction was finished under Nehemiah's leadership, using timbers procured from the royal forest by Artaxerxes's permission. Because of the danger from surrounding peoples, the workers had to be guarded and armed:

Half of my servants worked on construction, and half held the spears, shields, bows, and coats of mail. . . . Those who carried burdens were laden in such a way that each with one hand labored on the work and with the other held his weapon. And each of the builders had his sword girded at his side while he built.

(Nehemiah 4:16–18)

Jerusalem needed spiritual and moral as well as military fortification. In leading this triple task of reconstruction, Nehemiah was not alone. From Babylon came Ezra, a priest and scribe, bearing a broad mandate from the Persian monarch Artaxerxes to teach the Jews "the laws of their own God."

We do not know exactly when Ezra came to Jerusalem, and we are not even certain whether this was during Nehemiah's lifetime. The Bible says it was, but this claim, though supported by tradition, does not really conform with other facets of Biblical chronology. We do know that Ezra, who was learned in the Law of Moses, took his teaching responsibilities with the utmost seriousness. With the other spiritual leaders of the community, Ezra appeared in public before thousands of Jerusalemites, reading the

Torah in Hebrew and explaining it in Aramaic, so that all the people might hear and understand.

Ezra and his priestly colleagues denounced religious and moral laxity. In political terms, the government established by Ezra, with Persian blessing, was a theocracy, in which the priesthood held secular as well as religious power. But the genius of Ezra's reform was not only political. In reconstituting the people of Israel around the Law—supported, of course, by an ever-growing body of commentary and interpretation—Ezra was defining the identity of the Jews in a new way, not as a tribal or an ethnic group, not as citizens of a nation-state, but as "the people of the Law," the people of Torah. In their own land or in dispersion, with their own political institutions intact or living under the yoke of conquerors or oppressors, the Jews would constitute themselves as a community governed by the Law of Moses.

Judah remained within the Persian fold until 332 B.C.E., when Alexander the Great, the ruler of Macedonia, swept through Syria, Egypt, and Palestine on his way to the east. According to legend, the High Priest came out from Jerusalem to greet the Macedonian conqueror and then accompanied him to the Temple, where Alexander made sacrifice to the God of Israel. In truth, however, it is highly unlikely that there ever was such a meeting, and Alexander almost certainly took no part in Temple ritual. But he did earn the gratitude of the Judeans by suspending tribute from them during the first year of his conquest.

Alexander's empire had no clear heir. It is said that on his deathbed he bequeathed his conquests "to the best man," leaving it to his generals to determine who that man might

The candelabrum identifies this sarcophagus as that of a Jew in Roman times.

Ruins of the ancient city of Ostia, at the mouth of the Tiber River. Ostia, founded in the fourth century B.C.E., was a leading naval and grain port throughout the Roman period. RIGHT: remains of a first-century synagogue—the oldest in Western Europe—were excavated there in 1961.

be. They decided, after a struggle, to partition the empire, and two Hellenistic dynasties, the Ptolemies and the Seleucids, came to control most of it until Roman times. The Ptolemies were the descendants of Ptolemy Soter ("Ptolemy the Preserver," 367?–283 B.C.E.), one of Alexander's generals who, as king of Egypt, is best known to history for making Alexandria his capital and for establishing the Alexandrian library, the greatest repository of learning in the classical world. His successors ruled Egypt for 300 years, until, after the death of Cleopatra, Egypt became a Roman province.

The Seleucid dynasty began with another of Alexander's generals, Seleucus Nicator ("Seleucus the Conqueror," 358?–280 B.C.E.). The Seleucids, inheritors of Alexander's Asian holdings, including Syria, Persia, Babylonia, and much of Anatolia, remained in power until 64 B.C.E., when what was left of the dwindling Seleucid kingdom fell under the sway of Rome.

The Ptolemies and the Seleucids were in conflict over Judea. The Ptolemies controlled it from late in the fourth century until 198 B.C.E., when the armies of the Seleucid King Antiochus III ("Antiochus the Great," 242–187 B.C.E.), generally welcomed by the Jews,

ousted the forces of Ptolemy V (210?–181 B.C.E.) from Samaria and Judea. The Palestine campaign marked the beginning of the Seleucids' last great burst of military glory. With his Egyptian flank secured, Antiochus III marched through Asia Minor and, in 192 B.C.E., after the Romans had declared war on him, invaded Greece. There he was decisively defeated, despite the aid of the single most implacable foe of Roman expansionism, the Carthaginian general Hannibal (247–183 B.C.E.), who had fled to Syria in 196 after the Romans charged him with conspiring to break the peace they had imposed on Carthage five years earlier. Hannibal later committed suicide, and Carthage—a North African port and fortress near the present site of Tunis, and the seat of an empire that for centuries rivaled first Greece and then Rome for Mediterranean supremacy—was utterly destroyed in 146.

With the reign of Antiochus III and the Seleucid conquest of Judea, we stand on the verge of the Maccabean era and, with it, the open, violent conflict between Judaism and Hellenism—insofar as the oppressive and intolerant rule of the son of Antiochus, Antiochus IV, or Antiochus Epiphanes ("Antiochus the Illustrious," d. 168 B.C.E.), can be taken to represent Hellenistic civilization. The historic encounter between Greek and Jewish culture had begun as early as the fifth century B.C.E., the Age of Pericles, when Athenian coins bearing the heads of animals and gods—such as the Law of Moses prohibited the Jews from making—circulated as the main currency in Judah's expanding foreign trade. But the early impact of Periclean Athens on Judah was like the lapping of the surf on the Mediterranean shore. The power of Hellenism, carried forward by Alexander, the Ptolemies and Seleucids, and the legions of Rome, swept with the force of a tidal wave over the Jewish world.

This was true not only in Judea but also in the diaspora, notably in Egypt, where by the first century C.E. an estimated one million of the world's 8 million Jews were living. The influence of Hellenism on Jewish thought was particularly strong in Alexandria, the capital of Ptolemaic Egypt, where, beginning in the third century B.C.E., Hellenistic Jews began translating the Bible from Hebrew into Greek. Such a translation was essential if the Jews were to explain and defend their religion to the Gentiles, but it was also a way of ensuring that the decline in Hebrew literacy would not alienate the Jews from their own sacred books. This translation, which was almost certainly completed by the beginning of the first century C.E., is known as the Septu-

The triumph of Alexander the Great at the Battle of Issus (near present-day Iskenderun, Turkey) is depicted in this mosaic executed perhaps two centuries after his death in 323 B.C.E.

agint ("Seventy"), a name that originates in the legend that the translation of the Pentateuch, the Five Books of Moses, was completed by seventy (or seventy-two) scholars in exactly seventy (or seventy-two) days. By the time of Philo Judaeus (c. 20 B.C.E.–50 C.E.), this story has been further embroidered: now, it is said, the scholars all worked independently and, owing to Divine inspiration, arrived at translations that were identical in every way.

It is customary to discuss Greek and Jewish modes of thought in terms of contrast. Indeed, we have already referred to Jewish revelation versus Greek reason and to Jewish austerity versus the frank sensuality of Hellenic civilization. Plainly, Jews and non-Jewish Hellenes found much to disapprove in each other. Jews could not abide the cupidity of the Greek gods, the impiety of Greek theater, the lewdness of Greek festivals, and the nakedness of Greek athletic competitions. For their part, many Hellenes ridiculed Jewish worship of an invisible God, Jewish dietary laws, and Jewish clannishness and aloofness. It was not long before suspicion and distrust of Jewish distinctness took on the forms of overt anti-Semitism, as in this declaration by Cicero (106–43 B.C.E.), made at a time when Palestine had fallen under Roman control:

Even while Jerusalem was standing and the Jews were at peace with us, the practice of their sacred rites was at variance with the glory of our empire, the dignity of our name, the customs of our ancestors. But now it is even more so, when that nation by its armed resistance has shown what it thinks of our rule; how dear it was to the immortal gods is shown by the fact that it has been conquered, reduced to a subject province, made a slave.

Nevertheless, the Jews borrowed wholesale from the Greeks—not only in language but also in personal names, fashion, architecture, iconography, and literary forms. By the same token, Jewish monotheism and Jewish ethics excited the admiration of some Greek thinkers, who called the Jews "a race of philosophers."

Perfection through liberal education—the concept embodied in the Greek word *paideia* —was the primary means of Hellenization. The Greek educational ideal was not in itself objectionable to the Jews, who themselves would come to regard study as one of the highest goals of human life and the surest path to personal improvement, but there was much in the specific content and institutions of Greek education that the Jews could not accept. Moreover, *paideia* had political implications, for in Jerusalem, where the main drama of the Maccabean period was enacted, the goal of the Hellenizers was to transform a Jewish theocracy into a Greek-style *polis*. The most firmly committed Hellenizers were the upper classes, among them the priests. The High Priest Jason (Greek for Joshua), having bribed his way into office in 175 B.C.E., not long after Antiochus IV had ascended the Seleucid throne, established a Greek school virtually in the shadow of the Temple.

Three years later, rumors that Antiochus IV had died while campaigning in Egypt brought Jason back to Jerusalem, this time as the head of a 1,000-man army, to depose Menelaus. The rumors proved false, however, and Antiochus, who interpreted the ouster of Menelaus as an act of rebellion against Seleucid authority, took swift revenge. In rapid succession during the years 168 and 167, Jews were massacred, the Temple was looted, the practice of the Jewish religion was proscribed. Circumcision became punishable by death, as was Sabbath observance. The ultimate insult came in December 167, when, by order of Antiochus, an altar to Zeus was erected within the Temple, and the Jews were required to sacrifice swine flesh— unclean, of course, by Jewish law—to the god of the Greeks.

Discontent erupted into rebellion when the agents of Antiochus sought to compel the Jews to take part in pagan worship in the small town of Modi'in, northwest of Jerusalem. Leaders of the Jewish community there were Mattathias the Hasmonean, a man of priestly descent, and his five sons, John, Simon, Eleazar, Jonathan, and Judas, better known to history as Judah Maccabee, or "Judah the Hammer."

When Mattathias died in 166 B.C.E., Judah Maccabee became the leader of the Jewish rebels. The Maccabeans were far outnumbered by the Seleucid army. Knowing that the rebels could not risk a pitched battle, Judah, a brave fighter and resourceful strategist, relied on guerrilla tactics to achieve a military balance. The rebels surprised the Seleucid army near the fortress of Beth-zur, on the border between Judea and Idumea. Its commander, Lysias, was forced to retreat, opening the way for the Maccabeans to march north-northeastward to Jerusalem, reclaim the Temple Mount, and in December 164 cleanse and rededicate the Temple. It was a great victory for Judaism and for the Jewish spirit, commemorated today in the festival of Hanukkah.

But the struggle for Judea was only beginning. Although the Jews held the Temple Mount, the fortress of Acra, built near Jerusalem by Antiochus, remained in the hands of the Hellenizers. Not until 141 B.C.E., when the last Seleucid garrison was expelled from Acra, did the Maccabeans win full control of Judea. As for the sons of Mattathias, all five met violent death.

The victory of the Maccabee rebels consolidated the dynasty of the Hasmoneans—a priestly family that included Mattathias himself, his five sons, and all the rulers of independent Judea from the death of Simon, the last son of Mattathias to the Roman conquest seven decades later. Once the Seleucids had been expelled from Judea, the Hasmoneans embarked on a program of military and religious expansion; Samaria and Idumea were conquered and forcibly converted to Judaism, and by the beginning of the first century B.C.E. the Hasmonean empire was as large as David's had been. But Hasmonean rule was rife with corruption, court intrigues, and bitter political divisions. And all the while, under these less-than-worthy successors of Mattathias and Judah Maccabee, the Hellenizing process continued.

Nevertheless, there is another, brighter legacy of this period. Among those who joined Judah Maccabee after the revolt broke out at Modi'in were some members of the Hasidim ("Pietists"), a group that had led the intellectual and political struggle against Hellenization. One of the offshoots of the Hasidim was a party called the Pharisees (probably meaning "Separate Ones"). During the first century and a half of Roman domination, the Pharisees were only one of the four main religious-political factions. But after the devastation of Jerusalem and destruction of the Temple by the Romans, it was the Pharisees who would preserve and develop Judaism as we know it.

THE AGE OF ROME

The name of Rome has been mentioned with increasing frequency in these pages. The origins of the Roman Empire lie with Etruria, the empire of the Etruscans. The center of Etruscan strength was in the region now called Tuscany, between the Arno and the Tiber rivers, but by the sixth century B.C.E. the Etruscan empire extended northward into the plain of the Po River and southward into Latium, including Rome.

Rome threw off its last Etruscan monarch in about 510 B.C.E and embarked almost immediately on its own expansion program. At the start of the fifth century, Rome controlled about 350 square miles (907 sq. km) of territory; by the middle of the third century, about 10,000 square miles (25,900 sq. km) of land was under Roman domination, with another 42,000 square miles (109,000 sq. km) held by Rome's allies. By 200 B.C.E. the Roman Republic ruled the Italian peninsula, Sicily, Corsica, and Sardinia; more than three centuries later, during the reign of the "good emperor" Hadrian—the Jews had ample reason to dispute that epithet—the Roman Empire reached its territorial limits, encompassing the whole of Mediterranean Europe and North Africa, and extending from present-day Morocco and Portugal in the west to Lower Mesopotamia in the east.

How did Rome accomplish this military and administrative miracle? First, Rome ensured its control over conquered territory by constructing an efficient long-distance road system and by planting colonies of Roman citizens, usually retired military veterans, at strategic locations. Second, Rome dealt mercilessly with rivals and potential rivals: for example, at the conclusion of the Third (and last) Punic War, a war provoked by Rome, Carthage was not only razed but plowed over; salt was spread over the ruins as a gesture of contempt; and all settlement on the site was forbidden for twenty-five years. Third and most fundamental, Rome had manpower resources no rival could match. Since at least 1000 B.C.E., Italy had been Europe's second most densely populated region (Greece was the first); natural increase and the importation of slaves swelled Italy's population to 5 million by 200 B.C.E and to 7 million by the beginning of the Common Era. To feed this growing population, Rome needed the agricultural resources of North Africa, Spain, and other conquered lands; some 17 million bushels of wheat were unloaded each year at Ostia and sent by barge up the Tiber.

Even after the lapse of many centuries, the far-flung dimensions of the Roman Empire inspire our wonder. An Italian people with a culture borrowed from the Greeks conquered all the countries that border on the Mediterranean and incorporated them all into a single imperial structure. Even today, with all the advantages of modern communications, it would be difficult to organize and maintain such an empire. We have to think of a time in which it took two weeks for people and news to reach the capital from the outlying provinces. In addition to the handicap of distance there was the problem of diversity of peoples, tongues, cultures, faiths, thought, and conduct. The problem was how to involve all these people in allegiance to the Roman Empire, thus minimizing the prospects of revolt.

This could not be achieved by making Romans of them all, by trying to impose the stamp of Roman culture upon them. It could be achieved only by giving them a large measure of autonomy, by leaving them free to develop their own faith and thought and ways of life and expression. But underlying this diversity were two unifying elements—Roman law and Roman power. There was a universal law binding upon all the peoples of all the provinces in their relations with the outside world and with the Roman Empire itself. And in order to prevent revolt and secession, there was the sanction of overwhelming Roman military power.

The Romans were tolerant in their acceptance of diversity in culture, faith, and thought but very severe in the repression of revolt. For the Jews, as one of the subject peoples of the empire, there were two aspects of significance in the Roman attitude toward subject provinces and peoples. First, religion. The Romans were polytheists: they believed in the pluralism of gods. They therefore thought it natural that other peoples should have their own faiths, ceremonies, and religions. Moreover, the disposition of the Romans to give autonomy to subject provinces and peoples encouraged the Jews to develop a habit of independent communal

The Forum Romanum Magnum when it was new, as envisioned by the Italian artist Becchetti.

organization that was to be so characteristic of them throughout much of their history.

For more than four and a half centuries, Jewish history was enacted in the shadow of the Roman Empire. This was the center of world commerce, of world culture, and of world power. Jewish settlement was conspicuous as early as the first century. Excavations carried out in 1961 at the synagogue of Ostia, the oldest in Western Europe, revealed stone carvings whose symbols are still meaningful for Judaism today: a seven-branched candelabrum *(menorah)*, the ram's horn *(shofar)* sounded on the High Holy Days of Rosh Hashanah and Yom Kippur, the palm frond *(lulav)* and citron *(etrog)* that characterize the autumn festival of Sukkoth. Remnants of a ritual bath *(mikveh)* and of an oven for baking the unleavened bread *(matzot)* essential to Passover have also been found here.

Rome's first imperial rulers were anxious to cultivate the loyalty of their Jewish subjects at a time of growing unrest within Roman dominions. For reasons we shall soon examine, the Jews favored Julius Caesar (100–44 B.C.E.) in the civil war against Pompey (106–48 B.C.E), and Caesar returned the favor in many ways. He allowed the walls of Jerusalem to be rebuilt, exempted Judea from taxation during the sabbatical year, and allowed the Jews greater autonomy in communal affairs than was customarily granted to other peoples. The Jews were not required to worship the emperor as a deity, as were Rome's other subjects. They were even permitted to offer sacrifices and prayers for the emperor's well-being. Augustus (Gaius Octavianus, r. 27 B.C.E.–14 C.E.) permitted Jews throughout the empire to send money to support the Temple in Jerusalem. And Claudius (r. 41–54 C.E.) intervened when the civil rights and physical security of Jews in Alexandria and elsewhere were imperiled.

The lone exception to this early pattern of toleration and respect was Caligula (Gaius

Caesar, r. 37–41 C.E.), the mad emperor who reveled in torture, elevated his favorite horse to the status of consul, and apparently regarded the claims of his own divinity with the utmost seriousness. When, in 38 C.E., an intercommunal dispute arose in Alexandria, the anti-Jewish faction complained to the emperor that Jewish communal rights should be revoked because these "foreigners" had refused to place statues of Caligula in their synagogues. The leader of the Jewish mission was none other than the learned scholar Philo.

Literary documents are not the only evidence we have of Jewish life in imperial Rome. Artifacts, epitaphs, inscriptions, are also abundant. It is from ancient sites such as the catacombs, groups of underground burial chambers dating back to the early centuries of the Common Era, as well as from the writings of the period, that we get some impression of how Jews lived in Rome in these times. Each epitaph in the catacombs tells its own brief story:

To Amelius, a very sweet child, who lived two years, two months, five days . . .

Here lies Diophatus, the scribe of the Siburesians. In peace his sleep.

To Eulogia, most sweet mother, who lived eighty-one years

The inscriptions on these graves, including the names of those buried in them, are mostly in Greek, sometimes in Latin, very rarely in Hebrew.

As the Roman Empire expanded, important centers of Jewish life arose all over the area, but none could compare in size or importance with the Jewish community of Rome. Some estimate its size at 50,000 persons. The Jews were a very important community in Rome during the post-Hellenic period. They spoke Greek as the Romans did. They dressed like Romans. They looked like Romans. The question therefore arises: What kept them Jewish?

This question comes up time and time again as we follow the historic career of the Jews. And there is no doubt that the Biblical writings were the principal factor that kept the Jews Jewish. For these writings imparted to the Jews a sense of being a separate people in covenant with God, a belief in their own particularity that gave them a sense of identity. It was this that drew a sharp line between them and the polytheistic cultures all around them. And since they had pride and confidence in their very particular tradition, they wanted to impart it.

This brief survey of Jewish life outside Judea leaves us with the impression that these Jewish communities were relatively prosperous and generally unified in belief and outlook. This was not always the case: we have already seen evidence of conflict in Alexandria, and in the early second century C.E. we find Jewish rebellions in Egypt, Cyrenaica (northeastern Libya), and Cyprus. But for the most part, from 63 B.C.E to 73 C.E. —that is, from Pompey's capture of Jerusalem to the fall of Masada—life in the diaspora was far more stable and secure than life in Judea, where irreconcilable religious, political, and social conflicts were tearing the Jewish community apart.

Of the main religious-political factions in Judea, the Sadducees were the aristocrats and establishmentarians. Organized around 200 B.C.E., the Sadducees—whose name derives from Zadok, High Priest in the time of David and Solomon—were closely allied with the Temple rites and with the Hasmoneans. In religious matters they were rigidly observant, accepting as obligatory only those precepts that were written in the Torah and rejecting unwritten traditions—what Jews today call the Oral Law, or Oral Torah—as nonbinding. In secular matters, on the other hand, the Sadducees, the party of the privileged, were often allied with the Hellenizers,

a position that further isolated them from the Jewish underclass.

Consistently opposed to the Sadducees were the Pharisees, who became a distinct force in Judean life soon after the rededication of the Temple by Judah Maccabee. Far less rigid than the Sadducees in their outlook, the Pharisees regarded Jewish law as constantly evolving. For this reason, they held the Law of Moses and the Oral Torah equally binding and, if need be, equally subject to reinterpretation. Not surprisingly, the Pharisees were very much more sympathetic than the Sadducees to the emerging rituals of home and synagogue—perhaps, some scholars say, because these tended to undermine the hold of the priestly Sadducees on Judean religious practice. Both the Pharisees and the Sadducees affirmed the free will of man to choose to do good or evil, but the Pharisees also maintained (and the Sadducees denied) that good deeds would be rewarded and evil

Rigidly observant in religion but Hellenist in their cultural bent, the Sadducees were the aristocrats and establishmentarians of Jewish life in Judea.

deeds would be punished in a world that was to come.

The historian Josephus has left us a concise description of the differences between Pharisees and Sadducees:

Pharisees are friendly to one another and seek to promote concord with the general public, but Sadducees, even toward each other, show a more disagreeable spirit, and in their relations with men like themselves they are as harsh as they might be to foreigners.

No one better exemplified the Pharisees' devotion to education—and to the principle that knowledge of the Law should be open to all and not just to aristocrats and priests—than a poor woodcutter who came from Babylonia to Jerusalem to learn Torah from the leading Pharisaic teachers of his day. Many stories are told about this woodcutter, whose name was Hillel, and Jewish tradition has lovingly preserved his sayings and teachings:

Be of the disciples of Aaron, living in peace and pursuing peace, loving mankind and bringing them near the Torah.

If I am not for myself, who will be for me? And if I am only for myself, what am I . . . ?

A heathen said to Hillel, "If you can teach me the whole Torah while I stand on one foot, you can make me a Jew."
    The rabbi replied: "What is hateful to you, do not do to your neighbor. This is the whole Torah; the rest is commentary. Go and study."

Hillel's version of the "golden rule" echoes the Biblical injunction:

Thou shalt love thy neighbor as thyself.
                                    (Leviticus 19:18)

The gentle spirit of Hillel can also be heard in the voice of another Jew, one born at Nazareth during Hillel's lifetime. When asked which commandment of the Bible was most important, this teacher, whose Hebrew name was Joshua, answered, first, the prayer Shema Yisrael, "Hear, O Israel, thy Lord is our God. The Lord is one" (Mark 12:29).
    And the preacher from Galilee continued:

The second is . . . , Thou shalt love thy neighbor as thyself. There is none other commandment greater than these.
                                    (Mark 12:31)

So spoke Jesus of Nazareth, probably in the year 29 C.E. Though he denounced the Pharisees (and the Sadducees, too), Jesus to a large extent shared the Pharisaic outlook. In the following chapter we shall have much more to say about Jesus' teachings, about his crucifixion at the hands of the Romans, and about his followers' reinterpretation of his mission and significance after his death. At this stage, we should take note of the fact that the ministry of Jesus did not begin until after his encounter with another Jew, who, like Jesus, won a wide following among Judeans and was executed by the Roman authorities.

This man, whom some contemporary observers likened to the prophet Elijah, was John the Baptist. He preached the imminence of the coming of the Messiah and called upon all Jews to purify their souls through confession and baptism. We do not know for certain whether John the Baptist belonged to the Essenes—a group that rivaled the Sadducees and Pharisees in Roman Judea—but he must have had close ties with them or with some similar sect.

Only a few decades ago, our sources of information about the Essenes were confined to the writings of Josephus, Philo, and a Roman scholar, Pliny the Elder (Gaius Plinius Secundus, 23–79 C.E.). Josephus, who lived for three years with an Essene hermit, left a detailed description of the asceticism, discipline, and dedication of the Essenes.

The sensational discovery in 1947 of seven ancient scrolls, written in Hebrew and Aramaic on parchment and papyrus, in the caves of Qumran, at the northwestern tip of the Dead Sea, expanded and revolutionized our knowledge of the Essenes, whose sacred scriptures these may have been. These first finds, together with the tens of thousands of fragments found later, made up the library of the Qumran Brotherhood, including two copies of the Book of Isaiah, other Biblical texts and commentaries, various apocalyptic writings, and the Dead Sea sect's *Manual of Discipline*. This manual, written as a guide for the "children of light," speaks of the conflict, ever since God created man, between the spirit of truth and the spirit of perversity, between the Fountain of Light and the Wellspring of Darkness. For the "final age," when truth will triumph over perversity and each person will be judged according to which of the two spirits he chose to follow, the Qumran brethren prepared a battle manual, *The War of the Sons of Light and the Sons of Darkness*.

In withdrawing to their desert communes, in abjuring Hellenistic fashion for their robes of white, the Essenes hoped to stand aside from the major conflicts of their own time in preparing for the time to come. But this was impossible. The Essenes, who emerged in the second century B.C.E. and might never have numbered more than 4,000, disappeared from Jewish history soon after the destruction of the Second Temple. As for the Qumran Brotherhood, its desert community was wiped out, sometime between 68 and 70 C.E., by the Roman army that devastated Judea.

The Zealots—the fourth major force in troubled Palestine—crystallized as a distinct political group early in the first century C.E. and, like the Essenes, vanished within a few years after the Temple fell. Unlike the Essenes, however, the Zealots made no effort to remain aloof from Judean politics. Quite the contrary. Whereas the Pharisees, Sadducees, and Essenes all in their own way sought to accommodate themselves to the political reality of Roman power, the Zealots insisted that no Jew living in the Holy land had any business paying tribute to Rome and acknowledging its emperor as his master. That was apostasy, they said. And if withholding tribute from Rome meant war, then the Zealots (whom Josephus, betraying his Roman bias, called *Sicarii*, or Dagger Men) were fully prepared to wage it. But before the Zealots confronted Rome, they first waged ruthless war on their Judean rivals:

They assassinated men in the broad light of day and in the very heart of the city. Chiefly at festival time, mingling with the crowds, they stabbed their enemies with the daggers concealed under their cloaks. Their victims dead, the murderers joined in the general

Cristo Guerriero (Christ Militant), an early medieval mosaic from the Chapel of the Archbishop in Ravenna. The Latin reads: "I am the way, the truth, and the life" (John 14:6).

expressions of indignation. This plausible behavior prevented their exposure.

(Josephus II 159–60)

There was much truth in the Zealot claim that Roman rule was an insult to Jewish dignity. The Zealots could point, for example, to the sordid circumstances under which Jerusalem first capitulated to Rome. After Pompey had conquered Syria and put an end to the dynasty of the Seleucids, two rival Hasmonean claimants to the Judean throne, Hyrcanus II (c. 103–30 B.C.E) and Aristobulus II (d. 49 B.C.E.), each pressed Pompey to take his side. The supporters of Hyrcanus opened the gates of Jerusalem to Pompey and his men, who thus entered the city entirely un-

Scholars are still debating whether the Dead Sea Scrolls are the key to the mysteries of the Essenes. This fragment, one of the Thanksgiving Psalms, is written in Hebrew square characters and is now displayed at the Shrine of the Book in Jerusalem.

their temple. It is a fact well known that he found no image, no statue, no symbolical representation of the Deity: the whole presented a naked dome; the sanctuary was unadorned and simple. By Pompey's orders the walls of the city were levelled to the ground, but the temple was left entire.

Pompey treated Judea as a conquered state. Hyrcanus was permitted to serve as High Priest, but the administration of Judea was entrusted to Antipater II (d. 43 B.C.E) a converted Jew. Under Pompey's provincial reorganization, Judea was severed from the Mediterranean, and most of its Transjordanian holdings were also stripped away. Judea's status changed to that of a "free" (though still tributary) state under Julius Caesar, who not only allowed the Jews substantial religious and judicial autonomy but also restored to Judea the port city of Joppa (Jaffa), which Pompey had made part of a Syrian province. No wonder that when Caesar was slain in the Roman Senate in 44 B.C.E., at the foot of a statue of Pompey, he was mourned by the Jews more than by any other people.

Through clever political maneuvers, Antipater II managed to survive and even to augment his power during the civil war between Pompey and Caesar. But a year after Caesar's murder, Antipater died, and during the period of resulting confusion and conflict, Antipater's son Herod ("Herod the Great," r. 37–4 B.C.E) emerged as king of Judea.

Like his father, Herod was an astute politician, but he is more renowned for his cruelty toward rebels and rivals; among the murders he arranged were those of his second wife, Mariamne the Hasmonean (d. 29 B.C.E.) and their two sons, Alexander (d. 7 B.C.E.) and Aristobulus (d. 7 B.C.E.), whom he accused of plotting his assassination. But Herod also achieved enduring fame as a builder, so that the rabbis could later say, "He who has not seen a building by Herod

impeded. Aristobulus was arrested, and his supporters, who had taken refuge on the Temple Mount, were besieged and slaughtered. It was at this time, in 63 B.C.E., that the pagan general strolled brazenly into the Temple's inmost sanctuary, the Holy of Holies. Pompey's act, a profanation in Jewish eyes, was portrayed by the historian Tacitus (c. 55–120 C.E.) from a Roman perspective:

Pompey was the first Roman that subdued the Jews. By right of conquest he entered has not seen a beautiful building in his life." As Judea once again expanded its territory, Herod launched monumental construction programs on a scale not seen in Palestine since Solomon's day.

Historians differ as to how Herod's Jewish subjects viewed the great Temple he built. Josephus says that the Jews were filled with joy when the Temple was finished. But some modern writers are doubtful. How, they ask, could the Jews have rejoiced at the sight of Herod's Temple when they knew from the Bible that King David had been denied the privilege of building the House of God because his hands were too bloody? If David's hands were too bloody, what then of Herod's? Plainly, however grandiose his plans, however exquisite his craftsmanship, Herod was morally unfit for the task he assigned himself. And when Herod erected a golden eagle—the symbol of imperial Rome—at the Temple gate, the more radical Jews, seeing it as proof that Herod served not God but Augustus, tore it down at the cost of their own lives.

After Herod's death, and a brief period of transition under his son Archelaus (d. 16 C.E.) Judea became a province of Syria and was ruled for six decades by "procurators" responsible to the Syrian governor. The fourteen men who held the office of procurator between 6 and 66 C.E. were, as a class, rapacious in their greed and merciless in their exercise of power. One of them was Pontius Pilate, during whose term (26–36 C.E.) Jesus was crucified.

The Judean war was not a straightforward struggle against a foreign empire. The Jews had bitter grievances against Rome, but they were also in conflict with their Gentile neighbors. Moreover, the Jews themselves—as always—were torn by political and class differences. There were riots in the diaspora, with pagans attacking Jews, Jews attacking pagans, and *sebomenoi* assaulted from both sides. (The *sebomenoi*, or God-fearers, worshiped the Jewish God and practiced the Jewish Sabbath without becoming fully Jewish.) The Jewish rebels won some early victories against imperial troops, but knowing that Rome was sure to send in reinforcements, they organized a government in Jerusalem and divided the country into seven military districts, of which the most vulnerable was the Galilee. Command of the Galilee district was assigned to a priest of Hasmonean descent, Joseph ben Mattathias—the same Josephus whose *Jewish War* is our prime source for what happened during those turbulent and tragic years.

The family tree of the Caesars, a patrician Roman clan whose name became synonymous with imperial rule both in ancient Rome and, later, in Germany (kaiser) and Russia (czar).

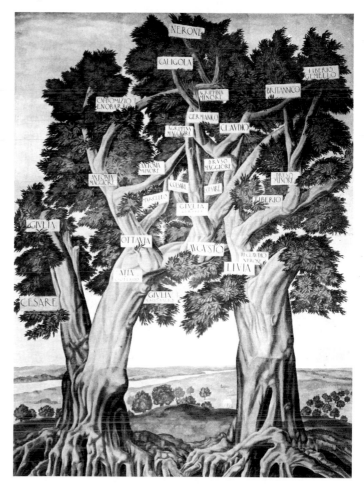

Ons auons mousti a nens trespasser des closes qui ont au notume & duuant este faictes en pourueant ala memo rethyr a la mort & la pyc de ceulr qui les lironv. Car a royme alecandre. Or ceulr qui escripuant hystoires ou ra racomptons les closes qui seusurier compteut closes anaennes il conui et ne tendons a nulle autre close for ent pour lanacunete mettre ou faire

This illumination by the French artist Jean Fouquet (1416?–1480) of Josephus's Antiquities of the Jews *displays one of the more shameful episodes of Jewish history—when the Roman general Pompey strolled unhindered into the Temple's inner sanctum, the Holy of Holies.*

where the Jewish captives bearing the *menorah* from the Temple were dragged into the Forum?

If for many Roman writers this was just another of the many revolts of tribes and provinces that had to be put down, it was not like that in Jewish history. In Jewish history, this is a turning point. It is the point

from which the dominant theme of Jewish life is the diaspora, the condition of being dispersed, of being scattered. The Jews were to develop a special talent for living in diaspora. For being scattered and yet maintaining cohesion with each other. For being separated from their homeland and yet not forgetful of it. For being able to build autonomous centers of Jewish life under whatever government they happened to be living.

It must not be assumed that diaspora begins with the events commemorated by the Arch of Titus. For a long period before, the Jews had been scattered far and wide throughout Babylonia and the Greek and Roman worlds. But from the time commemorated by the Arch of Titus, this becomes the central fact of Jewish history. Palestine was no longer the physical home of most of the Jews, although it always retained its symbolic and its magnetic quality.

Jews continued to live in Judea under foreign rule for two centuries, until many or most of them emigrated for economic reasons. The era of wandering had now begun. The history and the destiny of the Jews would now be inseparably bound up with those of the Roman Empire, and there would be great repercussions of this for the Western world.

MASADA

Jewish resistance did not end with the devastation of Jerusalem. Bands of Zealots held out in fortresses scattered throughout Judea, but nowhere longer than at Masada, overlooking the western shore of the Dead Sea. Led by Eleazar ben Yair, the Zealots had controlled the fortress since the early days of the Judean revolt, and especially from 70 to 72 C.E. had used Masada as a base for raids against the Romans. Not only did the rock-fortress occupy a strong defensive position,

with its powerfully fortified summit 1,300 feet (about 400 meters) above sea level, but Herod the Great had also installed an elaborate water system and extensive storage facilities and living quarters. Many months passed before the soldiers of the Tenth Legion, under the command of the Roman governor Flavius Silva, were able to erect a siege tower high enough to allow their iron battering ram to reach the fortress walls. But early in May of 73 C.E. they breached Herod's walls and set fire to a wooden barricade the Zealots had hurriedly thrown together. Then the Romans retired for the day, confident that total victory would be theirs the following morning.

At daybreak, when the Roman troops entered the fortress, they saw and heard nothing but what Josephus calls a "fearful solitude." They saw no sign of the enemy until, entering one of the buildings, they found the mounds of dead bodies—960 in all, men, women, and children. Only two women and five children survived. The rest of Masada's defenders had chosen to commit suicide rather than submit to Roman captivity. To this resolve, says Josephus, they were urged by the eloquence of their leader, Eleazar:

Since we, long ago, my generous friends, resolved never to be servants to the Romans, nor to any other than to God Himself . . . the

The rock-fortress of Masada—was it a symbol of Jewish spiritual resistance, or an emblem of submission to the rule of Rome?

time is now come that obliges us to make that resolution true in practice.

Let our wives die before they are abused, and our children before they have tasted of slavery. And after we have slain them, let us bestow that glorious benefit upon one another mutually, and preserve ourselves in freedom, as an excellent monument for us.

As for those who are dead in the war . . . we should esteem them blessed. For they are dead in defending, and not in betraying, their liberty. But as to the multitude of those who are now under the Romans . . . who would not make haste to die before he would suffer the same miseries with them?

And where is now that great city, the metropolis of the Jewish nation? It is now demolished to the very foundations. Some old men lie upon the ashes of the Temple. And a few women there are preserved alive by the enemy, for our bitter shame and reproach. Now who is there that resolves these things in his mind, and yet is able to bear the sight of the sun . . . ? Let us make haste to die bravely.

One of the unresolved dilemmas of Jewish history is whether Eleazar actually spoke these words, or anything like them. The Masada excavations led by Yigael Yadin from

October 1963 to May 1964 and again from November 1964 through April 1965 did uncover some circumstantial evidence lending credence to Josephus's story. In a small cave on the southern cliff, twenty-five skeletons, including those of women and children, were found; perhaps these were the remains of Masada's defenders, heaped there by the Romans. Yadin attached the greatest significance to the discovery of eleven ostraca, or potsherds, each bearing a single name (in one case, Ben Yair, presumably Eleazar), which may have been used in casting lots as to who should kill the others and then himself. But for the speeches of Eleazar (and, for that matter, the manner of the Zealots' death) there was no confirmation, and some modern scholars have suggested that Josephus, following the practice of many ancient writers, fabricated Eleazar's eloquence and perhaps much else that happened here.

And if we do take Josephus's story at face value, how shall we interpret the meaning of these events? Should the Jews have borne the Masada suicides as a badge of shame or an emblem of spiritual triumph? Did the Zealots' policy of warring against Rome till the bitter end serve or impede the cause of Jewish survival? In the Zealots' own time, many voices called for accommodation with Rome. From the mid-second century to the late 1800s, those voices would chart the Jewish future.

CONCLUSION

The Roman Emperors Vespasian and Titus thought so highly of their achievement in crushing the Jewish revolt that they had coins struck with the inscription "Judea Capta." Captivity had already been the Jewish fate for six and a half centuries. Between the destruction of the Temple of Solomon in 586 B.C.E. and the destruction of the restored temple in 70 C.E., the Jews had known four conquerors—Babylon, Persia, Greece, and Rome.

Rome was the harshest and cruelest of them all, and for a century Jewish life seethed with guerrilla warfare and sporadic revolt. But in the end there was no course but resignation. What was the point of military and political resistance? Indeed, for Jewish pacifists like Johanan ben Zakkai or the monks of the Dead Sea caves, resistance fighters, militants, and Zealots were not so much heroes as men of little faith, unwilling to put their patient trust in God's ultimate dispensation.

In any case, there were ways of compensating for the lack of military valor and political responsibility. One way was the apocalyptic dream. There were the Jewish monks, pacifists and ascetics, in their Dead Sea caves writing a scroll called *The War of the Sons of Light and the Sons of Darkness* in which they described a cosmic struggle between supernatural forces.

More constructive than these distant dreams was the tenacious study of the Torah, the holy literature. For this a Jew needed intellectual freedom; he did not need national sovereignty. Indeed, the very absence of military activity and of political responsibility seemed to sharpen intellectual and spiritual energies. A typical product of these times was the literature of the Mishnah, a detailed study of and commentary on the Biblical texts, written in balanced, lucid, precise Hebrew prose.

But as we have seen, the central theme of the Jewish condition was now *galut*. This Hebrew word, which means "exile," did not necessarily imply absence from the land of Israel. Indeed, the Jews who lived on in Galilee still thought of themselves as in exile, because although they were on holy soil, their lives were without balance, without

dignity, and without immediate hope of redemption. They were even forbidden by the
Roman emperors from visiting the Temple
Mount. *Galut* meant sterility, *galut* meant humiliation, *galut* meant alienation. But this
was only one side of the coin. The other side
was the new freedom of the Jews to diffuse
their culture and to transmit their ideas into
history. Their identity no longer depended
on a particular place. It could take expression
in the power of principles and ideas; it could
be expressed in synagogues and academies
and in literature.

The Jews had very little influence on the
civilizations of Babylonia and of Persia. But
with Greece it was another matter. We find
the great philosopher Philo of Alexandria, a
contemporary of Jesus of Nazareth, engaging
in discussion on the possibility of harmoniz-
ing Hebrew prophecy with Greek philosophy. Rabbinic Judaism also was to have a far
greater influence than Titus could ever have
imagined. Not directly: the Jews had little talent and little instinct, indeed, no power for
conversion. They could not impose their
ideas upon others. But who could have predicted when Titus struck his coin what a
powerful influence the Jewish captives were
going to have through the penetration of universal culture in the rise and expansion of
Christianity?

*The Roman emperors Vespasian and Titus
thought so highly of their own achievement in
crushing the Jewish revolt that each had coins
struck with the inscription "Judea Capta"; the
three coins shown here were minted during Vespasian's reign (69–79 C.E.). During the next century, the Jewish rebel leader Bar Kokhba would
issue his own coinage celebrating the liberation of
Jerusalem and the rebirth of Israel.*

4.
The Shaping of Traditions

THE FIRST 500 years after the birth of Jesus are notable for growth, change, and adaptation, both in Judaism and in Christianity. The Jews of Galilee and especially of Babylon created a monumental source of Jewish culture, the Talmud. They wrote commentaries on the Bible, and then commentaries on the commentaries, and then they wrote commentaries on all of that. Thus they produced a rich, copious, voluble, chaotic, but vivid body of writing, of literature, legend, and law. A page of the Talmud in Hebrew and Aramaic goes on and on, without any periods or commas or other punctuation. The Talmud cannot be read. It has to be learned, or studied—and "study" or "learning" is just what the Hebrew word Talmud means. The Talmud became a complete culture in itself, the primary theme of life and devotion for traditional Jews all over the world. It is also an intellectual instrument, sharpening the critical faculty and analytical power of its devotees. In the course of time, the study of the Talmud became consecrated as an act of virtue, a symbol of devotion to God.

Meanwhile, the Christian world was in full and dynamic expansion. It would first convert Jews, then Gentiles, and finally spread throughout the Mediterranean world. Under the apostle Paul, a man of Jewish birth, Roman citizenship, and Greek culture, Christianity would make masses of converts, irrespective of their previous faith.

Christians and Jews had something in

Bet She'arim attained special importance toward the end of the second century C.E., when Judah ha-Nasi settled in the city and it became the hub of the patriarchate and the meeting place of the Sanhedrin, of which he was president.

Christianity's Jewish roots emerge clearly in this illumination from the fifteenth-century Flemish Book of Hours, which shows an Old Testament figure, Jesse, the father of David, dreaming of his descendants, culminating in the Messiah.

common. They were each persecuted by the Roman Empire. But who should be converted to Christianity in the fourth century but the Roman Emperor Constantine himself? By the fifth century the entire Roman world had become formally Christian, and no other faith was tolerated. Christianity was now the "Establishment," while the unconverted Jews remained the eternal dissidents, the perpetual minority. But from these five centuries they had carried away a new mobility for themselves and a new flexibility for their ideas and culture. These ideas and culture were no longer tied down to an Ark of the Covenant or to a Temple in Jerusalem. The Jews could now move forward in any direction, wherever books of the Bible and of the Talmud could be found.

There are several important stories to be told in this chapter. The first is the dispersion of the Jewish people to every corner of the Roman world, and even beyond it. The second is the reconstruction of Judaism and the separate development of Christianity after the fall of the Temple. The third is the growing divergence and bitterness of feeling between the two faiths. These three stories are enacted against the backdrop of a disintegrating Roman Empire, the creation of a new social and political order in Europe, and the ascent of a new empire—that of the Muslim in western Asia, Arabia, and the Mediterranean. Of Jewish life in the empire of Islam, we shall speak briefly in this chapter and at greater length in the next.

We return to the year 73 C.E.

Masada, the last outpost of the Zealots, has fallen. The Temple, which had been the power base of the Sadducees for more than two and half centuries and the heart of Jewish religious ritual for most of the previous thousand years, has been destroyed. The Essene brotherhoods, small in membership but boundless in faith, have been obliterated. On the imperial throne sits Vespasian, conqueror, on his own and through his son Titus, of Judea.

How would a nation survive so utterly destroyed, its people scattered to the wind? The persistence of the Jewish people is a mystery unparalleled in the story of civilization. There is no simple answer to this mystery of a people dispersed to the far corners of the earth, carrying somehow with it the seeds of its own survival, retaining its own identity wherever it takes root. No matter how foreign the soil, the Jewish people lives to flower and renew itself from generation to generation. Part of the answer to this enigma may lie in the dispersal itself—the scattering of the Jewish people which is called in a single word *diaspora*.

The word comes from the Greek for "scattering," and it was used to define the spreading and resettlement of many peoples in the ancient world. There is a similar word, *diaspore*, for the pod of many seeds in the milkweed, or butterfly plant, which has grown in Israel since ancient times. This diaspore scatters its seeds in far directions. The milkweed now grows and flowers, with some variations, in almost every part of the world.

There is something symbolic in this. We must remember that at the time of the destruction of Jerusalem, more than half of all the Jews of the world were not living in Judea. Many were established in Babylonia, in other parts of the Middle East, and in various communities of the Roman Empire. It would take a thousand years to see and grasp that the war with Rome, which ended with the expulsion of the Jews from their land, had paradoxically saved them from the fate that awaited other civilizations. For the Jews were exiled into survival. Once their homeland was lost, only the diaspora could save their identity. Thus, the diaspora became the essential condition for the preservation of their identity and creativity, which would have perished if they had stayed on to be massacred in Judea.

But if their resettlement in other lands enabled the Jews to survive physically as a people, there was something deeper that permitted them to survive creatively, interacting with other civilizations while developing and fashioning their own tradition. What lifted the Jews from obscurity into a

The priesthood of Aaron, the Ark of the Covenant, and sacrificial animals are depicted in this Dura-Europos fresco dating from the third century C.E. By this time, however, synagogue worship had irrevocably supplanted the sacrificial cult.

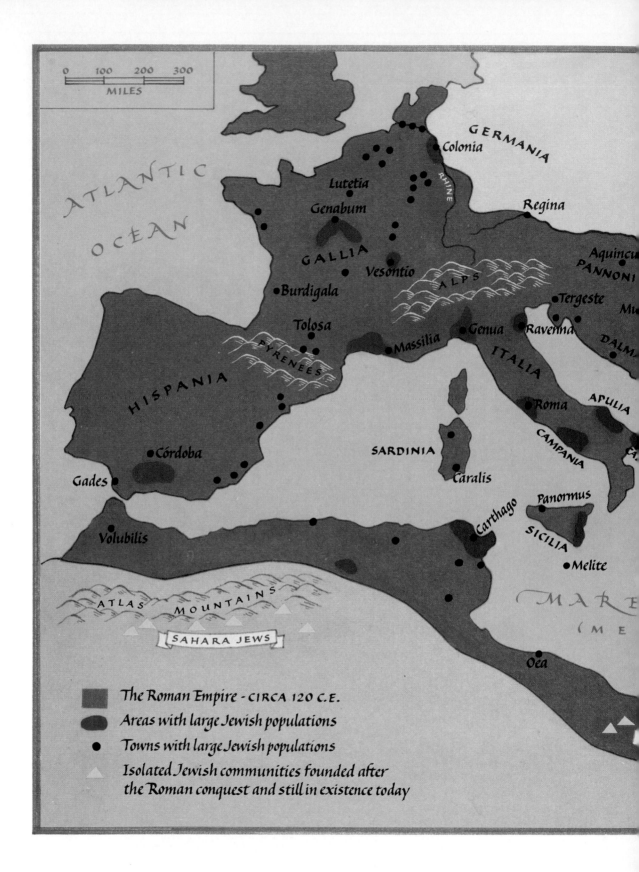

ATLANTIC
OCEAN

GERMANIA

Colonia

RHINE

Regina

Aquincu
PANNONI

Lutetia

Genabum

GALLIA

Vesontio

ALPS

Tergeste

Mu

Burdigala

Genua

Ravenna

DALMA

Tolosa

PYRENEES

Massilia

ITALIA

HISPANIA

SARDINIA

Roma

APULIA

CAMPANIA

Córdoba

Caralis

Gades

Panormus

Carthago

SICILIA

Volubilis

Melite

ATLAS
MOUNTAINS

MARE

(ME

SAHARA JEWS

Oea

The Roman Empire - CIRCA 120 C.E.

Areas with large Jewish populations

• Towns with large Jewish populations

▲ Isolated Jewish communities founded after
the Roman conquest and still in existence today

0   100   200   300
MILES

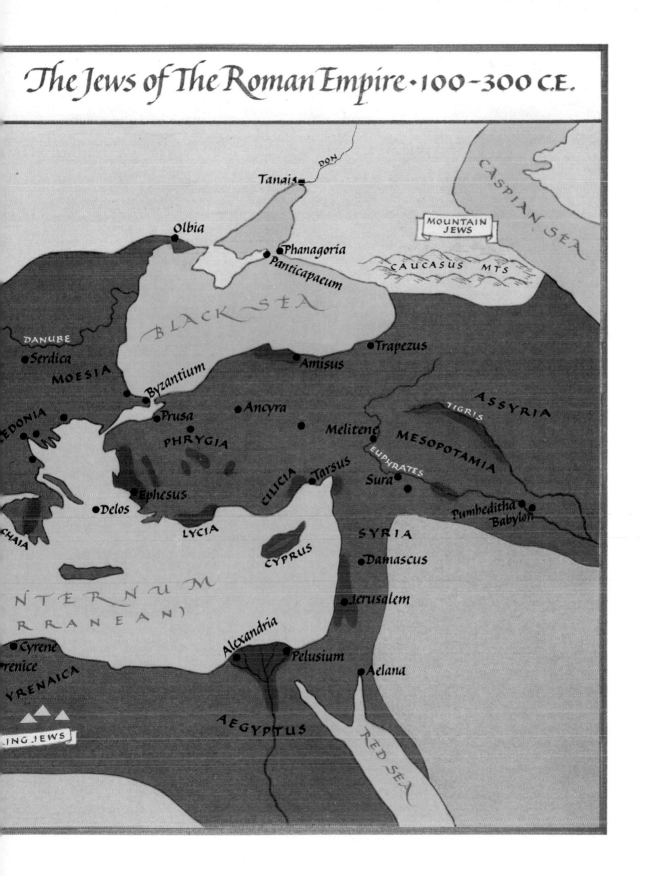

The Jews of The Roman Empire · 100–300 C.E.

DON

Tanais

Olbia

Phanagoria
Panticapaeum

CASPIAN SEA

MOUNTAIN JEWS

CAUCASUS MTS

BLACK SEA

DANUBE

Serdica

MOESIA

Trapezus

Amisus

Byzantium

ASSYRIA

Prusa

Ancyra

TIGRIS

Melitene

MESOPOTAMIA

EDONIA

PHRYGIA

EUPHRATES

Tarsus

Sura

CILICIA

Ephesus

Delos

LYCIA

SYRIA

Pumbeditha
Babylon

CHAIA

CYPRUS

Damascus

NTERNUM

RRANEAN)

Jerusalem

Cyrene

renice

Alexandria

Pelusium

Aelana

YRENAICA

ING JEWS

AEGYPTUS

RED SEA

central and permanent place in history has sometimes been called a passion for meaning. As we shall see, underlying this passion for meaning was the invisible power of the body of law and tradition called the Talmud.

At the beginning of the Christian Era, the Jews of Palestine accounted for a minority of world Jewry, as they do today. According to one estimate, based on a medieval report of a census conducted by the Emperor Claudius in 48 C.E., some 7 million Jews lived within the bounds of the Roman Empire; probably another million lived outside the jurisdiction of Rome, most of them in Mesopotamia, under Parthian rule. Of the empire's Jews, no more than 2.5 million—roughly one in three—lived in Palestine, with Asia Minor, Egypt, and Syria each accounting for another million. These are, of course, very crude estimates, and it is possible that the number of Jews in Palestine was much smaller. Some demographers contend that Palestine's total population—Gentile as well as Jewish—was only about 800,000 at this time.

With geographic dispersion came economic diversification. By 300 C.E. we find Jewish bakers and shippers in Italy, Jewish olive growers in Spain, Jewish slave traders in Germany, Jewish farmers and herdsmen in Mesopotamia. Many Jews dwell in urban communities, but there is also a strong rural representation, and there are even isolated Jewish settlements in the Atlas Mountains and in the Caucasus. Ancestors of the Falashas are already established in Ethiopia, and in the Greek colonies along the Black Sea we find Jews living on the fringes of the land that would later be known as Russia.

Judea, and especially Jerusalem, played a much larger role in Jewish life than purely demographic and economic factors would suggest. While the Temple stood, diaspora communities were bound to support the sacrifices and the priests who performed them. At festival time—during Sukkoth, Passover, and Shavuot—thousands of pilgrims would stream into Jerusalem from Italy and Greece, Cyrenaica and Egypt, Syria and Galilee, Arabia and Mesopotamia.

The mass pilgrimages stopped with the destruction of the Temple, but Jerusalem retained its special place in Jewish minds and hearts. Jewish tradition abounds with tales and expressions that show—and would help preserve—Jerusalem's centrality in Jewish life, even in the era of its physical decline:

Ten portions of beauty descended to the world. Jerusalem acquired nine and rest of the world one.

There is no wisdom like the wisdom of the Land of Israel. There is no beauty like the beauty of Jerusalem.

Jerusalem is the light of the world . . . and who is the light of Jerusalem? God.

Bleak as the Jewish prospect might have appeared in 73 C.E., the Jews could still find some reason for hope. Their exiled ancestors had returned to Jerusalem barely five decades after the Babylonian conquest. Why should this second exile last any longer than the first? The words of Second Isaiah must have been as comforting to the Jews of Roman times as they had been more than six centuries earlier:

For a small moment I have forsaken thee; but with great mercies shall I gather thee.

(Isaiah 54:7)

Moreover, the Jews had by this time developed a proud military tradition. What Jewish patriot could forget the imperial conquests of King David, the spectacular triumph of the Maccabees over the army of Antiochus IV, the protracted resistance of Judea to the legions of Vespasian and Titus? Perhaps, as in the time of the Judges, God would send a new warrior-hero to guide them. Or per-

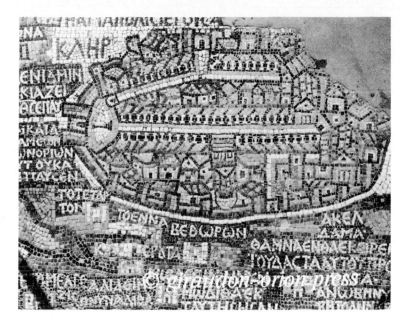

A sixth-century mosaic map of Jerusalem and the Judean hills.

haps, as the prophets had foretold, an "anointed one," a Messiah, would lead the children of Israel back to the Promised Land.

The fact is that within six decades after the fall of the Temple, Israel had its new military leader, and the city of Jerusalem was once again, if only briefly, the capital of a Jewish state. That military leader, Simeon ben Kosiba (d. 135 C.E.), was and remains one of the most controversial figures of Jewish history. His admirers called him Bar Kokhba, "Son of a Star," a name with messianic overtones. His detractors labeled him Bar Koziba, "Son of a Liar." Among those who hailed Bar Kokhba as the Messiah was Rabbi Akiva (c. 50–135 C.E.), the foremost sage and scholar of his time.

Bar Kokhba's charismatic powers and his singleminded harshness fascinated the rabbis. According to the Talmud, he required that his soldiers unhesitatingly cut off at least one of their own fingers as a mark of loyalty and valor. The Talmud records how the sages pleaded with him, "How long will you continue to turn all Israel into maimed men?"

The rebellion that Bar Kokhba would lead had its seeds in the decision by the Roman Emperor Hadrian (Publius Aelius Hadrianus, r. 117–138 C.E.) to build over the ruins of Je-

rusalem a Roman city called Aelia Capitolina in his own honor, at the site of Herod's Temple. While Hadrian was in Judea and Egypt, in 130–131 C.E., the Jews bided their time, planning tactics, stockpiling weapons and supplies, and sending emissaries throughout the diaspora to gather support for the coming struggle. Among these emissaries was Akiva, who traveled as far west as Gaul (France) and as far east as Babylonia. When the revolt began, in late 131 or early 132 C.E., the Roman Tenth Legion, caught by surprise, was forced to abandon its encampments near Jerusalem. Under Bar Kokhba's leadership, the rebels established a provisional government, made plans to rebuild the Temple, and in the interim resumed the ritual sacrifices at a temporary altar on the Temple site. A new calendar was proclaimed and new coins were issued. One such coin bears the inscription "Shimeon [Bar Kokhba] President of Israel" on one side, "Year One of the Redemption of Israel" on the other.

Inevitably, Hadrian sent in reinforcements, under the command of Sextus Julius Severus, the governor of Britain. In late 134 or early 135 C.E., the Jewish rebels were driven from Jerusalem. Bar Kokhba and his men dug in at the fortress of Betar, about seven miles southwest of the capital; but by late summer Betar had fallen, Bar Kokhba was slain, and Akiva had been imprisoned and tortured to death. Except for sporadic fighting in the hill country, the Bar Kokhba rebellion was crushed.

After the war, Hadrian proceeded with his plans for Aelia Capitolina, which Jews were forbidden to enter on penalty of death. The names Judea and Jerusalem were expunged from the map of the empire. The city and its surroundings were colonized with Gentiles, and Judaism's most basic practices—circumcision, celebration of the festivals, observance of the Sabbath, the study and teaching of Torah, even the possession of a scroll of the Law—became capital crimes.

The fall of Betar marks a decisive break in Jewish history. The Jews no longer held any real hope of reclaiming Jerusalem or rebuilding the Temple. There would be no more Jewish rebellions. There would be self-defense against massacres and pogroms, but more than 1,800 years would pass before the Jews would again rule anywhere in Palestine and be masters of Jerusalem. During those eighteen centuries the Jews would be a minority everywhere they lived, including the land of Israel, where for most of this period the Jewish population cannot have numbered more than a paltry 5,000.

The final cessation of ritual sacrifice and of Temple worship also meant a decisive change in Jewish religious practice. For this transformation, however, the Jews had been well prepared by their experience during the Babylonian exile and their subsequent development of synagogue rituals and autonomous communal organizations. Tradition ascribes the principal role in the remaking of Judaism to Johanan ben Zakkai, a Pharisaic spiritual leader in the line of Hillel. In 68 C.E., as Roman troops stormed through Judea and Jerusalem was torn apart by civil strife, Ben Zakkai urged his fellow Judeans to submit to

Vespasian, warning that continued resistance would result in the loss of their city, their Temple, and their lives. Perceiving finally that the Zealots preferred death to submission, and that they were prepared to kill him and his disciples rather than risk his delivering Jerusalem into Vespasian's hands, Ben Zakkai arranged for his pupils to bear him out of the city in a coffin, as though he were dead. He then interceded with the Roman emperor on behalf of an entire generation of sages and scholars, the leading Pharisees of his day. Specifically, Ben Zakkai sought and obtained Vespasian's permission to establish an academy for the study of Judean law at Yavneh, between Jerusalem and the coast (near Rehovot in modern Israel). He established a religious court, or *bet din* (literally, "house of judgment"), to regulate the calendar and rule on other spiritual and secular matters. Establishment of this *bet din*, which helped diffuse Pharisaic Judaism not only in Palestine but throughout the diaspora, was only one of many ways, practical as well as symbolic, in which Ben Zakkai reinvested Yavneh with much of the cultural and political influence that Jerusalem had formerly exercised.

Ben Zakkai was succeeded as president of the *bet din* and patriarch of Judea by Rabban Gamaliel II, the great-great-grandson of Hillel. During Gamaliel's tenure, the *bet din* was reconstructed as the Great Sanhedrin, recognized by Rome as the supreme political, judicial, and religious body for Jews within the empire. It was Gamaliel who determined, with the consent of the Sanhedrin, that decisions on matters of Jewish Law (*halakhah*) should follow the principle of majority rule. It was at Yavneh, under both Ben Zakkai and Gamaliel, that the textual integrity of the Bible was preserved. This period also saw a new translation of the Hebrew Bible into Greek, the introduction of alphabetic devices to clarify the pronunciation and meaning of the Hebrew text, and a revision of the Biblical canon, including the admission of Ecclesiastes to the Bible.

Nevertheless, the suppression of the Bar Kokhba revolt marked an end to the supremacy of Judea in Jewish religious life. For the next several centuries, the leading centers of Jewish study and authority would be in Galilee and Mesopotamia. Reflecting this bifurcation is the fact that we have not one but two great compilations of Jewish law and learning—two versions of the Talmud. The Babylonian Talmud, vast in size and encyclopedic in scope (as in the Hebrew phrase *Yam ha-Talmud*, ''ocean of the Talmud''), was compiled between 200 and 500 C.E. at Sura, Nehardea, Pumbeditha, and the other rabbinic academies of Babylonia, where Jews had lived continuously at least since Nebuchadnezzar's time. The second version is

The image of Bar Kokhba that emerges from the bundles of his letters and related documents found in the Judean desert, not far from Qumran, is one of a stern military commander seeking to rule Judea with the power and authority of an emperor.

The brutal suppression of the Bar Kokhba rebellion by the Emperor Hadrian, depicted in this marble bust, marks a decisive break in Jewish history. More than 1,800 years would pass before Jews would again be masters of Jerusalem.

often called the Jerusalem Talmud, but this is a misnomer, since it was compiled predominantly in Caesarea, Tiberias, and Sepphoris. About one-third the length of its Babylonian counterpart, the Jerusalem Talmud is accordingly less complete and much less authoritative. Both versions of the Talmud have the same starting point, however: each takes the form of a commentary on the Mishnah, which was codified in Galilee around 200 C.E under the direction of Judah ha-Nasi (d. 217? C.E.).

Judah himself studied at Usha, where the Sanhedrin convened after the eclipse of Yavneh. He then moved to Bet She'arim. During his tenure, the patriarchate, which was already a hereditary office and had taken on some of the trappings of royalty, reached its height of prestige and influence, not only

Two Talmudic sages, Rabbis Gamaliel and Elea-zar, as portrayed in the margins of a sixteenth-century Cretan Haggadah.

among the Jews of Palestine and the diaspora but also among the rulers of Rome.

After Judah's death, the Palestinian patriarchate gradually became ineffectual, carried on by what one historian has called a "monotonous succession of Gamaliels, Judahs, and Hillels." However, scholarship continued to flourish in Galilee and especially in Babylonia, with whose sages Judah had maintained friendly ties and to whose Jewish leader, the exilarch, Judah had paid due respect. The redactors of the Mishnah, under Judah's leadership, saved for posterity not only the Oral Law (*halakhah*) as it had developed up to the time of Hillel but also the teachings of the rabbis (*tannaim*) during

the first two centuries of the Common Era, when Rome twice laid waste to Judea. The disciples of Judah and their students (*amoraim*) would now provide an extended commentary on the work of their predecessors. This commentary, called *Gemara*, embraces not only *halakhah* but *aggadah*—the proverbs, parables, anecdotes, and brief historical and biographical sketches that afford the Talmud its principal literary interest.

It is difficult to picture what Jewish life would have been like for the last fifteen centuries without the Talmud. Its appeal to the Jewish imagination is quite different from that of the Bible. It has none of the Bible's universal appeal; indeed non-Jews seldom have any understanding of it, certainly no affection. It belongs to the intimate recesses of the Jewish consciousness. The Bible conveys the idea of eternity, whereas the Talmud was a daily companion, dealing with things that are homely and practical and concrete. For generations of Jews in the ghetto it was the faithful mirror of an ancestral civilization in Babylon and Judea. For centuries Jews lived their lives in conformity with its experiences and idioms and tested their intellectual attainments in accordance with its precepts. The Talmud opened a door to a full, vivid, bustling Jewish life, which often seemed more real to Jews than their actual experiences centuries later. It is hard to think of any other body of writing that cast such a spell beyond its own context of time and place.

As we study the Talmud we learn more and more about the rabbinic mind and about the sages and scholars who with their families and contemporaries are buried at Bet She'arim. The rabbis were both rational and poetic. We find meticulously precise legal texts side by side with all sorts of bits and pieces of legend and superstition. But whatever their mood, the rabbis were always obsessed with Torah. They wanted to give their students a sense of divine salvation. But the path to it lay through study and study and more study, until their students began to see the form, shape, dimensions of the cosmic order and the place of the Jew within it.

This very original and unsystematic method of teaching was once described by a rabbi in a commentary on Genesis. "It is all like an impenetrable thicket of reeds. What does a clever man do? He cuts a path and enters. And then he cuts more reeds and penetrates further. In the end he has made a clearing, and all begin to enter by following his path."

Among the concerns of the rabbis was the Hebrew calendar. A long passage in the Mishnah deals specifically with the question of how to be sure the new moon has been sighted, a matter that involves deciding which witnesses are competent to testify that they have seen it.

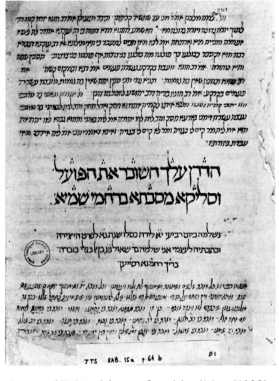

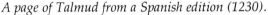

A page of Talmud from a Spanish edition (1230).

Traditional Jewish life has always been regulated by the Hebrew calendar. It is a lunar calendar, and a precise knowledge of the cycles of the moon is needed to set the days of celebration of the festivals and holy days prescribed by the Bible. In ancient times the appearance of the new moon was communicated to the diaspora communities by the fastest means then conceivable. A chain of signal fires would be set up on high hills, stretching from the Mount of Olives in Jerusalem clear across the vastness of the great desert all the way to Babylonia, creating a line of beacons to telegraph the news of the beginning of the new month.

The lighting of the signal fires was prohibited by Rome in the fourth century, and new means were devised to calculate the calendar. But if these beacons were extinguished in the centuries that followed, the fires of faith were fed by a passion for learning and

Built in Rome around 114 C.E., Trajan's Column commemorates the emperor's conquest of Dacia, in Central Europe, about eight years earlier. Soon Trajan would face another military challenge—the Jewish "Diaspora Rebellions" of 115–117.

meaning, an ethical and religious tradition that would never die where Jews lived. In all the lands of the diaspora, Jews faced the unending dilemma of being part of and yet apart from the societies in which they found themselves. In the Talmud they found an enduring beacon of light, visible from the most distant and exotic lands, to guide and unite them, in preservation of their identity and their age-old tradition.

CHRISTIANS AND JEWS

Except for some episodes of persecution during the fifth century, the Jewish community in Babylonia seems to have remained relatively stable and spiritually and intellectually fruitful. Not so in the West. We have concentrated on Rome's internal disorders—the Jewish revolts of 66–70 and 131–35 C.E. (there was another revolt in the intervening years, the Diaspora Rebellions of 115–117)—but the external threat was also growing, and during the reign of Hadrian, at the height of its territorial expanse, Rome began literally to build a wall in Britain and Germany to hold off barbarian invaders. But the walls were breached, and the empire crumbled: in four centuries the city of Rome had been repeatedly sacked, and barbarians claimed most of Europe.

These events held far-reaching implications for the Jews, whose settlements by this time extended all the way up the Rhine, perhaps as far as the North Sea. And yet it was a spiritual and theological revolution that most profoundly transformed the position of the Jews—a revolution set in motion by the life and death of Jesus of Nazareth.

It is said that Jesus preached at Capernaum, on the shores of the Sea of Galilee. The synagogue there was built some 200 years later, perhaps on the ruins of the one where Jesus told his parables as he sought a following among the major Jewish centers of Galilee.

More than one writer has remarked that Christianity began as a Jewish sect. What, aside from belief in Jesus as the Messiah, served to distinguish these first synagogue-going Gentiles from the synagogue-going Jews? The truth is: nothing. For Gentile as well as Jew, the Temple in Jerusalem was still the center of worship. Gentiles as well as Jews observed Jewish ethics, followed Jewish leaders, and hoped for deliverance by a Jewish Messiah. The astonishing thing is that within only a century, Christianity would blossom into a separate religion, and less than two centuries later would become the state religion of Rome.

So here was Jesus, the Jewish teacher, with his many followers, perceived as a threat by the Romans and by some among the Jewish leadership who were fearful of political chaos and who also opposed Jesus' messianic

The village of Capernaum, on the shores of the Sea of Galilee, was a leading Jewish community in the time of Jesus and an important center for the growth of Christian belief. The remnants of this Capernaum synagogue date from the late second century C.E., when Judaism and Christianity were developing side by side.

In a scene from *The History of the Savior* depicted in a series of mosaics at Ravenna, Jesus appears before the Roman procurator Pontius Pilate, who graphically "washes his hands" of the case. Centuries of bitter controversy surround the question of what roles the Roman secular and Jewish religious authorities played in the Crucifixion.

claims. In the traditional Jewish view the Messiah was to be a man—a messenger of God, a redeemer with Divine attributes, but still a man. It was the concept of Jesus as the Son of God that must have been deeply shocking to those elements of Judaism that took pride in the abstract nature of divinity. Jewish doctrine had been built on the belief in a God who had no form, a universal God who could not be seen.

In the long view of history, the ethical affinity of Judaism and Christianity emerges as more significant than the historic conflict. But no historian can possibly allow his ecumenism to lead him into such sentimentality as to ignore the fact that this was a sincere confrontation of ideas on matters of the utmost importance to many.

When Jesus led large numbers of people into Jerusalem and called for reform, the Romans saw the seeds of another uprising of the kind they had suppressed many times before. The details of the arrest and trial of Jesus are difficult to disentangle, but he was finally crucified by the Romans. For almost 2,000 years, the Christian perception has often been that the Jews were in some way collectively responsible for Jesus' death. In 1965 the Second Vatican Council sought to modify that perception, holding in blame only those who in Jesus' time directly pressed for his death, and deploring the hatred, persecutions, and outbreak of anti-Semitism directed against the Jews at any time and from any source. Between the time of Jesus and our time, there would be almost continuous persecution of the Jews by Christian powers throughout the world, for reasons so complex that they have never been fully identified. But in these same 2,000 years, Christianity would spread throughout the world, bringing with it many of the fundamental beliefs of the Jewish faith from which Jesus derived his belief and doctrines.

In its infancy, Christianity managed to at-

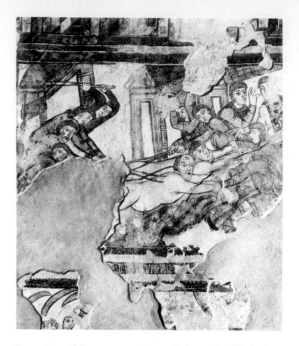

Rome's ruthless persecution of the early Christians did not halt the spread of Christianity, and veneration of martyrs came to have an important part in popular Christian worship. An Italian fresco dating from the ninth century.

tract followers despite a persecution by the Romans as relentless as any the Jews had endured. By 64 C.E., these early Christians were the empire's chosen scapegoats, singled out, as Tacitus tells us, as the cause of the great fire of Rome, which some suspected the Emperor Nero of having kindled so that he could enjoy the glory of building a magnificent new capital.

The martyrdom of Christians was not a sufficient satisfaction for Rome. The aim of the Roman Empire was to extirpate Christianity entirely. Christian tradition holds that most of Jesus' original disciples died as martyrs. The philosopher-emperor Marcus Aurelius, who held a low opinion of the Jews (though a high opinion of their patriarch, Judah ha-Nasi), was an especially ruthless persecutor of the Christians; by the time his reign ended, in 180 C.E., veneration of martyrs had come to play an important part in popular Christian worship. In the year 250 the Emperor Decius (201–251) instituted the first universal, systematic persecution of Christianity, seeking through terror and torture to compel the Christians to sacrifice to pagan gods. In many cases Christian martyrs were buried in Jewish cemeteries, and some Christians found shelter in Jewish synagogues. As late as 303 the Emperor Diocletian (245–313) ordered the churches to be torn down, the Christian scriptures confiscated, the clergy imprisoned and tortured—measures that must have had a fearful ring to Jews then and raise ominous echoes in Jewish hearts today.

And yet, only a decade later, the war against the Christians ended suddenly and astonishingly during the reign of Flavius Valerius Aurelius Constantinus, better known to history as Constantine the Great (306–337). He is one of the great figures in the history of Christianity. He began his reign as the head of an empire in which Christianity was the only religion officially outlawed and ultimately was converted and baptized, thus paving the way to the merger of the Roman state and Christian Church (it is as though the King of Saudi Arabia suddenly converted to Judaism). Overnight, Christianity became transformed from an oppressed minority sect into the state religion of the world's largest empire.

The victory of Christianity through the conversion of Constantine had negative effects for the Jews. Until then, they had been one of many peoples in the great mosaic of the Roman Empire. In the year 212 they had won citizenship; but a century later, when Christianity had become the official religion of Rome, there was a gradual effort to reduce their status. Judaism was not outlawed as paganism was. But there was an attempt to create for Judaism a state of legal inferiority. Roman emperors from Constantine onward promulgated laws prohibiting conversion to Judaism, on penalty of death. Intermarriage between Jews and Christians was also pro-

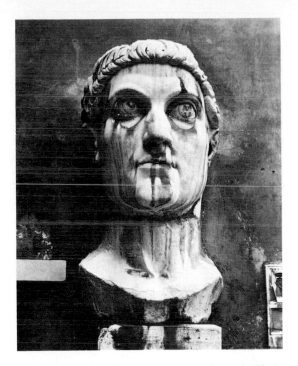

Constantine the Great, who transformed Christianity from an outlaw faith into the favored religion throughout imperial Rome.

hibited. Moreover, Jews were not allowed to own slaves, as Christians were.

To be quite fair, we should point out that these restrictions were not applied to the Jews alone; there is mention of their being applied to Samaritans and other sects as well. The object of these restrictions was not to oppress other sects and minorities for the sake of oppression, but rather to protect Christianity against intellectual and spiritual competition by other religions. Christianity still had to fight for its place in the hearts and minds of the peoples of the empire, and it was not disposed to leave its competitors free and equal in the field. But whatever the motivation for these restrictions, their effect was ominous, their precedent, dangerous. To put the matter simply, Jews under Roman rule passed almost overnight from minority status in a pagan empire to minority status in a Christian empire—a revolution all the more perilous for the Jews because of the increasing animosity between the two faiths since Jesus' time.

However much we emphasize the Christian debt to Pharisaic ethics and acknowledge the Church's recognition that—in the words of Vatican Council II—"she received the revelation of the Old Testament through the people with whom God in His inexpressible mercy concluded the Ancient Covenant," the fact remains that Christians and Jews faced irreconcilable differences on many key questions. Was Jesus the Messiah? Was Jesus the Son of God? Did faith in Jesus supersede the commandments of Mosaic Law? Had Christians replaced Jews as God's chosen people? These were all Jewish questions. There was no doubt in the mind of the Church fathers that Christianity's main purpose was to convert the Jews. Some maintained that anyone could accept Jesus as the Christ and thus become a Christian. But Paul believed otherwise. For Gentiles, he felt, it would be enough if they accepted Jesus as the Messiah and worshiped the Supreme Lord as their God. But Jews would have to meet more stringent conditions. They had, in fact, to cease being Jews.

There is something uniquely tragic in the relationship between Judaism and Christianity across the centuries. On the one hand they are linked by a kinship as strong as between mother and daughter. Deep and manifold affinities of origin, idiom, conceptual outlook, and moral values draw them together. But despite or, perhaps, because of their common roots, they have been torn apart by the savage intolerance of the daughter faith toward the mother, and by the reciprocal disdain and defiance with which the older creed defended its identity and its original sources of conviction. The real barriers are drawn not between Judaism and Christianity but between those who uphold and those who deny the role of faith and spirituality in their contest with atheistic and nihilistic materialism. Yet it is only in this century that any real ecumenism has developed in their relation to each other, and even

today the scars of past torments continue to cloud their dialogue. In most of history Christianity has resented the refusal of Jews to accept its claim of progress and innovation, while Christians have declined to pay filial tribute to the parent sources from which their faith has sprung. The belief that Christians have replaced Jews as God's elect remains a part of Christian doctrine to this day. Vatican Council II reaffirmed that "the Church is the new people of God," even as it condemned the teaching that the Jews were "rejected or accursed as if this followed from the Holy Scriptures." But the truth is that the ashes of the Temple had scarcely cooled when Christian proselytizers began citing the destruction of Jerusalem as a sign that God had withdrawn His blessing from the Jews. In any event, the rabbis attributed the fall of the Second Temple, as they did the destruction of the first, to Israel's failure faithfully to live by the precepts of Torah:

The first Temple was destroyed because of the sins of idolatry, harlotry, and murder. The second, in spite of Torah studied, commandments and deeds of love executed, during its existence, fell because of groundless hatred, and this teaches us that groundless hatred is a sin that weighs as heavily as idolatry, harlotry and murder.

In defining Church doctrine and practice, the Christians sought increasingly to distance themselves from Judaism and from the Jews. In about 300 c.e., a Christian council in Spain, the Council of Elvire, forbade Catholic parents to allow their daughters to marry heretics or Jews, on penalty of five years' excommunication. Social contacts with Jews were also forbidden:

If any person, whether clerical or one of the faithful, shall take food with the Jews, he is

The Road to Calvary, by the fourteenth-century Sienese master Simone Martini.

Fifteen centuries after the collapse of Rome, signs of the imperial achievement remain throughout Western Europe, the Mediterranean region, North Africa, and the Near East. ABOVE: in Cumberland, England, a stretch of Hadrian's wall. OPPOSITE PAGE, FROM LEFT: in Jordan, a triumphal arch in honor of Hadrian; in Algeria, another triumphal arch, this one glorifying Trajan; and in Tunisia, an amphitheater façade.

papacy. By virtue of that authority, it was he who formulated the policy of the Church toward the Jews, a policy that remained consistent, by and large, for all subsequent generations. It was never a completely favorable policy, but under the influence of pontiffs such as Gregory, there was a certain sufferance, and the Jews were protected with some minimal legal rights.

Gregory gave this policy its most explicit expression in his letter of June 598 to Victor, the bishop of Palermo, who had seized a synagogue without papal authorization:

Just as one ought not to grant any freedom to the Jews in their synagogues beyond that permitted by law, so should the Jews in no way suffer in those things already conceded to them.

Gregory's legalistic formula would often be quoted by later popes, and it was the willingness of Gregory and his papal successors to adhere to Church law that enabled Jews throughout Christian Europe to appeal to the pope whenever they were victimized by anti-Jewish outbreaks.

Gregory's impact on Church history extends far beyond his policy toward the Jews.

Tradition credits him with reshaping the Latin liturgy and reforming church music; and the system of plainsong developed by the Church of Rome is named "Gregorian chant" in his honor. Gregory gave the teachings of Augustine the stamp of orthodoxy, and he was the first pope to make belief in purgatory an essential of the faith. He also asserted papal authority in Spain, and he

The Empire in the West succumbed to barbarian invaders at the end of the fifth century C.E., but the Empire in the East—the Byzantine Empire—endured for almost a thousand years longer. This mosaic, at Ravenna, shows Emperor Constantine IV (r. 668–685), known as Pogonatus, the "Bearded One" (fifth from right).

the clergy, maintain public worship, and aid the poor.

One of Gregory's major edicts was his insistence on monasticism and celibacy for priests. Since the Talmudic era, Judaism had seen nothing especially virtuous in abstaining from marital relations, choosing instead to follow the Biblical commandment "Be fruitful, and multiply." The early Christians, on the other hand, in extolling the virtues of the spirit as against the evils of the flesh, came quite naturally to regard the highest form of earthly life as one that practiced self-denial. The "father" of Christian monasticism, Saint Anthony (c. 250–350 C.E.), a Coptic Christian of Egyptian birth, gave up his possessions at the age of twenty and by thirty-five had taken up the life of a hermit. Eventually he gathered around himself a group of like-minded men, each of them improvising his own rituals and exorcising his own demons.

More important for European history than these tendencies was the establishment of monasteries. The first true monastery was founded in Egypt about 318 C.E. by a monk named Pachomius, who required its members to follow the uniform rules of life and conduct he had devised. The ideal of life in common under the leadership of an abbot reached its highest stage of development about a century and a half later under the guidance of Saint Benedict of Nursia (480?–543?). At the age of twenty, Benedict too became a hermit, but in 529 (the traditional date) he founded, on the hill of Monte Cassino, midway between Naples and Rome, the monastery to which he gave his now famous Rule, the *Regula Monachorum*. Each monk was required to take the customary vows of poverty, chastity, and obedience. But the true guiding principles of the Benedictine monastery were moderation, industry, and order. Each activity—sleeping, eating, working, reading, praying—had its appointed time, for, said Benedict, "idleness

launched the missionary campaign that eventually brought Britain into the Roman fold. As the single most powerful figure in Italy, he negotiated directly with the Lombards, conceding their conquests in the north but maintaining the independence of Rome and its environs. And as the leading administrator of Church landholdings in Italy, Sicily, northern Africa, and southern France, he controlled much of the food supply of the Mediterranean world; he used the income from these lands to defend Rome, support is the enemy of the soul." And so, while the Rule held sway in both spirit and letter, the industrious monks became known as the best farmers in Europe, and they also earned respect as artisans for their weaving, glassmaking, and brewing. Moreover, in the absence of stable town life and effective civil government, the monasteries offered charity to the poor, hospitals for the sick, and sanctuary for the wayfarer. (For poor relief, medieval Jewry looked not to such Christian institutions, of course, but to its own synagogues.) Islands of literacy in a sea of ignorance, the monasteries maintained libraries, offered a haven for scholars, and labored to preserve the scriptures sacred to the Judeo-Christian heritage.

Before he became pope, Gregory I had resigned his office as prefect of Rome, divested himself of his possessions, and entered the monastery of Saint Andrew; at the time of his election to the papacy, he was the abbot of Saint Andrew, which had embraced the Benedictine Rule. Gregory thus became the first Benedictine monk to hold the Church's highest office.

During the seventh and eighth centuries the great diaspora continued to spread, scattering the seeds of Jewish survival throughout the entire Frankish empire, to Gaul and Spain and to parts of what are now Italy and Germany. The Emperor Charlemagne (742–814), as we shall see, was both a conqueror and a political genius. He had a remarkably strong influence on the life of his time. Despite his support for many Jews, the voices of the militant priests during his reign and in the subsequent period became increasingly shrill in denunciation of the Jews.

This virulent anti-Jewish rhetoric was not yet shared by the general populace. In the towns and villages in which they lived side by side with a few Jewish families, there was a relatively friendly relationship. Christianity was gradually penetrating the masses of the people. Many Christians were lax in their observance. They were quite happy to mingle some Jewish elements with their Christian observance. There were Christians who celebrated the Jewish Sabbath and who observed the Jewish festivals.

By this time, the Church had resolved most of the problems it had faced with the heretical religious movements—that is, the movements that had refused to accept the doctrine and authority of the Church. In the eyes of the militant priests—and not all priests were militant—the Jews were the last remaining major group within Christian Eu-

A scene from the life of Gregory the Great, skillfully depicted by an artist of the late Carolingian period. According to legend, when Saint Gregory paused for a long time while dictating his homilies on Ezekiel, one of his scribes impatiently pushed aside a curtain and saw the divine source of Gregory's inspiration—the dove of the Holy Ghost.

rope that was still outside the bounds of Christian orthodoxy. The notion that the Jews were somehow responsible as a people for the death of Jesus had now become an accepted part of the Christian tradition. Time had obliterated the fact that the early Christians were Jews, that Jesus himself was a Jew. And time had obliterated any consciousness that the Crucifixion of Jesus by the Romans was the response of Rome to a defiance of its authority. Nevertheless, the anti-Jewish sentiment expressed in the rhetoric of the militant priests was not yet reflected in any major overt activity against the Jews. And under Charlemagne and his immediate successors they had a relatively easy lot.

By any measure, Charlemagne is the commanding European figure of the early Middle Ages and one of the great monarchs of history. Nevertheless, there is something peculiarly evanescent about his achievements. When he became ruler of the Franks his kingdom already encompassed most of present-day France, West Germany, Austria, and the Low Countries; to these he added Bavaria, the Lombard kingdom in Italy, the buffer zone (or "march") between Christendom and Muslim Spain, and after a long and bitter struggle, the north German land of the Saxons, whom he converted to Christianity with brutal compulsion. And yet, within thirty years of Charlemagne's death, his empire had been dismembered along lines so heedless of national differences and natural boundaries as to plague Western Europe up to our own era. On Christmas Day, December 25, 800, Pope Leo III had crowned Charlemagne emperor of the West, an office that conferred upon him an almost apostolic responsibility as defender of Christendom, the Constantine of his age. Yet what did this title really mean? We owe to Voltaire the remark that the Holy Roman Empire was "neither Holy, nor Roman, nor an Empire"—a gibe that has since become one of the clichés in the writing of European history. Cliché

though it may be, there is truth in Voltaire's sally, for the Holy Roman Empire never did function as an effective political entity.

What then of the so-called Carolingian Renaissance, the rekindling during the reign of Charlemagne of the lamp of learning? There is no doubt that Charlemagne proved himself a wise and far-sighted ruler in recognizing the need for literate people to spread the faith, minister to the faithful, and maintain his kingdom.

Charlemagne himself was an assiduous pupil—when he was not off on horseback winning or governing his kingdom. He liked Augustine's holy books and was fascinated by astronomy. And yet, though he could read Latin and understand some Greek, he never mastered the script that is one of the crowning achievements of the age: in short, he could barely write his own name. As for Carolingian culture, it pales before what the Hebrews, Greeks, and Romans had accomplished, and what the Arabs—whom some have called the Greeks' true heirs—were about to achieve.

There were battles, of course, and the winning of people. There was the mastery of a religion, and—kindly with reason and faith, or brutally with the sword—there was the spreading of the word of Charlemagne's God. There was his need of and decency toward the Jews, and all the rest of what he did to the world and the world did to him. But all at once, Charlemagne the emperor was an old man: he was seventy-two. With misgivings and, evidently, the realization that the Carolingian empire would never be the same, he made his son Louis emperor. Louis was later to be known as Louis the Pious. Shortly thereafter, Charlemagne died. It seemed fitting that he be buried in the church he had built at Aachen. The inscription over his sepulcher tells his story:

Beneath this tomb lies the body of Charles, the great and orthodox emperor, who nobly

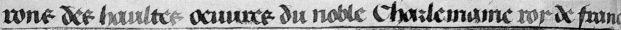

De plusieurs batailles que Charlemame eut alencontre

increased the kingdom of the Franks and reigned prosperously for forty-seven years. He died in his seventies in the year of the Lord 814, in the seventh indiction on the fifth day before Calends of February.

Charlemagne is crowned Holy Roman Emperor, December 25, 800. The title survived until 1806, but Charlemagne's own great kingdom was dismembered within thirty years after his death.

For the Jews of the European diaspora, Charlemagne was the stuff of legend. They would talk of the ways the emperor had favored their people—of how, as a gesture of thanks to the loyal Jews of Narbonne, on the Gulf of Lions along the south coast of France, he had appointed a Jewish "king" to rule that city. There is more than a grain of truth in such tales. But the reality is far more complex, and not fully comprehensible until we have considered the situation of the Jews in France and Germany and, in Chapter 5, under Muslim rule.

On German soil in medieval times, a specific branch of Jewish culture emerged as early as the eighth century. Under Charlemagne and his son Louis the Pious, the Jews were protected because of the services they could render to trade and finance. The Jews of northern France and western Germany

called that region, for some reason, by the Biblical name of Ashkenaz. Later the term *Ashkenazim* came to denote all Jews whose culture originated and developed in this part of Europe, as distinct from the *Sephardim*, whose culture originated and developed in Spain and the Mediterranean.

The original Ashkenazi Jews were economic pioneers, men of great mercantile enterprise. They were also deeply devoted to learning. Their scholarship concentrated mainly on Jewish and Talmudic studies, as distinct from the Jews of southern Europe, who put the emphasis of their research and learning on secular subjects. Throughout the Middle Ages the Ashkenazi Jews were to suffer great anguish and persecution, but they were to originate, develop, and transmit a legacy that would profoundly affect the course of Jewish history down to our own times.

Like the figure of Charlemagne himself, the origins of Ashkenazic Jewry are obscured by legend. Jews had settled along the Rhine in Roman times, but the impetus for the development of Talmudic scholarship among Western European Jewry came with the arrival in Germany of the Kalonymos family, probably sometime in the ninth century; Jewish tradition ascribes this migration to Charlemagne's call to the learned Rabbi Kalonymos of Lucca, Italy, to come to Mainz (Mayence).

Charlemagne was also interested in the Jews' diplomatic and commercial connections, for by virtue of their dispersion, the Jews were uniquely well qualified to serve as a vehicle for the Carolingians' limited contacts with non-Christian lands to the south and east. When Charlemagne sent an embassy in 797 to the Caliph Harun al-Rashid (literally, "Aaron the Upright"), the Muslim caliph of Baghdad, a Jew named Isaac served as interpreter; of all the principals among the envoys, Isaac alone survived the trip home, bringing with him to Charlemagne's court a present from the caliph—an elephant, until then unseen in Europe. And when Charlemagne wanted exotic foods from the Holy Land, he named a Jew as his imperial purveyor.

Events have now brought us to the beginning of the ninth century. During the reign of Charlemagne the word "Jew" had taken on a new meaning. Not only did it signify "merchant" to many, but it also meant one who was trustworthy and knowledgeable. Certain of the merchants were known as Radhanites, a term of uncertain origin (some have suggested that the word stems from a Persian root meaning "they know the way").

Popular history is surprisingly neglectful in failing to point out that 500 years before the famous explorer Marco Polo, Jewish merchants traveled thousands of miles to the distant corners of the world over trade routes they themselves had created, carrying with them goods they had purchased in Europe. By the year 800, when Charlemagne was crowned emperor of Rome, the Jews of Europe had already established regular trade routes by way of North Africa and the Middle East to regions as far east as present-day India, Russia, and China.

The diaspora of the Jews had begun almost 1,400 years before Charlemagne in the exile of Babylon. Some 700 years later the Romans had destroyed Jerusalem, and the scattering of the Jewish people seemed to be complete. But now, in the ninth century, as if in response to some instinct for survival, some foreknowledge of events to come, the diaspora reached out still further, spreading its small seeds to the most distant and unknown corners of the world.

We know from documents of the reign of Louis the Pious that Jews were becoming increasingly important to French and German commerce—so important, in fact, that the market day in Lyons, by then a significant center of Jewish settlement, was switched from Saturday, the Jewish Sabbath, to the middle of the week. Another, more negative indicator of rising Jewish influence was the torrent of anti-Jewish polemics that began issuing forth from two radical prelates of Lyons, the Archbishop Agobard (779–840) and his successor Amulo, who have been called the "fathers of medieval anti-Semitism." Here is Agobard complaining to his sovereign about the way in which the emperor's kindness to the Jews moved them to arrogance:

The Jews, abusing the naivete of the Christians, deceitfully pride themselves on being dear to your heart, because of the patriarchs from whom they are descended. . . . They exhibit orders and warrants bearing your gold seal and containing words that I cannot believe to be true. They display the dresses that their wives, they claim, have received from your family and from the ladies of the palace; they boast of having received from you, contrary to the law, the right to build new synagogues.

There is no evidence that Louis the Pious was swayed by these polemics. And when Agobard took it upon himself to compel the Jews of Lyons to attend Christian missionary sermons in their own synagogues, and sought to baptize Jewish children without their parents' consent, Louis summoned him to the imperial court to answer for his unlawful actions.

Under Archbishop Amulo the drumbeat of anti-Jewish agitation grew still louder:

Cursing the infidelity of the Jews and seeking to protect the Christian people from contagion, I have thrice publicly asked that our faithful draw aside from them, that no Christian serve them either in the cities or in the villages, letting them perform their labor with the help of their pagan slaves; I have also forbidden the eating of their food or the drinking of their liquors. And I have published several other severe injunctions, in order to tear out the evil by the root and to imitate the example of our pious master, shepherd, and predecessor Agobard.

In the spirit of these words a collection of anti-Jewish canons was submitted in 845–846 to the king of France, Charles the Bald (Charles I, 823–77), for his approval. Charles, however, refused to ratify them. Perhaps, like Charlemagne and Louis the Pious, he took a tolerant view on religious matters; we know, for example, that he appointed a Jew named Judah to the high office of imperial ambassador. Or perhaps the Jews were simply too important to his kingdom's economy to risk offending them; after all, they were essential suppliers of exotic commodities from the Muslim world and of slaves from Eastern Europe. (The English word "slave" actually derives from the ethnic term "Slav," for the Slavs, not yet Christianized, could be traded and owned as slaves by Jews as well as Christians.) Or it may be that in the administrative chaos that followed the creation

The reign of Louis the Pious, Charlemagne's son and successor, brought increasing prosperity to Jews in French and German commerce. This portrait of Louis is the oldest preserved manuscript illumination of a Carolingian monarch.

of the Kingdom of France through the breakup of the Carolingian empire, Charles simply regarded such anti-Jewish laws as unenforceable.

Whatever the reason, the Ashkenazim remained in relative prosperity under Charles the Bald, and for another 125 years after his death. Meanwhile, in Spain, North Africa, and the Near East, under the new and energetic empire of Islam, the Jews of the diaspora would once again enter the mainstream of world power and culture.

CONCLUSION: THE NEW AGE

By the seventh century the world of the Jews had grown by dispersion. Their communities extended from Persia to Morocco to Spain, from Central Europe to the Sahara. Christianity was now the religion of the Roman world, but the Jews were still a persecuted minority. And yet their central idea had triumphed: the idea of the unity of God and, therefore, the coherence of nature and of human destiny. That idea lived on in their own Biblical texts and Talmudic writings, and, through Christianity, was to become the normative principle of the Mediterranean world. Between Jews and Christians there was antagonism, but between Judaism and Christianity there was a deep underlying consensus. That consensus would now be enlarged. A vigorous, militant assertion of it would spring out of the blazing parched sands of the Arabian Peninsula.

We must remember that when Titus devastated Jerusalem in the year 70, the Jews had fled in all directions, some of them to the south and to the east. The Jews in Arabia cultivated the date palm and practiced their crafts as goldsmiths and silversmiths. The Bedouin tribes among whom they lived had a lofty poetic tradition. But their poetry told of love and hate, of war and heroism and hunting, with very little reflection on human destiny. The Bedouin Arabs were fascinated by what they heard from the Jews about Abraham and Moses and the prophets who came after. They liked the simplicity, the purity, the transcendent sweep of what they learned from the Jews about the one living God. The Arabs called the Jews the "people of the Book."

In Arabia, a young, vigorous Arab, Muhammad, pondered deeply on what he had heard about the Hebrew and the Christian writings. He developed his own ideas about a prophetic tradition from Abraham and Moses to Jesus, a tradition of which he believed himself to be the divinely appointed successor. But he did not succeed in persuading his neighbors, the Bedouin Arabs of the tribe of Qureysh in Mecca. In the year 622 he fled from their mockery and persecution to Medina. The flight of Muhammad to Medina in the year 622 is the starting point of a new calendar. The year 1984 is the year 1404 of the Hejira, or Hijra, the flight of Muhammad.

Muhammad had reason to hope that he would have better fortune with the Jews of Medina. But they too rejected his message. As so often in Jewish history, the refusal of Jews to be converted made them the target of a new hostility. But Muhammad was not a man to be easily thwarted. He collected an army of 10,000 men and marched to Mecca, which he conquered. What now happened is almost beyond belief. The armies of Muhammad and of his successors, the caliphs, captured Damascus, Jerusalem, Egypt, Baghdad, and Persia, one after another.

A hundred years after the death of Muhammad, his faith, Islam—which means resignation to God, or Allah—dominated vast areas from India all the way to Morocco and Spain. The advance of the Arab armies was halted only in the year 732 by the armies of the French Emperor Charles Martel at Tours and Poitiers in southern France.

Henceforward, the religious life of humanity is dominated by three faiths, each proclaiming the unity of God: Judaism, within its own intensely cultivated garden; Christianity, dominant in Europe; and the new faith, Islam, a new civilization, indeed a whole system of thought, government, and social behavior. The adherents of this new faith would scale great heights in literature, philosophy, art, architecture, mathematics. The ensuing generations would be the Arab age. The essential insights of Jewish experience had taken root in a new and fertile soil, and the harvest would be abundant beyond any dream.

The Passion of Christ, a wood panel by the fifteenth-century Flemish artist Hieronymus Bosch. In Christian iconography, the pelican (center) symbolizes redemption through suffering.

ومنهُم جبرٱيلُ

قال ذُابّجةُ اميرُ الرُّوحِ وخازنُ القُدسِ ويُقالُ لهُ انّهُ الرُّوحُ الامينُ والرُّوحُ القُدسُ
والنامُوسُ الاكبرُ وطاوسُ الملائكةِ جاءَ في القُرانِ انّ اللّهَ تعالى ادعُكُم بالّذي
سمعَ اهلُ السّماءِ جبرٱيلَ صلصلةَ جرِّ السِّلسلةِ على الصّفوانِ فيصعقُونَ ولا يزالُونَ كذلكَ
حتّى ياتيهِم جبرٱيلُ فاذا مضى فزِعَ عن قلُوبِهم فالوا يا جبرٱيلُ ما ذا ما لدبِّكَ
فيقُولُ الحقَّ فهو الحقُّ الحقُّ وجاءَ بالقُرانِ النّبيَّ صلّى اللّهُ عليهِ واله وسلّمَ
قال لجبرٱيلَ انّي احبُّ ان اراكَ على صُورتِكَ فقالَ انّكَ لا تُطيقُ قالَ .

5.
The Age of Faith

THERE IS much color and drama in the interplay of the Jews with the two great faiths, Christianity and Islam, that had sprung from the Law of Moses. Islam was not just a religion to be practiced in the mosques on Fridays. It is a comprehensive civilization, reaching into every avenue of human experience. And unlike early Judaism and Christianity, Islam from the beginning possessed great temporal power. Moses and Jesus never commanded armies or ruled territories, but Muhammad and his followers did both.

What is the truth about the Jewish condition under Arab rule? Most Jews lived in the East, in Babylonia, but what befell them there may be typical of their experiences later in Egypt and in Spain. There is no pretense of equality. For Islam, Jews may be the "people of the Book," but they are not believers, and therefore they cannot aspire to the highest political and military rank. There is sporadic persecution. There are no prolonged periods of assured stability for life and property. But there are compensating elements. The Muslim rulers interfere very little with the internal life of the Jewish community. There is a large measure of autonomy. The heads of the diaspora, called "exilarchs"— Jewish leaders whose families claimed descent from the House of David—exercise full control over their adherents. There is freedom of movement, freedom of occupation. And Jews although not reaching the highest rank, achieve positions of administrative and economic significance.

OPPOSITE

A miniature of the Archangel Gabriel, who appears as a heavenly messenger in both the Hebrew and the Christian Bible and is venerated by Muslims as the spirit who revealed the sacred scriptures—the Koran—to the Prophet Muhammad.

The Alhambra of Granada represents an enduring tribute to the genius of Islam.

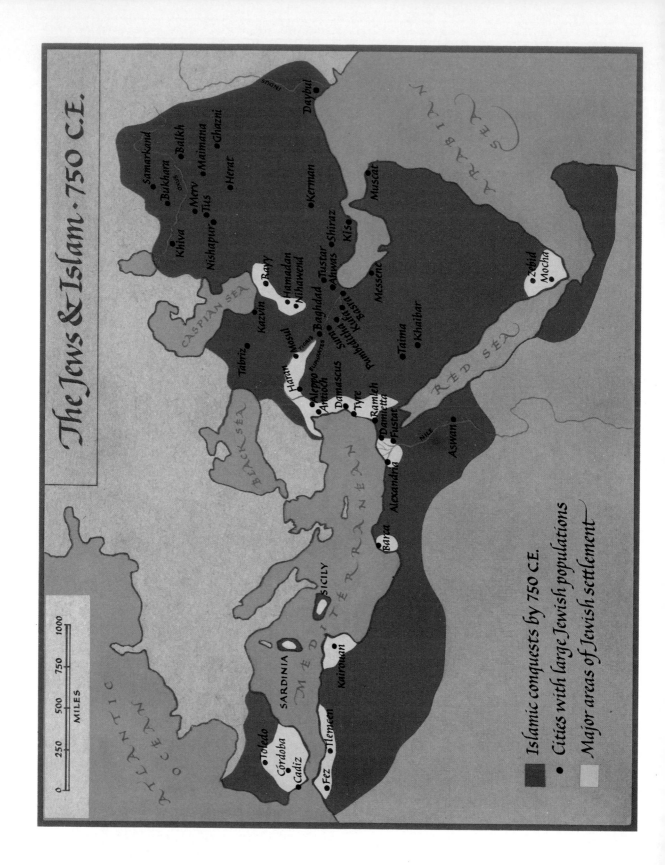

The Jews & Islam · 750 C.E.

Islamic conquests by 750 C.E.

• Cities with large Jewish populations

Major areas of Jewish settlement

MILES
0   250   500   750   1000

ATLANTIC OCEAN

Toledo
Córdoba
Cadiz
Fez
Tlemcen
Kairouan
SARDINIA
SICILY
MEDITERRANEAN
Barfa
Alexandria
Damietta
Fustat
NILE
Aswan
Ramleh
Tyre
Damascus
Antioch
Aleppo
Haran
Tabriz
BLACK SEA
CASPIAN SEA
Kazvin
Mosul
TIGRIS
EUPHRATES
Baghdad
Sura
Nihawend
Hamadan
Rayy
Khiva
Nishapur
Tus
Merv
OXUS
Bukhara
Samarkand
Balkh
Maimana
Ghazni
Herat
Kerman
INDUS
Daybul
Muscat
ARABIAN SEA
Shiraz
Ahwas
Tustar
Kis
Messene
Pumpeditha
Pumbeditha
Basra
Khaibar
Taima
RED SEA
Zebid
Mocha

Above everything else, life under Arab rule offered wide scope for creative spiritual energies. How else can we explain the heights of creative energy, of literary grace and aesthetic perfection exemplified in the eleventh and twelfth centuries by Solomon ibn Gabirol, Moses ibn Ezra, and Judah Halevi, all in Spain; and in Egypt by Moses ben Maimon—Maimonides, or Rambam—who also was born in Spain. In some places in the Arab empire, the Jews reached spiritual heights they had not scaled under Christian rule in the diaspora and would never know again until the emancipation of European Jewry in the nineteenth century and the development of American Jewry in the twentieth.

Underlying every conflict and prejudice separating Jews from Muslims was the unifying theme of allegiance to the authority of an exclusive God. What Jews recited in the second of the Ten Commandments—

Thou shalt have no other gods before me
(Exodus 20:3)

—reechoes from every minaret:

There is no god but Allah, and Muhammad is the emissary of God.

And in the first chapter of the Koran we find God referred to in Hebrew terms:

Praise to God, who is the Lord of the Worlds [Rab-al-Ālimīn], the ruler of the Day of Judgment [Yōm al Dīn].

These are in their origin Hebrew words, and are Hebrew ideas.

And so, in the medieval world, we have the confrontation of three great faiths. But how different is their condition! Two of them, Christianity and Islam, are firmly established as the state religions of great empires. Judaism, the first of them, must fight for its identity by force of spirit alone.

The intricacy of Islamic art is typified in this decorative page from an eleventh-century Koran.

THE WORLD OF ISLAM

In European history, the period extending roughly from the fifth through the fourteenth centuries is called the Middle Ages, a term originating in the Latin *medium aevum*, from which the adjective "medieval" derives. The humanists of the Renaissance tended to regard this entire period as a deep, dark chasm of ignorance and superstition, separating the enlightened classical civilizations of Greece and Rome from their own extraordinary era. No one who has studied the poetry of Dante and Chaucer, who has attended the piquant motets and splendid Notre Dame Mass of Guillaume de Machaut, or who has stood in awe before the Gothic spires of Chartres, Amiens, Reims, and Notre Dame de Paris can possibly share such a view. Especially when applied to the period from about 1150 to 1450, the idea of a Middle Age, of a merely transitional civilization, grossly underestimates the cultural accomplishments of European Christendom.

The idea of a Middle Age is misleading in another way. It suggests that while European culture languished, the world itself remained in a period of stagnation, waiting for the Renaissance to get civilization moving again. Nothing could be further from the truth. In Latin America, the Maya, Inca, and Aztec peoples were retracing the path from temple culture to urban society which the peoples of Mesopotamia had taken 2,000 to 3,000 years earlier. Emerging from the highlands of what is now Guatemala, the classic Maya civilization of Central America reinvented hieroglyphics, built magnificent ceremonial centers, and devised a calendar whose intricacy and accuracy demanded a sophisticated grasp of astronomy and mathematics. By the fifteenth century, on the eve of European conquest, two peoples predominated. In Mexico lived the Aztecs, who, despite the lack of a written language, had developed a complex network of trade and tribute; their religious life was devoted to supplying their principal deity with some 10,000 human sacrifices a year. In South America the Andean lands from present-day Ecuador to Chile were the home of the Incas, gifted empire-builders and administrators who had mastered techniques of land terracing, irrigation, metalworking, and (to a surprising extent) medical surgery.

Africa's first empires emerged during this same period, partly under the impetus of contact with Muslim lands across the Red Sea and along the Mediterranean. The West African empire of Ghana, flourishing from the eighth to the eleventh centuries, was succeeded by that of Mali, stretching from the Atlantic across the great bend of the River Niger. The trans-Sahara trade, though perilous, carried a steady supply of luxury goods and salt to the African interior, in exchange for slaves, leather goods, and gold.

Paper money, invented in China during the later Middle Ages, was a direct outgrowth of two other Chinese innovations. Paper made of mulberry bark had appeared in China as early as the second century C.E., and block printing was developed during the eighth or ninth century. The Chinese had also invented movable type by the eleventh century, or some 400 years before a German printer named Johann Gutenberg produced his first Bible. China is also credited with two other important inventions, the mariner's compass and gunpowder, although the Chinese used the latter for fireworks rather than firearms. All these discoveries probably reached Europe through Muslim intermediaries.

Between 600 and 1200 C.E., the population of China more than doubled, from an estimated 45 million to 115 million; in Europe, during this same period, the population increased much less rapidly, from 26 million to 58 million. Throughout these six centuries, Europe's share of the world population averaged 15 percent, compared with 70 percent for Asia as a whole.

As we thus survey the development of civilization from a global perspective, we can see that during the early Middle Ages, Christian Europe was lagging behind. No building in Christendom bears comparison with the Temple of Shiva at Prambanan, or with the great mosques of Córdoba and Damascus. While Chinese cartographers were drawing detailed maps of the world around them, Eu-

Bahram V (r. 420–40), the Sassanian king depicted with a bow in this Persian manuscript, began his reign by persecuting the Christians, but after losing a war with Rome in 422, he agreed to extend to Christians the same degree of tolerance that Zoroastrians would henceforward receive from the Roman emperor. The Sassanians ruled Persia until the mid-seventh century, when Arab conquest replaced Zoroastrianism with Islam, and Persia came under the rule of a caliph.

ropean mapmakers—faithful to Scripture, if not to the geographical realities—were still portraying Jerusalem as the center of the world, and the Nile, Ganges, and Euphrates as outflowing from the Garden of Eden.

But neither China nor Europe boasted the city that was, in all likelihood, the world's most populous by 814, the year of Charlemagne's death. That city was in the Middle East, in the heart of the Muslim empire. It was founded in 762 on the west bank of the Tigris, not far from the ruins of the ancient Persian capital Ctesiphon, in a region that had been since the end of Talmudic times the preeminent political and intellectual center of world Jewry. Abu-Ja'far' Abdullāh al-Mansūr (d. 755), the caliph who established this city as his capital, called it Madinat al-Salam, "City of Peace." By the ninth century, the population of Baghdad and its suburbs may have exceeded 2 million.

During the first six centuries of the Common Era, the population of the Arabian Peninsula more than doubled, from an estimated 2 million to at least 5 million. In particular, the population of the barely habitable Arabian interior (present day Saudi Arabia) is believed to have increased from one million to 2.5 million, a level not to be exceeded until our own century. Perhaps the most we can say is that resources were scarce and willing warriors were plentiful, but it was the message of Muhammad that galvanized the Arabs to action.

How shall we account for the revolutionary power of Islam, which conquered more territory more rapidly than any other mass movement in human history—and which, in today's Middle East, retains an extraordinary ability to rouse its adherents to passionate commitment? There is, of course, Muhammad's uncompromising insistence on absolute submission to the will of Allah, as revealed through His prophets. Among these Muhammad included the prophetic figures of both the Old and the New Testament,

from Abraham through Jesus. But the last and the greatest of all the prophets—*the* Prophet, as Muslims call him—was said to be Muhammad himself. God's revelations to Muhammad comprise the Koran (Al-Qur'ān, or "The Reading"), the holy book of Islam, whose 114 chapters, or *sūrahs*, embody codes governing religious, civil and commercial, and military affairs. In this respect the Koran resembles the Torah, the revelation to Moses. And like the Torah, the Koran has inspired commentaries upon commentaries —thousands of them—and a body of traditions (*Hadīth*) or established precedent (*Sunna*) that, variously codified, has enabled Islam to adapt its fundamental creed to changing times and circumstances.

Beyond these general characteristics of Muslim belief, there were special circumstances that contributed to Islam's unprecedented expansion. The first of these is the fact that unlike Christianity, which began life as a Jewish sect, Islam was from the very outset an independent religious movement. Unfettered by ties to Judaism, which had political links with Persia's Sassanian kings (rulers of much of Arabia at this time), or to Christianity, whose political center was Byzantium, Islam was free to sustain—and to draw sustenance from—the rising tide of Arab nationalism. Although the Koran proclaims that military action must be retaliatory rather than aggressive, it makes plain in repeated admonitions that Islam is a fighting faith:

Fight . . . until persecution is no more, and religion is for Allah.

Relent not in pursuit of the enemy. If ye are suffering, lo! they suffer even as ye suffer, and ye hope from Allah that for which they cannot hope.

As Arab conquerors sped on camel and horseback across North Africa and the Near East, compelling idolaters to choose "Islam or death," it is apparent that the line separating aggressive from defensive war must have been drawn quite liberally. As for the Bedouins who carried the burden of the fighting, the Koran promised that their willingness to sacrifice themselves in this world would surely be rewarded in the next.

Muhammad brought a message not only of political but of social revolution, a gospel that echoes the teachings of the Hebrew prophets. Nor should we neglect to mention the unique role played by the Koran. The Prophet himself could neither read nor write, and his revelations were transcribed by secretaries. Compiled by his followers shortly after his death, the Koran was the first Arabic book and as such had incalculable social, cultural, and educational as well as religious impact. Literacy in Arabic soon meant, quite simply, the ability to read Islamic scripture. The Koran holds the key to the evolution of Arabic script and prose style, much as the Bible translations of Martin Luther (1483–1546) and of the group of scholars commissioned by King James I (1566–1625) would later shape the development of German and English thought and expression.

We should not underestimate the Jewish and Christian presence in Arabia during Muhammad's lifetime. Jews had been living in northern Arabia at least since the Roman era, and their numbers must have increased after the destruction of the Second Temple and the suppression of the Bar Kokhba rebellion. Early in the sixth century, Judaism was briefly adopted by the royal house of the Yemenite kingdom of Himyar. Muhammad may have met many Christians and Jews in Mecca, his birthplace, which was on the caravan track from Yemen; and he would also have come into contact with the "people of the Book" on the way to Syria, for Muslim tradition holds that he accompanied caravans along that route.

It is sometimes said that the Koran sanctions holy war (jihad) only against idolaters,

Coins, which first appeared in China and in the Aegean region before 700 B.C.E., were barely known in Arabia in the time of Muhammad. The Syrian dinar (left) is a copy of a Sassanian coin; the silver dirham is based on a Byzantine model.

but the fact is that this is not entirely true:

Fight against such of those who have been given the Scripture as believe not in Allah nor the Last Day, and forbid not that which Allah hath forbidden by His messenger, and follow not the religion of truth, until they pay the tribute readily, being brought low.

(IX, 29)

In 632, shortly before his death, Muhammad instructed his representative in Yemen that this tribute (jizya) should take the form of a poll tax. In practice, this meant that Jews and Christians (as well as Zoroastrians) would not be compelled to embrace Islam, as the pagans invariably were, but they would be required to acknowledge the Muslims' political supremacy, on terms not unlike those which other imperial conquerors had imposed on their subjects. War was permissible as long as the Jews continued to resist, but if they were willing to submit—as they soon were, even before Muhammad and his army had conquered Mecca—the Koran required that their religious practices and communal institutions be respected.

When Muhammad arrived at Medina on September 22, 622, did he truly expect the Jews to accept him as their prophet, or at least to look with favor upon his mission to bring pagan Arabs into the monotheistic fold? When he began to pray while facing in the direction of Jerusalem, as the Jews did, and when he adopted the Jewish practice of fasting on Yom Kippur, was this because he was deeply impressed by their piety, or was this merely an opportunistic attempt to curry Jewish favor? Whatever Muhammad's motives and expectations may have been—and there is no unanimity concerning them—the fact is that his reception among the Jews of Medina ranged from indifference to hostility and, among Jewish scholars, open ridicule. Such indignities Muhammad could not forgive. Within five years, he succeeded in having most of Medina's Jews banished or slain. Some of the survivors settled in Khaybar, about seventy miles to the north. Besieged in 628, the Khaybari Jews capitulated after a struggle, on terms that set the pattern for the surrender of Jewish oases throughout northern Arabia.

The regulations that collectively made Jews and Christians the protégés (*dhimmīs*) of Allah are usually called the Covenant of Omar ('Umar) and attributed to the caliph Omar I ('Umar ibn-al-Kkattāb), during whose reign from 634 to 644, Muslim armies defeated the Sassanians and conquered Palestine, Syria, and Egypt.

The Covenant of Omar requires that Jews undertake to respect the supremacy of Muslims, to avoid imitating them, "to rise from our seats when they wish to sit down"—and to follow other practices of deference and self-abasement. As early as the eighth century, Jews and Christians were required to identify themselves through the clothes they wore and in many other ways as subject peoples. By the fourteenth century, Jews were commonly required to wear yellow, Christians blue, and Samaritans red; badges had

become standard equipment; and non-Muslim women were required to wear shoes that did not match, in combinations of black with white or red.

Generalizations about Jewish life under Islam are dangerous, in view of the great size of the Arab empire, the long time span involved, and the weakness of caliphate rule during much of this period. The fact is that the covenant laws were inconsistently enforced and obeyed. Dress regulations were often accepted and even welcomed by Jewish leaders, who saw them as barriers to assimilation and, therefore, as aids to the survival of a distinctly Jewish community. Nevertheless, these precedents were available to any Muslim ruler who, for religious, political, or economic reasons, wanted to humiliate his Christian or Jewish subjects.

Wherever the Muslims conquered new lands, they found well-established Jewish communities. In Palestine, Persia, Syria, Egypt, North Africa, Spain—Jews had been living from 500 to nearly 2,000 years. But the Arabs, who were eager to learn, also found many other civilizations to learn from. Alexandria, which fell to the Muslims in 638 and again in 646, had long been a repository of Greek learning, and the study of geography, astronomy, mathematics, and medicine had all flourished there. Mesopotamia offered not only storehouses of Persian and Jewish tradition but also a still vital Syriac culture.

Equally important, Muslim merchants and diplomats served as conduits of commerce and culture between those lands that the Arabs did not subdue. In 798 ambassadors of Harun al-Rashid concluded a treaty of alliance with China's T'ang rulers. From China the Arabs learned how to make paper; there were paper mills in Baghdad in Harun's lifetime. From India the Arabs learned the numerical system we call Arabic, the same numbers most of the world uses to this day. From Persia and Byzantium the Arabs acquired the art of the decorative mosaic, al-

For centuries, the *Maqâmât (Assemblies)*, a collection of picaresque tales in rhyme by Abu Muhammad al-Qasim al-Hariri (1054–1122), held prestige and popularity in the Arab world second only to that of the Koran. These illuminations from a thirteenth-century version show, ABOVE LEFT: the sultan's guard; ABOVE RIGHT: Al-Hariri's roguish hero, Abû Zaid, preaching in the Mosque of Samarkand; and, RIGHT: a passenger boat plying the Tigris River.

The Great Mosque of Samarra, Iraq, is the largest in the world, covering more than 400,000 square feet. Construction of the shrine began in 847, and the staged minaret was added the following year.

ence that performances of medieval European music increasingly acknowledge.

The period from the tenth through the twelfth centuries marks what some historians have called the "Renaissance of Islam." It is not a coincidence that this era, in which Islamic arts and sciences achieved their highest expression, was also a period of commercial expansion, in which Jews shared along with Muslims.

THE "GOLDEN AGE"

The rise of Islam brought a revival of Jewish fortunes in Jerusalem, where relatively few Jews had lived since the second century C.E. From Hadrian to Constantine, Jerusalem—then called Aelia Capitolina—was a small Roman town to which Jews were allowed limited rights of pilgrimage and in which a sizable Christian community gradually developed. After 326, when Constantine's mother, Saint Helena, visited the city, Jerusalem developed a more aggressively Chris-

The Al-Azhar Mosque of Cairo, although rebuilt over the years, has occupied the same site since 970 C.E., shortly after the Fatimids established their new capital at Al-Kahira.

though the technique of ornamenting furniture and interior surfaces with bits of enamel, glass, and stone dates back to ancient Egypt and Mesopotamia.

A brief list of English words of Arabic ancestry indicates the range of Muslim skills and interests: in mathematics, *algebra, algorism,* and *zero;* in the sciences, *alchemy* and *alcohol;* in art and architecture, *arabesque* and *minaret;* in textiles, *damask* and *muslin;* in leather crafts, *cordovan* and *morocco.* Nothing conveys to us the genius of Islam quite so well as its distinctive architectural style, with its colorful geometric patterns, Arabic script motifs, characteristic horseshoe arches, and domes of various types. Spanish-Arabic poetry and music had a palpable influence on the troubadours of Provençal—an influ-

tian character. Christian tradition ascribes to her pilgrimage the discovery of the "True Cross" in a crypt beneath the fallen temple of Venus. On this site, held to be the burial place of Jesus, Constantine erected the original Church of the Holy Sepulcher, which has itself passed through several incarnations.

Much of what we know about the Golden Age we owe to the recovery of a huge cache of letters, legal papers, literary works, business accounts, and other public and private records deposited by Egyptian Jews of the eleventh and twelfth centuries in the storeroom (*genizah*) of a synagogue in Fostat, the old city of Cairo. The existence of this Cairo *genizah* was known in Western Europe at least as early as 1753, but it was not until the late nineteenth century that European and American Jewish scholars began systematically to decipher and catalogue its contents.

As long as the caliphs made their capital in Damascus, the Jewish community in Jerusalem remained relatively secure. Jews were allowed to pray near the Temple site, and a new synagogue and school were built in the same vicinity. It was during this period, in all likelihood, that the Talmudic academy of Tiberias was relocated to the City of David.

Jerusalem's fortunes ebbed once again

Music has been woven inseparably into the fabric of Jewish life since Biblical times. ABOVE: five musicians—playing, from left, the tabor and pipe, violin, lute, bagpipes, and kettledrums—grace a fifteenth-century Barcelona Haggadah; BELOW: numerous tiny figures, many playing musical instruments, crowd the Hebrew letters of a German Jewish prayerbook produced in 1471.

The golden Dome of the Rock, still the most brilliant jewel of the Jerusalem skyline, was built in 691 on the site from which Muslims believe Muhammad ascended to heaven. The Rock is said to be the stone of Solomon's Temple on which the Ark of the Covenant stood.

after 750, the year in which the Umayyad caliphs—descendants of the caravan merchant aristocracy, the *Umayya*—were overthrown by the Abbāsids, a diverse group of rebels whose leaders traced their ancestry to Abbās (d. 652), Muhammad's paternal uncle. When the Abbāsids moved their capital to Baghdad, Jerusalem suddenly found itself at the periphery of Islamic power, and the influence and security of the city's Jewish community correspondingly declined. By the end of the century, Jerusalem had been overrun by the Fatimids, a North African caliphate rivaling the Abbāsids and claiming descent from Muhammad's daughter Fatima. The next conquerors were the Seljuks, founders of the Turkish empire; and finally, in 1099, came the Crusaders.

This ceaseless fighting took its toll of Jerusalemites of all faiths, but non-Muslims had to bear the additional burden of the *jizya* and other taxes. As so often happened, the impoverished Jews of Jerusalem turned to their more prosperous brethren in the diaspora. In this eleventh-century letter from the Cairo *genizah,* a certain Solomon the Younger, head of Jerusalem's Yeshiva of the Pride of Jacob, thanks the leading Jews of Fostat for their generous support in terms that would be familiar to diaspora Jews to this day:

A letter from our envoy has arrived related how you helped and aided him; how you encouraged the people to help their poor brethren time after time; and you informed them with touching words of their misery, their helplessness, and this heavy burden which has weighed like a yoke upon its inhabitants. . . .

This fourteenth-century Haggadah, probably from Barcelona, shows the Passover story being read to worshipers in a Sephardic synagogue.

. . . it is a duty for all Israel to support those who live in Jerusalem and to be a tent peg for them in time of need. Everyone who champions their cause will be entitled to share in their joy.

Support from the diaspora, however generous, could not save the Jews from the disaster that befell them when the Crusaders entered Jerusalem, after a six-week siege, on the night of July 14, 1099. Those Jews who escaped massacre by the Christian invaders were sold into slavery or held for ransom. The slaughter of its Muslim and Jewish defenders left the city severely depopulated, and as a remedy, Christian Arabs were resettled in what was formerly the Jewish quarter.

Then came yet another reversal of fortune.

In November 1187 the Crusader Kingdom fell to the armies of Saladin (Salāh-al-Dīn Yūsuf ibn-Ayyūb, 1138–1193), the Egyptian sultan who overthrew the Fatimid dynasty and cultivated Maimonides as a court physician. The Jews once again returned to Jerusalem, and the Western Christians were banished. But this, too, was only temporary. During the next four decades four more crusades were mounted. Worse still, in 1244 a horde of Khwarizim Turks rampaged through the city, and only sixteen years later it was sacked by the Mongols. When the Spanish Jewish scholar Nahmanides (Moses ben Nahman, or Ramban, 1194–1270) arrived in Jerusalem in 1267 he found only a ruin:

Great is the solitude and great the devastation, and, to put it briefly, the more sacred the places, the greater their desolation. Jerusalem is more desolate than the rest of the country; Judea more than Galilee. But even in this destruction it is a blessed land. It has about 2,000 inhabitants; about 300 Christians live there who escaped the sword of the Sultan. There are no Jews. There are only two brothers, dyers by trade, who have to buy their ingredients from the government.

Another two and a half centuries would pass before a Jewish presence in Jerusalem could be successfully reestablished.

In power, prosperity, and prestige, Jerusalem's loss was Babylonia's gain. By the time of the Muslim conquest, Jews had been living in Babylonia for well over a thousand years. Here, near the banks of the Euphrates, stood two great academies of Talmudic learning, Sura and Pumbeditha, described by one modern writer as the "Oxford and Cambridge of Mesopotamian Jewry." The Sura academy was founded early in the third century by Abba Arika ("Abba the Tall," d. 249), also known as the Rav, or "Teacher"; a native of Babylonia, Abba had studied Torah in Palestine with Judah ha-Nasi. The Pumbedi-

tha academy was established a few decades later by Judah bar Ezekiel (d. 299), of whom the Talmud says, emphasizing the continuity of Jewish tradition, "On the day Judah ha-Nasi passed away, Judah [bar Ezekiel] was born." During the Talmudic period, the head of each academy was elected by its rabbis. But from the sixth century, when the leader of each academy assumed the title of Gaon, the two Geonim were usually appointed by the exilarch.

During the period of Sassanian rule, the exilarch was recognized as the governor of Persian Jewry, but his influence spread much wider, especially after the Jewish patriarchate in Palestine was abolished by Theodosius (r. 379–395), emperor of the East. With the coming of the caliphate the exilarch could claim to represent all Jews within the domain of Islam, although his administrative authority was still confined to Iraq and Persia. Contributing to the exilarch's prestige under Islamic rule was the fact that the Muslims, unlike the Persians, honored David as one of their prophets. The exilarch when the Muslims conquered Babylonia was Bustanai ben Haninai (c. 618–670). Bustanai, to whom all subsequent exilarchs under Arab rule traced their ancestry, himself claimed descent from

Arabs offering tribute to the Byzantine emperor.

David. The exilarchate exercised its broadest power during the first half century of Abbasid rule, but when the influence of the Baghdad caliphate began to wane, the potency of the exilarchate declined with it.

The exilarch's counterparts in religious matters were the Geonim, who became *ex officio* the intellectual leaders of diaspora Jewry. The academies they headed served as the supreme courts of Judaism, interpreting and resolving contemporary legal questions in the light of Torah and Talmud. Each year, thousands of Jews made the journey to Sura and Pumbeditha, where lectures were given and rulings issued. The Geonim would dispatch their written opinions (called *responsa* in Latin, *teshuvot* in Hebrew) to halakhic questions submitted from afar.

Despite the prestige of the Babylonian Gaonate, the fact is that relatively few men who held the title of Gaon ever made a significant mark on Jewish history. One reason

Although Granada of the Golden Age is remembered chiefly for its Muslim monuments, such as the Alhambra, Jews lived in the city long before the Moors arrived, and in the time of Samuel ha-Nagid, Jews were a majority of the population.

for this was that the exilarchs, who named the Geonim, usually chose these office holders for political motives rather than on considerations of scholarship. Moreover, the office tended to be hereditary, with only a half-dozen families supplying the Geonim for both Sura and Pumbeditha.

The outstanding exception to this pattern was the Gaonate of Saadia ben Joseph (882–942), better known as Saadia Gaon. Born in Egypt, Saadia was already accomplished in Torah and secular subjects when he left his native land to study at the Talmudic academy of Tiberias in Palestine. He reached Babylonia in 922 and immediately joined the Pum-

A sixteenth-century depiction of the Reconquista, in which King Alfonso X of Spain (r. 1252–1282) lead his forces in battle with the Moors.

beditha academy, succeeding to the Sura Gaonate six years later. A master of Hebrew, Saadia wrote three treatises on the language and did the first translation of the Hebrew Bible into Arabic. Most of his writings, though on Jewish themes, were Arabic originals—an indicator of the extent of Jewish social and economic integration under Islam after three centuries of Arab rule.

Saadia's *Book of Opinions and Doctrines* attempted to prove that there was no irreconcilable conflict between the evidence of reason and the teachings of Judaism. Here Saadia was facing one of the central intellectual problems of his day. This was an era when the Jews, as never before in their history, participated fully in the secular sciences, not just in medicine but in mathematics, geography, astronomy, and navigation.

Could a Jew immerse himself in these scientific currents without denying the beliefs and traditions that made him Jewish? Saadia's answer was an unequivocal yes. He held that reliable tradition—which in rabbinic Judaism meant Torah, oral as well as written—was as indispensable a source of knowledge as were sense impressions, self-evident principles, and syllogistic inferences. As sources of knowledge, Saadia maintained, reason and revelation did not confute but rather complemented each other. Thus we can see the Sura Gaon as a great reconciler, balancing the claims of science and religion, of Arabic culture and Jewish belief.

Saadia's most frequent antagonists were the Karaites (literally, "people of the Scriptures"), a name given in the ninth century to a number of heterodox Jewish sects that were united primarily by their denial of the authority of the Oral Law and their rigid adherence to the Bible. The Karaites pointed, for example, to the Biblical prohibitions governing the Sabbath. The Oral Law, codified in the Talmud but not restricted to it, maintained that while no fire could actually be lit on the Sabbath, a fire kindled before the Sabbath eve might be left burning. The Karaites denied this—a denial that, as the Rabbanites (the followers of oral, or rabbinic, tradition) pointed out, left the Karaites' homes dark, chilly, and cheerless.

For the most part, the dispute between Rabbanites and Karaites was an internal quarrel, with both factions treated alike as Jews by the outside world; only in nineteenth-century Russia were the Karaites distinguished from the remainder of the Jewish population and granted special legal and social privileges, which they exploited to the disadvantage of their orthodox brethren. Today, Karaism has only a few thousand adherents in Israel and elsewhere.

JEWS IN SPAIN

The Spanish era is one of the most extraordinary chapters of Jewish history. The story has a central figure. During Saadia's lifetime, and in the three decades following his death, a Cordoban Jew, Hasdai ibn Shaprut (c. 915–975), laid the foundations in Muslim Spain for a Jewish cultural flowering that would far surpass that of Babylonia.

Jews had been living in Spain since Roman times, subject to religious persecution and social ostracism. From the fourth century onward, the Visigoth rulers vacillated in their policy toward the Jews, sometimes imposing economic sanctions as an incentive to "voluntary" conversion, at other times resorting to forced baptisms and outright expulsion. Meanwhile, the Muslims were making their way across North Africa and penetrating the Mediterranean. The conquest of Alexandria in midcentury immediately gave them the benefit of that city's great shipyards, and by 680, Arab vessels had begun to raid the Spanish coast. As the Muslim threat mounted, the rumor that Spanish Jews planned to appeal to the Arabs to rescue them from Christian persecution began to grow. In 694 the Visigoth king Egica convened a council and denounced the Jews as traitors to the realm. Suddenly they were slaves: all Jews who could not escape lost their possessions along with their freedom. It is hardly surprising, therefore, that when the Muslims finally did invade Spain in 711, the Jews not only welcomed them but fought alongside them and administered the cities they conquered.

Before the Muslims could launch an invasion of Iberia, however, they first had to subjugate the Maghreb. Sixty-five years elapsed between the fall of Tripoli (644) and the conquest of Tangier (709), during which time the Arab armies encountered fierce and continuing resistance from the Berbers of North Africa. Berbers were converted to Islam and served in large numbers in the army that conquered Spain. By 718 the Muslims controlled almost the entire Iberian Peninsula, which they called al-Andalus.

The Muslims, who settled mainly in southern and central Spain, made their impact on Spanish life not by force of numbers but by

The changing fortunes of Spanish life are reflected in the history of Córdoba and its most famous religious edifice. On the site where first a Roman temple and then a Visigothic church once stood, the Moors erected the great mosque, resplendent with columns of marble, jasper, and onyx and lit by 4,000 brass and copper lamps. With the reconquest of Córdoba in 1236, the mosque was consecrated as a church. Today it serves as a cathedral.

the power of their culture. During the first three centuries of Islamic rule, the entire population of Spain probably did not exceed 4.5 million. The Arab invaders and their descendants were a small minority of a minority—only 20 percent—in a complex ethnic mix that also included Berbers, Muslims of native Spanish stock (Muwallads), Christians of the south (Mazarabic Christians) as well as the north, and slaves of Slavic or black African lineage. Jews made up an estimated 6 to 10 percent of the population overall, but perhaps twice that proportion in the urban centers of southern Spain, where the Arab minority was also concentrated. Jews undoubtedly fared better for longer under the Muslim caliphs than under the Christian

The year 1066, an ominous point in Judeo-Spanish history, was even less propitious for the Saxons in England. It was in 1066 that William the Conqueror—shown exhorting his knights in the famous Bayeux Tapestry (c. 1073–1088)—landed on British shores, defeated a Saxon army, and assumed the English crown.

kings. During the first 300 years of Islamic rule, when the fighting between the Christian and Muslim societies was confined to the north, Muslim agriculture, trade, and technology brought prosperity to southern Spain.

Politically, Spain was an isolated enclave at the extreme western flank of the Islamic empire. The Abbasid revolt of 750, which so altered the course of Baghdad's history and that of Babylonian Jewry, affected Spain only indirectly: as a result of the Abbasid persecution of the Umayyads, Abd-er-Rahman I, a member of the Umayyad family, fled from Damascus to Spain, arriving there in 755 and establishing himself as emir (from the Arabic *amir*, "commander") of Córdoba shortly thereafter. This Cordoban offshoot of the Umayyad dynasty did not attain dominance over its provincial rivals until the advent of Abd-er-Rhman III (891–961). He became emir in 912 and, having subdued the recalcitrant Arab and Berber chieftains, declared himself caliph in 929—an act that ushered in the Golden Age of Muslim Spain and likewise proved decisive for Jewish history.

Abd-er-Rahman's accomplishments as caliph are justly celebrated. He defeated the armies of the northern Christian kingdoms of León and Navarre. He seized part of Morocco for his caliphate. He established Córdoba as Europe's chief seat of learning. From the standpoint of Jewish history, however, his most far-reaching act was to elevate Hasdai ibn Shaprut, his court physician, to the office of director of the customs department and to the role of trusted adviser and emissary. It was Hasdai who conducted the delicate negotiations that led to the conclusion of peace treaties with León and Navarre in the late 950s.

Just as Abd-er-Rahman, in placing himself on a par with the caliphs of Damascus and Egypt, established Muslim Spain's political autonomy, so Hasdai ibn Shaprut, as leader of the Jewish community of Muslim Spain, deliberately sought to end his people's subservience to Babylon. He named as rabbi of Córdoba the learned Moses ben Hanokh (d. c. 965), who headed a *yeshiva* (rabbinical academy) and wrote *responsa*, so that Spanish Jews would not have to send to Sura and Pumbeditha for answers to halakhic questions. Hasdai befriended poets and supported scholars. A practicing physician, he also patronized the sciences and the other learned professions.

At the same time, Hasdai did not scorn the

intellectual resources of Babylon. He bestowed gifts on Sura and Pumbeditha, and he exchanged letters with Saadia Gaon's son, who sent Hasdai a biography of his famous father. Hasdai had an enormous curiosity about how Jews fared in every corner of the diaspora. One of the most celebrated surviving documents of the Golden Age is the letter he wrote through his secretary, Menahem ben Jacob ibn Sarūq, to Joseph, king of the Khazars. He has heard, writes Hasdai, of a Jewish kingdom called Khazaria, about a fifteen-day sea journey from Constantinople. At first he doubted the report, which was brought to Córdoba by Persian emissaries. But now, he tells Joseph, this news has been confirmed by Byzantine ambassadors, who tell him of the Khazars' Jewish king.

Hasdai first offers the Khazar king a description of his own land, which he calls Sefarad, of the king who rules it, and of the steps that Hasdai has taken to arrange for the delivery of his letter, written in Hebrew sometime between 950 and 960. Next comes a barrage of questions that Hasdai entreats Joseph to answer.

What is your state? What is the name of your land? What tribes inhabit it? What is the manner of government, how kings succeed one another, whether they are chosen from a certain tribe or family, or whether sons succeed their fathers, as was customary among our ancestors when they dwelt in their own land? . . .

Who were the Khazars and where did they come from? Today we know that the Khazars, a nomadic people of Turkic stock, reached the Volga-Caucasus region from Central Asia not later than the sixth century C.E. By the end of the seventh century, the Khazars had fought the first of two wars along their southern border with the empire of Islam; the Khazars' own empire had by this time expanded westward to the Crimea, initiating a period of unbroken contact with Byzantine civilization and of sporadic involvement in the imperial politics of Constantinople. How, then, had the Khazar kings come to be Jewish? Not, as Hasdai supposed, because of any descent from or contact with the "ten lost tribes." Originally, Joseph tells him, the Khazars were pagans, and they remained so until a king named Bulan, "a wise God-fearing man . . . expelled wizards and all idolaters from the land, and trusted in God alone."

Probably in 965, but surely within Hasdai's lifetime, Russians from the state of Kiev (already regarded as a threat to Khazaria in Joseph's letter) invaded the empire and sacked Atil. Arabic sources indicate that Khazar leaders then appealed to a neighboring Islamic state but were told that the price of assistance was Khazaria's conversion to Islam. Thus, according to Muslim historians,

A fourteenth-century Passover seder, as depicted in a Haggadah from Barcelona.

the kingdom that had embraced Judaism around 740 suddenly abandoned it less than two and a half centuries later. But even this drastic step could not save Khazaria. What the Kievan Russians began, the savage Polovtsi nomads finished, and by the end of the eleventh century the Khazar empire was no more.

As important for Jewish life as the direct historical role of Khazaria may have been, its symbolic significance was even greater. The idea that a powerful king, able to choose freely among the world's great faiths, would select Judaism over Islam or Christianity must have been cheering to a people who saw the growth of their religion constricted by prejudice and political circumstance. The hold of Khazaria on the Jewish imagination also highlights the sense of incompleteness that characterizes the most thoughtful Jews of the Golden Age. This theme, expressed as a longing for freedom from foreign rule in Hasdai's letter, takes proto-Zionist form in the poetry of Judah Halevi (1085?–1140):

My heart is in the east, and I in the uttermost
    west—
How can I find savour in food? How shall it
    be sweet
to me? How shall I render my pledges and
    vows, while
yet Zion lieth beneath the fetter of Edom,
    and I in
Arab chains? A trifle would it seem to me to
    leave
all the good things of Spain—
Seeing how precious it would be to behold
    the dust
of the desolate sanctuary.

Halevi incorporated the story of Khazaria into his philosophical dialogue originally entitled, in Arabic, *Kitāb al-Hujja wal-Dalīl fī Nasr al-Dīn al-Dhalīl* (*The Book of Argument and Proof in Defense of the Despised Faith*) but now more familiar, in Hebrew, as *Sefer al-Kuzari* (*The Book of the Khazars*). In this influential polemic, which purports to be an account of

how the Khazar king chose Judaism over the other religions, Halevi champions the rabbinic view not only against Christianity and Islam but also against Karaism and Aristotelian rationalism. It is noteworthy that in the final pages of the *Kuzari*, completed as Halevi prepared to make the dangerous journey to the Holy Land, which he seems never to have reached, the rabbi, having convinced the king of the merits of Judaism, announces his own intention of leaving Khazaria for Jerusalem. There alone, says the rabbi (speaking for Halevi), can the life of a Jew be completely fulfilled.

Underlying this nascent Zionism was an acute awareness of the vulnerability of Spanish Jews. Following the decline of the Córdoba caliphate early in the eleventh century, Muslim Spain entered an era of political fragmentation, during which numerous Arab and Berber principalities competed for cultural, commercial, and military supremacy. In the short run, this was a boon for educated Jews, who provided the Muslim princes with a steady supply of scribes, scholars, physicians, and political and financial advisers. Over the long term, however, the costs of political instability were high. A whole Jewish community might be uprooted when a prince was toppled through conquest or court intrigue.

The political upheavals of the eleventh and twelfth centuries cast a shadow over the careers of most Jewish notables of the Golden Age. When Berbers conquered Córdoba in 1013, one of the many Jews forced to flee the city was a young scholar named Samuel ibn Naghrela (993–1056). Samuel, who had studied Jewish law with Hanokh ben Moses and was fluent in both Hebrew and Arabic, settled in Málaga, where he opened a spice shop.

Samuel was brought to the court of Granada, where he successively held the posts of tax collector, secretary, and assistant vizier to the Berber King Habbūs. After Habbūs died,

Samuel became vizier (as well as military commander and most trusted adviser) to Habbūs's son Bādīs, whose accession to the throne Samuel had helped maneuver. When Samuel led Bādīs's army into battle for the first time in 1038, he had already been leader (*nagid*) of Spanish Jewry for more than a decade. It is astonishing to think of a Jew, Samuel ha-Nagid, commanding a Muslim army through seventeen years of Spanish combat and compiling a manual of Jewish law so as to make Spanish Jewry independent of the Geonim in Babylon. In addition to fulfilling these public duties, Samuel was also one of the leading Hebrew poets of the Golden Age.

Samuel was also a patron of other poets, notably Solomon ibn Gabirol (1020–1057?). Probably born in Málaga, Gabirol was raised in Saragossa, where, by his own account, he was ugly, sickly, and weak. He might have come to Granada in 1048, during Samuel's viziership—but in any event, his panegyrics to Samuel leave little doubt that the *nagid* was one of his sponsors. With astonishing virtuosity, Gabirol adapted into Hebrew a panoply of Arabic motifs, meters, and verse forms. Although he has been called the major religious poet of Spanish Jewry, his most characteristic note (rare in Hebrew poetry) is a self-concern that ranges from self-pity to a kind of arrogant swagger.

The further we go into the eleventh century, the more pervasive become the signs of uprootedness and instability. One of Solomon ibn Gabirol's early patrons, Jekuthiel ben Isaac ibn Hasan, an adviser to the Saragossa court, was deposed and executed under mysterious circumstances in 1039. Samuel ibn Naghrela's son Joseph ha-Nagid (1035–1066), who succeeded his father as vizier of Granada before he turned twenty-one, was accused by Muslims of using his office to benefit Jewish courtiers unduly. As arrogant as he was talented, Joseph was assassinated on December 30, 1066, as the result of a palace intrigue

The title page of the Guide for the Perplexed, *the last of Maimonides's monumental works.*

In the English-speaking world, 1066 is remembered as the year in which William, duke of Normandy, known as William the Conqueror, landed on British shores, defeated an army led by the Saxon King Harold II in the battle of Hastings, and was crowned king of England on Christmas Day. For the history of Spanish Jewry, however, the year 1066 has an ominous ring. On December 31 of that year, the day after the murder of Joseph ha-Nagid, a Muslim mob stormed through the Jewish quarter of Granada—the first, but certainly not the last, recorded case of Muslim persecution of Spanish Jews. The poet and philosopher Moses ibn Ezra (1070–1137?) was forced to leave Granada after its conquest in 1090 by the Almoravides. His protégé Judah Halevi fled Granada for the same reason. After the coming of the Almohades, Maimonides (1135–1204) likewise fled, following a route that would take him from his native Córdoba through Spain (and perhaps Provence) to Morocco. The Golden Age was not all that golden.

Moses Maimonides and his family endured persecution not only in Spain but also in Morocco, which they fled in 1165. After living for about five months in Acre, the family headed southward to Jerusalem and Hebron, and from there to Egypt. Following a brief stay in Alexandria they settled at Fostat, which had been founded by Muslim conquerors a decade after the death of Muhammad and which had been the capital of the Fatimid caliphate since the tenth century. Such proximity to the seat of Islamic power in North Africa must have been an advantage to Maimonides, as it had been for the Jewish leaders of Babylonia and Andalusia. But power seeking was probably not the reason why he came to Cairo. More likely, Rambam saw Cairo, with its well-organized Karaite community, as a formidable challenge to his talents as a Talmudist.

The early years at Fostat seem to have been among the most fruitful and happy of his career. His brother David's success in the gem trade allowed Maimonides to devote full time to writing, studies, and community duties. In 1168 he completed his first major work, the *Commentary on the Mishnah (Perush ha-Mishnah)*, not only a history of the Oral Law but also a learned comparison of Aristotelian and rabbinic ethics. Five years later, however, the death of his brother completely changed his outward circumstances. This was a blow from which Moses, thirty-eight years old at the time, never really recovered.

Maimonides was now faced with the time-consuming necessity of earning a living. He thought it improper to support himself by teaching Torah. "Better . . . to earn a drachma as a weaver or tailor or carpenter," he wrote in 1191, than to depend on the exilarch for a license to be a rabbi.

Maimonides chose to earn his living as a physician, a profession that was not uncommon among the leaders of Golden Age Jewry. Hasdai had been a physician; so had Judah Halevi. Judah ben Saul ibn Tibbon (c. 1120–1190), the translator of *Kuzari* from the original Arabic into Hebrew, practiced medicine after leaving Granada for southern France; his son Samuel ben Judah ibn Tibbon (c. 1160–1230), who prepared the Hebrew translation of Maimonides' *Guide for the Perplexed,* was also the translator of several medical texts. (The medical profession, incidentally, was open not only to men; the Cairo *genizah* documents mention several women doctors. Most likely these women, being unable to afford the costly apprenticeship in scientific medicine, held the lower rank of "medical practitioner.")

Maimonides mastered medicine as he mastered many fields of knowledge—through tireless study. By 1185 he had become a leading physician at Saladin's court, as well as personal physician to the vizier al-Fadil.

Maimonides is the most remarkable figure in post-Biblical Jewish history. He offers the clearest picture of his varied communal responsibilities in a vivid letter that he wrote to Samuel ibn Tibbon in 1199, when Maimonides was in his mid-sixties. This oft-quoted document, written in order to discourage Samuel from coming to visit him, describes a daily routine that would stagger many a younger man:

I dwell at Misr [Fostat] and the Sultan resides at Kahira [Cairo]; these two places are two Sabbath day's journey [about a mile and a half] distant from each other. My duties to the Sultan are very heavy. I am obliged to visit him every day, early in the morning; and when he or any of his children, or any of the inmates of his harem, are indisposed, I dare not quit Kahira, but must stay during the greater part of the day at the palace. It also frequently happens that one or two of the royal officers fall sick, and I must attend to their healing. Hence, as a rule, I repair to Kahira very early in the day, and if nothing unusual happens, I do not return to Misr until the afternoon. Then I am almost dying with hunger. I find the antechamber filled with people, both Jews and Gentiles, nobles and common people, judges and bailiffs, friends and foes—a mixed multitude, who await the time of my return.

I dismount from my animal, wash my hands, go forth to my patients, and entreat them to bear with me while I partake of some slight refreshment, the only meal I take in the twenty-four hours. Then I attend to my patients, write prescriptions for their various ailments.

In consequence of this, no Israelite can have any private interview with me except on the Sabbath. On this day the whole congregation, or at least the majority of the members, come to me after the morning service, when I instruct them as to their proceedings during the whole week; we study together a little until noon, when they depart. Some of them return, and read with me after the afternoon service until evening prayers. In this manner I spend that day.

A page of the Mishneh Torah (1180), Maimonides's great codification of Jewish law, in an edition published in Spain in the 1400s.

What is remarkable is that Maimonides should have been able to shoulder the burdens of his medical practice, leadership of Cairo Jewry, a flourishing correspondence, and the writing not only of medical treatises but also of the works on which his enduring fame depends—the *Mishneh Torah* (*Repetition of the Law*), completed in 1180, and the *Guide for the Perplexed*, finished a decade later. In compiling the *Mishneh Torah*, his Hebrew masterwork, Maimonides suffered from no modesty of purpose. His intention, he proclaims, is to codify and rationalize the Talmud and all the rulings and commentaries of the Geonim. Maimonides claims unashamedly that his work makes direct study of the Talmud and of Geonic writings unnecessary. The influence of the *Mishneh Torah* on Jewish practice and halakhic scholarship has been incalculable. One index of its enduring interest is that hundreds of commentaries have been written about it—an ironic compliment for a work its author believed would be the only code required "for ascertaining any of the laws of Israel."

In the *Guide for the Perplexed*, composed in Arabic, Rambam had a different purpose—the attempt to harmonize reason and Scripture, an effort he had undertaken two decades earlier in the *Commentary on the Mishnah*. The *Guide* is addressed to that "religious man for whom the validity of our Law has become established in his soul and . . . actual in his belief," but who, having studied philosophy, is troubled by certain "equivocal, derivative, or amphibolous terms."

The *Guide* was the last of Rambam's monumental works. His death, on December 13, 1204, was marked by three days of public mourning in Fostat, a public fast in Jerusalem, and expressions of grief throughout much of the Jewish world. Maimonides lies buried at Tiberias, where, according to tradition, Johanan ben Zakkai and Rabbi Akiva also found their eternal rest.

"From Moses to Moses there was none like Moses." This popular slogan reflected the unique prestige of Rambam in post-Biblical Jewish history. His prestige grew with the passing years and was great enough to act as a counterweight to what in others would have been a cause for reproach. Jewish religious authorities have been generally reluctant to acknowledge the virtues of other faiths, and to admit that Judaism could ever exchange influences with previous or contemporary civilizations. Maimonides made no secret of his admiration of Aristotelian principles. He believed and proclaimed that there were common as well as disparate elements in thought and in Jewish beliefs. His name thus belongs both to orthodoxy and to ecumenism.

We face the paradox that Judaism and Hellenism celebrated their greatest affinities long after Hellenism had been eclipsed. Jewish thinkers in the Spanish Muslim period were largely engaged in translating and interpreting the Greek heritage to the dominant Muslim world. They sought a union between faith and reason, between revelation and humanism. Jews are vital for any understanding of the encounter between the Biblical and the Hellenistic legacies in the renascent Muslim culture.

While Maimonides inhabited the upper stratosphere of culture, more homely, populist figures in Jewish culture were bringing grass-roots Judaism to the knowledge of diaspora communities. The French Jewish scholar Rashi (Rabbi Shlomo Itzhaki, 1040–1105) wrote commentaries on the Bible and Talmud which reduced the most intricate texts to terms understandable by people of common speech and education. And Joseph Caro (1488–1575) codified the Talmud in almanac form in *Shulchan Aruch* (*The Prepared Table*). This made it possible for orthodox believers to observe the dictates of their religion without a heavy weight of learning or of interpretative skills. On the negative side, the *Shulchan Aruch* became so rigidly revered that it acted as a barrier to any kind of flexibility.

All in all, the degree of autonomous and uninterrupted cultural activity of the Jews in Spain arouses wonder. It contrasts sharply with the obtrusive, insistent invasion of Jewish observance by the Christian regimes that were to follow. Islam felt a keen sense of superiority. It despised the northern Europeans, whom one Arab geographer, Masudi, described as "uncouth, brutish and dull of understanding and heavy of tongue." It considered Jews unfit for salvation and unworthy of high political office. But Islamic rulers showed no disposition to invade the private sanctuaries of learning and speculation in which the Jews immersed themselves, and any replacement of Muslim by Christian rule was seen by Jews as a hostile turn of fortune.

In recognition of the profound influence that Aristotle's writings had on Maimonides, a fourteenth-century edition of the Guide for the Perplexed *shows the Greek philosopher seated on a chair covered with six-pointed Jewish stars.*

וינהגו צאן את עצמי קרובים אלעזר אליהם ויסיר אותם פעם ראשון
הראשון שאל מהם ויאמר אליהם לא שמעתם ולא ידעתם עמי
ויאמר אליהם תנה ונראה אשר נגד אשר אמר ישראל ויען כבל
אשר אמר ישראל אליהם ונשא את קול ויבכו אשר נגד כל עם
אשר אמר ישראל אליהם ונשא את קולם ויבכו אשר נגד כל עם
ויען כבל אשר אמר את הדבר אשר נגד כל עם ישראל ונשא
את קול ויבכו אשר נגד כל עם אשר אמר את הדבר ונשא את
קול ויבכו אשר נגד כל עם אשר אמר ישראל אליהם ונשא את
קול ויבכו אשר נגד כל עם ישראל אליהם ונשא את

ואשי יונק יקרא יקרא ויש נמצא
אמרי ותבלת מידך

PEDRO BERRUGUETE

Saint Dominic: The Destruction of the Books, depicted in the fifteenth century by the Spanish painter Pedro Berruguete. Book burning—not only of Jewish scriptures but also of works by Christian dissenters—was a common tactic of Christian zealots in combating heresy.

6·
The Crucible of Europe

URING THE golden age of the Jews in Spain and Egypt—an epoch extending, roughly, from 900 to 1200 C.E., from the birth of Hasdai ibn Shaprut to the death of Maimonides—Christian Europe began to experience a remarkable transformation. It is estimated that at the beginning of the eleventh century, the population of Europe, including the British Isles, western Russia and Turkey, and the whole of the Iberian Peninsula, reached 36 million, its highest point since the Roman era. By 1100, Europe's total estimated population was 44 million; by 1200, 58 million; by 1300, 79 million. At the pinnacle of the recovery, two out of every nine people on earth were Europeans—a proportion that would not be exceeded until the close of the nineteenth century, when Europe was at the zenith of its imperial power. In those times there was strength in numbers.

The ninth and tenth centuries witnessed the struggle of Western Europe to beat back invaders from all directions. From the south came the Saracens Europe's name for the Arab and Berber raiders from Islamic North Africa. After they had conquered Sicily in 827, the Saracens established bases in southern Italy and penetrated southern France. The turning point for Europe came in 972, when local forces ousted the Saracens from their French coastal stronghold. The increasing disunity of the Islamic empire and the simultaneous rise of Genoese, Pisan, Byzantine, and Venetian sea power ultimately broke the Muslim hold on the Mediterranean.

The most persistent and wide-ranging threat to Christian Europe during the ninth and tenth centuries came from the Vikings, or Northmen, renowned mariners of Scandinavian origin. We do not know precisely what impelled the Vikings on their missions of plunder and conquest, but overpopula-

The most brilliant of the Ashkenazim, and the most popular of all commentators on the Hebrew Bible, was Rashi, whose "house of study" (bet ha-midrash) *this may have been.*

tion, a shortage of arable land, superior maritime technology, and a mythos that glorified war and adventure may all have played a part. We do know that Vikings from Denmark and Norway repeatedly battered the British Isles and the Frankish empire. Especially in the latter, the inability of the monarch to shield his lands from such assaults led to an intensification of the developing feudal bond by which a lord pledged protection and land to his vassal, in exchange for which the vassal pledged allegiance and military service. In practice, this meant that the vassal supplied his lord with an agreed number of knights or a sum of money that would enable the lord to employ mercenaries in their stead.

Further complicating the impact of the Vikings in Western Europe was the fact that they did not rely exclusively on hit-and-run raids from their Scandinavian homeland. They also established bases in Ireland, Scotland, Wales, and northeast England, on the North Sea coast of Germany, and in northern and western France.

As we assess the role of the Vikings in European history, we should also bear in mind that they were traders as well as raiders. To Western Europe they offered furs, skins, and walrus tusks (Europe's main source of ivory), in search of which the Northmen sailed westward beyond Iceland and Greenland, reaching Vinland (Newfoundland and Labrador) by the year 1000. To the Muslims the Vikings proffered furs and slaves from northern Russia. The Northmen also mastered the waterways of Poland and Russia, conveying furs, swords, and slaves to Byzantium in exchange for silks and an abundance of silver.

The absorption of Vikings and Magyars from Central Europe into European Christianity was stimulating for the general recovery of Western Europe from 950 onward. The population spurt that accompanied this recovery was concentrated not along the Med-

iterranean, as during the Classical period, but in the European northwest. Drainage of marshes provided some new land, as in Flanders and in the Po Valley of northern Italy, but the prime engine of recovery was the clearing of the forests that up until the year 1000 had covered four-fifths of Western Europe north of the Alps and Pyrenees.

From the tenth and eleventh centuries onward, there are established Jewish communities in most of the major towns of Germany and France. The Jews were engaged mostly in commerce, in which they excelled. For some time they lived with their neighbors in relative tranquility. It was only later, when national states were established—in Germany under Frederick II, in France under Philip Augustus—that intolerance prevailed.

During the interval of relative harmony, the great Talmudic academies of Germany and France were able to develop intense intellectual activity. The most conspicuous figure is Rashi, the great commentator on the Bible and Talmud, who lived in Troyes in northern France. His grandsons Samuel ben Meir and Rabbenu Tam carried on his tradition. It is ironic that in later centuries this was the very area in northern France in which, as in so many other parts of Europe, the very study of the Talmud was proscribed by edict of the Church. Indeed, in the year 1240 whole wagonloads of the Talmud were publicly burned in the streets of Paris.

How shall we account for the descent of the Ashkenazim from their heights of scholarship and commercial prosperity into the maelstrom of murderous assault, forced baptism, confiscatory taxation, and arbitrary expulsion that made Jewish life so perilous in the late Middle Ages?

Such a complex phenomenon has no single cause. We might begin with the mutual antagonism of the Jews and the early Christians, the anti-Jewish resolutions of the early Church councils, and the fulminations of the

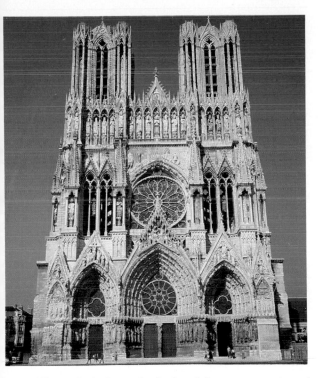

The Cathedral of Chartres, built in the twelfth and thirteenth centuries, was renowned for its stained-glass windows. A detail is shown here.

The cathedral was both the ultimate expression of medieval Christian belief and a tangible sign of the revival of town life and the growth of civic autonomy. *ABOVE*: the façade of the Cathedral of Reims, erected between 1225 and 1299.

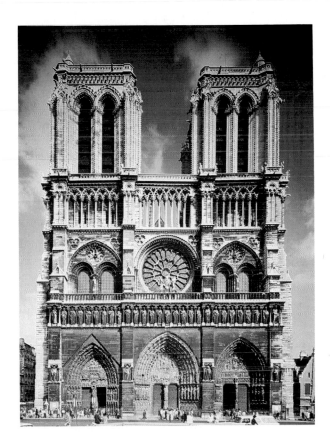

Notre Dame de Paris, begun in 1163 but not completed until early in the fourteenth century.

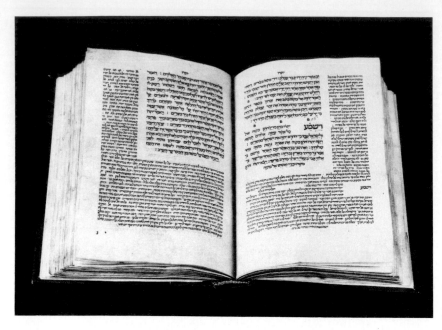

In a typical edition of Rashi, each page bears a brief Biblical text with Rashi's own commentary, as well as one or more commentaries on Rashi by his disciples.

ninth-century prelates Agobard and Amulo. All these elements exposed the Jews to the wrath of Church "reformers." For Western Christendom in the ninth and tenth centuries, the continued assaults of pagan Magyars and Vikings, as well as Saracens, were a destabilizing element. In this dangerous and uncertain climate, rumors abounded, and the Jews, who in eighth-century Spain had sided with the Muslims, were a common target. Nor, as we consider the Christian revival that swept across Europe in the tenth century, should we ignore the apocalyptic expectations that centered around the approaching years 1000—the presumed millenary of Jesus' birth—and 1033, then generally accepted as the one-thousandth anniversary of the Crucifixion. In this climate of Christian superstition, it was not very safe to be a Jew.

The event that crystallized this simmering anti-Jewish sentiment was the burning of the Church of the Holy Sepulcher in Jerusalem around 1009. The rumor quickly spread throughout Western Christendom that the Fatimid caliph had destroyed the church on the advice of the Jews of Orléans. In the resulting wave of attacks on the Ashkenazim, the Jews were expelled from Orléans for several years, and in 1010 the Jews of Limoges were forced to choose between expulsion and conversion.

Perhaps as part of the same wave of persecutions, an order expelling the Jews from Mainz was issued two years later. This year held special significance for the leading Jewish scholar of Mainz, Gershom ben Judah (c. 960–1028), for it was in 1012 that his son was forcibly converted to Christianity. We mention Gershom—who was known affectionately as Rabbenu ("Our Rabbi") Gershom—because there is a direct line of intellectual descent from his disciples to Rashi, who later paid him this reverent tribute:

Rabbenu Gershom, may the memory of the righteous and holy be for a blessing, who enlightened the eyes of the exile, and upon whom we all depend and of whom all Ashkenazi Jewry are the disciples of his disciple . . .

The alleged Jewish-Muslim plot to desecrate Jerusalem's Christian shrine was grist for the propaganda mill of the eleventh-century anti-Jewish chronicler Rodulfus Glaber. Glaber completed his *Five Books of Histories* about 1045 while he was living at the abbey of Cluny, and he dedicated his virulent tract to the abbot of Cluny, Odilo (994–1048). The typical Christian literature of this period is uniformly hostile both to Jews and to Judaism.

With the beginning of the Crusades, this anti-Jewish sentiment erupted into violence. The Crusades had no single motive: a convergence of political, economic, social, and religious factors produced this historical upheaval. There was the evident weakness of the Islamic world, which inspired Latin Christendom to believe that Jerusalem was ripe for the taking. There was also a great religious incentive: To each Crusader the Church offered a plenary indulgence—that is, full remission of all penalties either in purgatory or on earth previously due any sinner. But the prospect of eternal salvation was not the only great reward a Crusade promised. For the peasants a Crusade meant a chance of food, new land, and Eastern riches. For the lesser nobles a Crusade promised booty and glory, the opportunity to gain a fiefdom free of an overlord, an occasion to fight the

When Ottone Colonna ascended to the papacy in 1417 as Martin V, delegations of Jews, above, called upon him to offer their regards and to plead for reconfirmation of their traditional privileges, which Pope Martin readily upheld. Like many popes, Martin employed a Jewish physician and enjoyed favorable personal relations with Jews.

infidel instead of warring against each other, and what one writer called a "remedy for boredom." For the greater nobles, a Crusade offered relief from the lesser nobles' disruptive behavior. And for the monarchy also, the dispatch of the feudal nobility to the Holy Land meant a kingdom that was more stable and easier to manage—and a chance for the king to increase his landholdings and augment his authority.

The Church likewise coveted the lands that might be left by departing Crusaders, but it also had higher motives: to restore Europe's internal peace by diverting quarrelsome knights to the holy war against the Saracens, to reclaim Jerusalem for the Christian faith,

Jews suffered several partial or temporary expulsions from France, such as the one depicted in this chronicle of 1321, before their final, complete expulsion was decreed in 1394.

and to protect Christian pilgrims from Seljuk harassment. Of all these motives, the desire to wage war on the infidel and the quest for booty are the most salient to Jewish history, for each could—and did—spark attacks on Jews as well as Muslims.

When at the Council of Clermont on November 27, 1095, Pope Urban II (r. 1088–1099) issued his call for the First Crusade (1095–1099), he did not preach against the Jews alone. But the First Crusade inaugurated a terrifying era in Jewish history. The Christian chronicles deal explicitly with the question of why the Crusaders, ostensibly bent on reclaiming Palestine from the "Saracens," turned their fury against the Ashkenazim in Europe. "We desire to go and fight God's enemies in the East," declared the faithful who gathered at Rouen in the springtime of 1096. "But we have before our eyes certain Jews, a race more inimical to God than any other."

The Jews of Rouen, a French city nominally under the English crown, were the first target. The Crusaders dragged the Jews into church, and those who refused baptism were murdered. It was around this time that the Jews of France petitioned Peter the Hermit, who seems to have borne them no special animus, to use his good offices in their favor, in exchange for which they promised to supply food to all his followers. But Peter, who had traveled around northern and central France carrying with him, it was rumored, a letter from Heaven guaranteeing the success of the Crusade, apparently was unable to restrain the passions that his preaching had unleashed. According to one chronicler, Richard of Poitiers, the Crusaders "exterminated by many massacres the Jews of almost all Gaul, with the exception of those who accepted conversion." Although this claim cannot be verified, we do know that French Jews sent an urgent warning to their German co-religionists. The Rhenish Jews did not heed this warning, perhaps because of the trust

they placed in promises of protection they had secured from the German nobles and bishops.

It is not that the local churchmen were necessarily ill-intentioned. On May 3, 1096, Crusaders and Christian townspeople, inflamed by the religious revival, moved to attack the Jews of Speyer as they met in their synagogues for Sabbath prayer. Forewarned, the Jews dispersed early, but ten of them were caught by the mob on their way home and murdered, and one Jewish woman committed suicide. A Bishop Johann sent in his militia to restore order, punished some of the murderers, and gave the Jews sanctuary in his own castle—measures that prevented further massacres in Speyer but could neither undo the earlier damage nor halt the spread of violence to other German towns. Some 800 Jews died at Worms, mostly by their own hand. At Mainz, too, a local bishop offered protection, but he himself was driven away by an onslaught of burghers and Crusaders. In town after town the same ghastly pattern repeated itself. Within months, the massacres had claimed the lives of at least 5,000 Ashkenazim, out of a German Jewish population that, by one estimate, cannot have exceeded 20,000.

What alternatives were open to German Jewry in 1096? Forced by the Christians to choose baptism or death, some Jews did allow themselves to be baptized. Many of these unwilling converts continued to practice Judaism but in secret, until a truce proclaimed by Henry IV and the imperial nobility in 1103 allowed them openly to profess their Jewishness again. Whatever social stigma might have attached to these former apostates within the Jewish community, they had the force of rabbinic opinion to support the renewal of their Jewish ties.

Seven church councils were held at Clermont, the most important being in 1095, when Pope Urban II preached the First Crusade.

et austres saine lieux la enuiron.
Et les xpiens yushabitans a demou
rans . a que les austres pur culx
tyranniquement a inhumaine
ment tues . Ils auoient referue
en Infeliciteuse bie a fin que sur
eulx en loprobre du saint nom
xpien peussent contumer plus
souffreement leurs Insortablees

cruaultes . Et comment Il=
les tenoient en lup oprobrieuse
captiuite a seruiage . ou tresgraut
deshonneur a oprobre de tous
les xpiens . Concluant a mon
strant pur diuersee raisons tre
euidentes que le saint peuple
xpien ne debuoit plus souffrir
nenduree que ses saiuts lieux et

The Crusaders capture Jerusalem (July 15, 1099). What this fourteenth-century manuscript does not show is the indiscriminate slaughter of many hundreds of Muslims and Jews whose families had lived in the Holy City for generations.

Many Ashkenazim, echoing the Old Testament prophets, must have seen the coming of the Crusaders as a judgment by God on their own transgressions. "The sins of the Jews brought it about that the enemy overcame them and took the gate," wrote Solomon bar Samson. "The hand of the Lord was heavy against His people." It would seem that some Jewish communities chose not to offer concerted resistance in the hope that if they concentrated on piety, prayer, and repentance (rather than collective self-defense), the Lord of Israel would intervene to save them. But in fact, once the Crusaders attacked, the odds against the Ashkenazim were overwhelming. Even the most important German Jewish communities cannot

have numbered much more than 1,000. Count Emicho could muster more than a dozen Crusaders and local sympathizers for each Jew that stood in his path.

Another response—one with distinguished precedents in both Christian and Jewish history—was to elevate death to the level of spiritual resistance. The Jewish concept of *kiddush ha-Shem* (literally, "sanctification of the Holy Name") encompasses both prayer and righteous action as means of glorifying God, but in times of persecution its corollary of martyrdom comes to the fore. Indeed, from rabbinic times onward, the individual Jew was commanded to choose death —either at the hands of others or by suicide —rather than commit idolatry, unchaste acts (i.e., incest, adultery), or murder.

Accustomed by tradition to regard martyrdom as not merely commendable but mandatory under extreme provocation, the Ashkenazim held high praise for the pious Rachel, who, when the Crusaders stormed

Mainz, preferred to have her own children slain rather than see them forcibly baptized and raised as Christians. Three of her children—the boy Isaac, the two girls Bella and Matrona—submitted meekly to the slaughter. But the fourth child, Aaron, ran away, screaming, "Mother, mother, do not butcher me!"

When this righteous woman had made an end of sacrificing her three children to their Creator, she then raised her voice and called out to her son Aaron: "Aaron, where are you? You also I will not spare nor will I have any mercy." Then she dragged him out by the foot from under the chest where he had hidden himself, and she sacrificed him before God, the high and exalted.

There are many similar heartrending examples of self-sacrifice. For the Ashkenazim, *kiddush ha-Shem* had a communal as well as an intimately personal meaning. When persecution threatened the Jewish community, Jewish law and custom required the community to act as one—to band together for relief and assistance in time of peril, and under extreme conditions to die together when the preservation of individual life was no longer compatible with righteous action.

The Ashkenazim of France and Germany (and, in 1099, the Jews of Jerusalem) were not the only victims of the Crusades. There were armies of Crusaders across the water in England, where Jews had been living in limited numbers at least since the Norman conquest. We cannot conclude our consideration of *kiddush ha-Shem* without taking a look at the melancholy episode of the massacre at York. This outrage occurred during the Third Crusade (1189–1192), of which the English King Richard I (Richard the Lion-hearted, 1157–1199) was a principal. Heralding the new wave of mob violence was the sack of London's Jewish quarter in September 1189. In March 1190 an assault on the Jews of York began with a few isolated instances of plun-

When a local expulsion order was issued, the Jews had no choice but to pack their wagons, pull up stakes, and move to the next town that would have them. Sometimes Jews were expelled because the local nobleman no longer needed Jewish money lenders, sometimes because he had run up a debt he was unwilling or unable to pay.

der. Then came efforts at forced conversion. Those who were not massacred for refusing the sacrament besought the warden of the royal castle to protect them. He let them in, but then—possibly because of a misunderstanding—turned to the county sheriff, who was persuaded by the conspiring nobles to incite the townspeople to besiege the Jews in their temporary haven. All restraints were loosed, and anti-Jewish anger ran rampant.

Trapped in the royal tower, the Jews bravely hurled stones from an inner wall at their attackers as the siege machines were moved into place. With the end in sight, Rabbi Yom Tov ben Isaac of Joigny offered the Jewish brethren of York his spiritual counsel:

It is plainly the will of the God of our Fathers

The Jewish response to brutal persecution and mob violence was to elevate death to the level of spiritual resistance by embracing martyrdom (kiddush ha-Shem) when the only alternative was extreme dishonor.

that we do die for His holy Law. . . . Since, then, we ought to prefer a glorious death to a life of deepest shame, . . . since our Creator Himself now asks again for that life which He gave us, let us render it willingly and devoutly back with our own hands. . . .

And so they did.

To understand the ferocity of the Christian assault on the Jews during this period, we must grasp the tight interrelationship of power and ideas. Political legitimacy was linked to religious belief. A man's creed defined his social identity. He battled first for survival, then for recovery against the various pagan adversaries. The Christians felt

bound to project the exclusive rectitude of their faith. Their dominance was never secure in their own minds until Jewish scepticism and challenge were suppressed. It was not sufficient to obtain Jewish submission; it was necessary to bring about a Jewish confession of error. The Christian-Jewish relationship was thus suffused by a passion quite different from any interaction of Christians with other peoples in Europe during the Middle Ages.

At this time Western Europe was also undergoing an economic transformation with great effects for the Jews. The medieval economy suffered from a chronic shortage of currency. A trade imbalance that slowly drained Europe's gold stocks in exchange for Oriental luxury goods and spices further squeezed the cash supply. With the expansion of Western Europe's population, agriculture, and commerce during the twelfth century, the demand for money far exceeded that which medieval banking institutions such as the churches and monasteries could provide. To build a town, maintain an army, outfit an overseas trading venture—all these required substantial accumulation of capital and the willingness to accept deferred returns. Obviously, any person or institution that supplied capital for so chancy an enterprise as a foreign war or merchant expedition had a right to expect some return on the investment, if only to cover the risk of loss. Today, banks receive this return in the form of interest. But medieval churchmen denounced the taking of interest as "usury": in 1179, as the shortage of cash intensified, the Church decreed that usury was contrary both to Scripture and to natural law and punishable by excommunication.

Saint Thomas Aquinas (1225–1273) proclaimed that "to take usury for money lent is unjust in itself, because this is to sell what does not exist, and this evidently leads to inequality which is contrary to justice.

"In order to make this evident, we must

observe that there are certain things the use of which consists in their consumption: thus we consume wine when we use it for drink, and we consume wheat when we use it for food. . . . Accordingly, if a man wanted to sell wine separately from the use of the wine, he would be selling the same thing twice, or he would be selling what does not exist, wherefore he would evidently commit a sin of injustice. . . ."

Jews as well as Christians considered it compulsory to refrain from usury, whether in dealings with Jews or with non-Jews. So spoke Rashi on the brink of the First Crusade: "He who loans money at interest to a foreigner will be destroyed."

How then shall we account for the emergence of the stereotypical Jewish moneylender, the "Shylock" of European tradition? The answer, for Christians as well as Jews, lay in economic necessity. From Babylonian times onward, Jewish thinkers were driven by the exigencies of trade and finance to contrive legal fictions that would satisfy the Biblical command while permitting the community to prosper. Under similar pressures in the twelfth and thirteenth centuries, Christian Europe reacted in the same way. In Genoa, for example, the typical shipping contract provided for a partnership, or *accomendatio,* in which only one of the partners actually ventured abroad; the other, who stayed at home, raised the money and goods that made the venture possible. The Church forbade taking interest on the capital the second partner loaned the first, but it had no objection if the lender contracted to receive his deferred return in the form of a share of the profits. Christian capital was thus directed into shipping and other "creative," or profit-making, endeavors. However, there was another class of loan for which legal fictions were less readily available—loan for consumption, as in the case of illness or other unforeseen expenses. A loan to an impecunious king and prince was often of this type.

Then, as now (or at least until a few decades ago, when lending agencies and credit cards became more widespread), those who fell into debt turned to the pawnbroker: even a king might pawn his crown jewels. As in large-scale banking operations, the Italians were Europe's financial innovators. The generic name for a pawnbroker in Northern Europe was "lombard," a term that embraced Italians of Lombardy and other regions as well as the Jews. What made the Jews so prominent in this field was not belief or tradition but the lack of alternative economic opportunities. The founding of new towns, the rise of a new merchant class in Western Europe, the development of Italian and Hanseatic commerce—all tended to weaken the

---

Saint Thomas Aquinas (1225?–1274), the preeminent philosopher and theologian of the High Middle Ages, held that usury was unjust and therefore forbidden to Christians. In time, however, economic necessity won out over theological argument, and various legal fictions were contrived to allow the expansion of credit, without which no community could prosper.

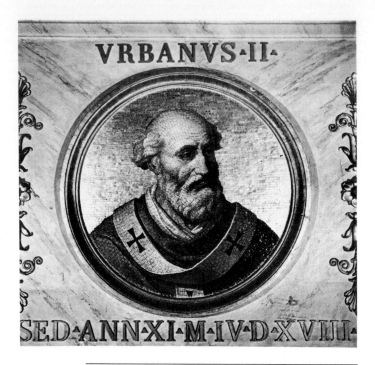

VRBANVS·II·

SED·ANN·XI·M·IV·D·XVIII·

A man of deep piety and humility who was also adroit in his handling of temporal power, Pope Urban II (r. 1088–1099) called the First Crusade but died before the news of the capture of Jerusalem could reach him in Italy.

position of the Jewish trader. Economically, as in so many other ways, the turning point was 1096. The murderous attacks of the Crusaders demonstrated to the Ashkenazim the vulnerability not only of their persons but also of their property. Wherever possible, they converted their wealth into gold or silver, which could be concealed or transported in the event of attack. It is not surprising that Jewish merchants, with their new cash reserves and their experience with credit financing, should have turned to the one profession that could—literally—place a sovereign in their debt. Here the strictures of the Church could not hinder them: theoretically, since the Jews were exempt from canon law, a Jew was free to lend at interest to a Christian, and a Christian was free to borrow at interest from a Jew. On the sole remaining problem, the negative stance of the Bible and Talmud, the rabbis proved flexible. "No

loans at interest must be made to the gentiles," they held, "if a livelihood can be earned in another manner." Nevertheless, their ruling continued, "at the present time, when a Jew may possess neither fields nor vines permitting him to live, the lending of money at interest to non-Jews is necessary and consequently authorized."

The changing economic role of the Jew is evident in the chronicles of the Second Crusade (1147–1149), the early days of which brought violence against the Jews. One notorious incident took place near Troyes during the holiday of Shavuot, May 8, 1147. The target was Rashi's grandson Jacob ben Meir, or Rabbenu Tam:

On the second day of the Feast of Weeks the French crusaders got together at Rameru, entered the house of our teacher Jacob (may he live long), took everything he had there, and even tore up the scroll of the Law in his presence. They got hold of him, led him out to the fields, condemned him because of his religion, and conspired against him to put him to death. Five times on the head they wounded him, and in doing so they said to him: "You are the greatest man in Israel; therefore we are taking vengeance on you because of him who was hanged [Jesus], and we are going to wound you just as you Jews inflicted five wounds on our God."

With the aid of a Christian knight (whom he bribed), Rabbenu Tam escaped his would-be assassins. Hundreds of Jews in Bohemia, Halle, and Carinthia were not so fortunate. Nevertheless, the bloodshed was not nearly so widespread as in 1096.

For this relative absence of violence, especially in France but also in the Rhineland (only a few Jews were massacred at Mainz and Worms in 1147), we may credit the preaching of the French ecclesiastic Saint Bernard of Clairvaux (1091–1153), the spiritual leader of the Second Crusade. Bernard made it clear that violence toward the Jews and seizure of their property would not be tolerated,

and when a Cistercian monk named Rudolf began agitating against them, Bernard himself went to the Rhineland to bring Rudolf under control.

"The borrower is servant to the lender," says the Biblical proverb. For the Jews of the later Middle Ages, however, the power to lend was a double-edged sword. Capital was a lever that Jews could use, at least in the short run, to find havens for settlement and to procure charters of protection from kings and princes. But as the social and religious isolation of West European Jewry deepened in the wake of the First Crusade, the Jews became ever more dependent on their feudal "protectors," and this in turn was a lever the Christian rulers could employ. In this asymmetrical relationship, the more a sovereign borrowed—or squeezed—from the Jews, the more vulnerable they became.

A brief survey of events in France and England during the twelfth and thirteenth centuries bears out this pattern. Philip II (r. 1180–1223), who carved out the modern French state at the expense of King John of England (r. 1199–1216) and to the considerable displeasure of Pope Innocent III (r. 1198–1216), began his reign by ordering the imprisonment of all Jews within his realm. He

A fifteenth century Flemish version of the battle for Jerusalem. By this time, the Holy City was once again in Muslim hands, and it would remain so for hundreds of years.

appears, however, to have been less interested in seeing his order carried out than in pocketing the ransom by which the French Jews procured their freedom. In April 1182, Philip ordered the Jews expelled—primarily, it seems, so that he could confiscate their holdings. Sixteen years later and again in need of funds, Philip removed the ban and offered to protect the Jewish usurers. This he did, not because his attitude toward Jews had changed—his dislike for the children of Israel appears to have been lifelong—but because the crown had now connived to regulate the lending business and to pocket its own share through taxes and duties.

In England, meanwhile, a small but cohesive Jewish community—perhaps not larger than 4,000—had developed in close association with the monarchy. Aaron of Lincoln (c. 1123–1186), the most important English capitalist of his day, supplied funds to the royal establishments of Scotland and England. When Aaron died, his entire estate was taken by the English crown. Nor were monarchs

onunc labia mca a
pnes. Et os mcu amu

Cathedral building, the "high technology" of the Middle Ages, mobilized an entire community's material and spiritual resources.

thority and a threat to a royal resource. On his way back from the Holy Land in 1192, Richard—who had concluded an inglorious peace that left Jerusalem under Saladin's control—suffered the further indignity of being captured by Austrian Duke Leopold V. Later imprisoned in Germany, Richard did not return to England until 1194, the Jews having raised a lion's share of his ransom. Richard's response to the York disaster was to proclaim an "Ordinance of the Jewry," establishing chests in the main towns for the storage of duplicate financial records and creating an office of *Presbyter Judaeorum* (archpresbyter), whose occupant, appointed by the crown, was responsible for organizing the Jewish community to serve the interests of the realm.

Not surprisingly, the English barons came to despise the Jews as instruments of royal oppression. A clause in the Magna Carta, the charter of liberties forced upon King John by his barons in 1215, limited the claims of Jewish moneylenders against the estates of landowners who had died in their debt. The outbreak in 1263 of the Barons' War, a rebellion by the nobility against King Henry III (r. 1216–1272), brought a wave of violence against the Jews of London, Canterbury, and other cities. Far from profiting by the royal connection, the Jews had in fact become steadily more impoverished as an "emergency" tax was levied upon them with oppressive regularity. When Edward I ("Longshanks," 1239–1307) assumed the English throne in 1272, the Jewish well had run dry. He made an unsuccessful attempt to ban usury entirely and to transform the Jews into a community of tradesmen and tenant farmers. This effort failed because the Jews did not receive the economic liberty and security that these roles demanded. Edward then issued an order of expulsion on July 18, 1290, the ninth of Av. The refugees headed for the European mainland, to Flanders, to Germany—and to France, where King Philip IV

his only clients. He also lent money to bishops, barons, and earls, and he helped finance the construction of at least nine Cistercian monasteries, the Abbey of Saint Albans, and the cathedrals of Lincoln and Peterborough.

The riots at York were a serious matter for Richard the Lion-hearted, not so much because of the Jewish lives lost as because the conspiracy of the nobles and the savagery of the townspeople were affronts to royal au-

("Philip the Fair," r. 1285–1314) greeted them in 1291 with an order prohibiting their settlement within his kingdom. As for the Jews already residing in France, Philip in 1306 ordered them imprisoned, seized their belongings, then had the Jews expelled. At this time the Jewish population of France may have been as high as 100,000; by 1500, after a series of readmissions, persecutions, and expulsions, and aggravated by the Black Death, only a few thousand Jews remained.

No rational examination of medieval politics, economics, or religious doctrine can fully explain the part Jews unwittingly played in the demonology of Christian Europe. We sense this in the lurid polemics of

A series of Crusades mounted after the Christians lost Jerusalem in 1187 failed miserably in their attempt to wrest the Holy Land from Muslim control. This illumination portrays the young followers of a Hungarian religious fanatic who sought unsuccessfully to free King Louis IX of France from Saracen captivity (1250–1254).

Rodulfus Glaber; we see it whole in the accusations made against the Jews by Christian fanatics during the later Middle Ages, slanders for which there exists not a shred of supporting evidence but that were nevertheless responsible for thousands of Jewish deaths. We might comfort ourselves with the thought that such slanders were entirely the

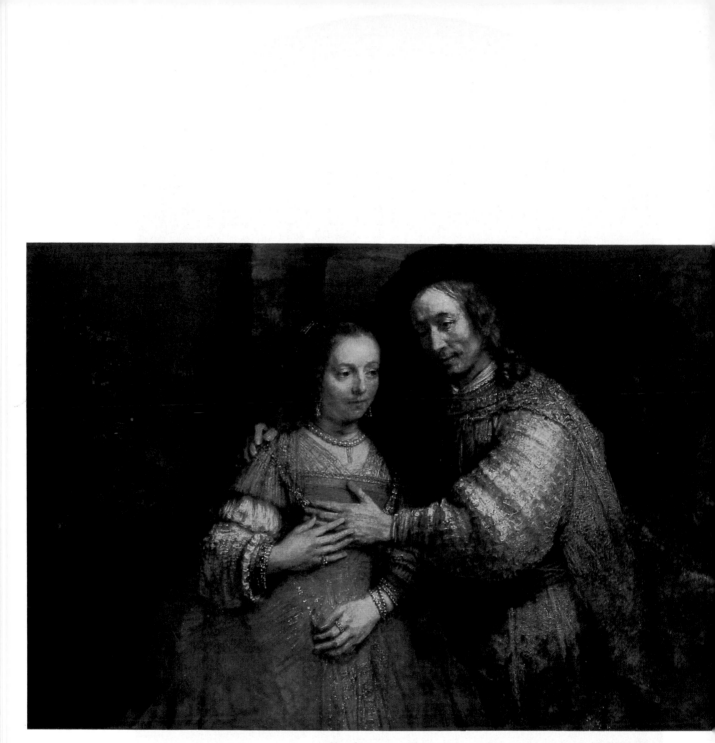

Tenderness, compassion, and the deepest sense of shared human-ity radiate from the works of the Dutch artist Rembrandt van Rijn, who lived for more than twenty years in Amsterdam's Jewish quarter. Rembrandt often used his neighbors as models, in both modern and Biblical scenes.

7.
Search for Deliverance

JEWS IN THE WEST
1492–1789

N O EVENT since the destruction of Jerusalem fourteen centuries before had shaken the confidence of Jews everywhere more than the expulsion from Spain. Expulsion was not a new experience; Jews had been expelled from France, England, and many cities in Germany. But none of these events had a traumatic effect in any way comparable to that of the sudden edict of banishment from Spain. Jews had never lived anywhere else as harmoniously or creatively as in Spain. They had taken an active part in the life of Spanish society while also cultivating their own particular legacy. They had been prominent in commerce, medicine, literature, and the arts. One out of every ten Spaniards had been Jewish or had descended from Jews. And now this flourishing community, the largest Jewish community in the world, had been eliminated with a single stroke of the pen. Jews everywhere were reminded of their acute and inescapable vulnerability.

Of the 100,000 or more Jews who left Spain during the summer of 1492, the overwhelming majority went to Portugal, whose Jewish community already played a prominent role in that nation's economic life. John II of Portugal (1455–1495) made the new arrivals pay for the privilege of settling in his kingdom. Wealthy Jews were taxed 100 cruzados, a substantial sum, for the right of permanent residence. Poorer Jews—a category that included most of the refugees—paid 8 cruzados a head for a stay of up to eight months; when the time limit expired, they were forced to find passage on a ship leaving Portugal or, failing that (for sailings were scarce), to convert to Christianity. Nor did the wealthy have a much happier fate. In 1496, King John's successor, Emanuel I (1495–1521), contracted a dynastic marriage with Princess Isabella, the daughter of Ferdinand and Isabella of Spain. As a precondition for

The original ghetto—a walled quarter where the Jews were closed in for the night by a gate that was locked at sunset—was born here in Venice in 1516, at the site of an old iron foundry. As an institution, the ghetto defined Jewish life in Venice and many other cities in Western Europe from the sixteenth through the eighteenth century.

the union, the Catholic monarchs insisted that Emanuel rid Portugal of the Jews, and on December 4, 1496, an expulsion decree was duly published. But Emanuel, reluctant to lose the Jews as an economic resource, soon changed his mind; instead of expelling the Jews, he would seek to convert them. On March 19, 1497, all Jewish minors were forcibly baptized. Their parents were then told to gather in Lisbon, where they, too, were detained and ceremonially converted. On April 21, 1499, emigration by this new crop of *conversos*—about 20,000 in all—was banned outright.

The term Sephardim encompasses those who left Spain and Portugal either as Jews or as *conversos*, as well as their descendants. For them the choice of a new land in the late fifteenth and sixteenth centuries was severely limited. Whole regions of Western Europe, including England and Wales, France and Provence, Sicily and Sardinia, and of course virtually all the Iberian Peninsula, were closed to legal Jewish settlement.

Hopes were dim in Germany, where Jews had been expelled from most cities and barred from most jobs; nor were Jewish prospects any better in Austria, Hungary, and Silesia. Among the few regions where Jews could settle openly and in significant numbers were the Ottoman Empire, Italy, and Poland. We shall consider each of these in turn.

The Ottoman Empire, which at its height in the sixteenth century embraced North Africa, the Aegean, Anatolia, the Crimea, the Near East, and much of Eastern Europe, takes its name from Osman I (Othman al-Ghazi, "the Conqueror," 1259–1326), who as leader of the Seljuk Turks conquered northwestern Asia Minor at the expense of the Byzantine Empire. Under Osman's successors, the Ottoman Turks consolidated their hold over Asia Minor and stormed the gates of European Christendom, conquering Walachia (now part of Romania), Rumelia (Bulgaria), and Serbia before the fourteenth century ended. Isolated and surrounded, the Byzantine capital, Constantinople (now Istanbul, Turkey), would surely have fallen to the Ottoman emperor, Bajazet, had not the Mongols intervened.

Paradoxically, the humiliating defeat that Bajazet suffered at the hands of the Mongol warrior Tamerlane (1336?–1405) signaled the subsequent Ottoman expansion. For Tamerlane was far more adept at conquest than at empire building. From the throne of Samarkand, now Soviet Turkestan, Tamerlane subjugated Persia and Mesopotamia and then launched assaults on the khanates established by his Mongol predecessors in Russia and Central Asia, as well as in Ottoman Turkey.

After Tamerlane's death (en route to China), the battered khanates were no match for the resurgent power of the Ottoman state, which was reconstituted during the reign of Muhammad I (1413–1421). Under Murad II (1421–1451) the Turks launched campaigns in Macedonia, Albania, Hungary, and Greece. On May 29, 1453, during the sultanate of Muhammad II (1451–1481), the Turks drove a final nail into the coffin of the Byzantine Empire, capturing Constantinople and making it their capital. Subsequent conquests resulted in a loosening of Venice's hold on Levantine commerce.

Through all their wars with Western Christendom, the Ottoman Turks held aloft the banner of Islam. In the reign of Selim I (1512–1520), the annexation of Syria and Palestine in 1516 and of Egypt in 1517 made this bond all the more firm, for it placed under Ottoman stewardship all the Muslim holy places in both Mecca and Jerusalem. The stage was now set for a revival of the fruitful partnership between Judaism and Islam, under the sultanate of Suleiman the Magnificent (1520–1566).

Wherever the Turks conquered—Algeria, Tunisia, Egypt, Palestine, Mesopotamia, the

Medicin Iuif.

Medicine, commerce, and banking and finance were the leading professions open to Jews in Constantinople during the reign of Suleiman the Magnificent (r. 1520–1566), when the Ottoman Empire reached the height of its power. Suleiman had many Jewish advisers, among them his court physician, Moses Hamon (c. 1490–1554).

Crimea, the Balkans—they found regions where Jews had been living continuously for hundreds of years. Some of these settlements had fallen on hard times. When Meshullam of Volterra visited Alexandria in 1481, he noted the decline both of the city and of its Jewish quarter:

Last, but not least, there are in Alexandria about sixty Jewish householders, with no Karaites or Samaritans among them, but only Rabbanites. Their habit of clothing is like that of the Ishmaelites. They wear no shoes but sit on the ground and enter the Synagogues without shoes and without trousers. Some Jews are there who remember that in their time there were about 40,000 householders, but they have become less and less, like the sacrificial bullocks of Tabernacles.

Another Jewish traveler, Obadiah da Bertinoro (c. 1490), found Jewish life in Jerusalem not greatly improved since Nachmanides visited the Holy City in 1267.

As for the administration of Jerusalem, Obadiah conceded that "the Jews are not

---

Book printing by movable metal type spread rapidly throughout Europe and the Mediterranean region during the second half of the fifteenth century. Hebrew printing was brought to Constantinople by Jewish exiles from Spain in 1493; this earliest known illustrated edition of the Passover Haggadah was produced in the Ottoman capital twenty-two years later.

On May 29, 1543, the Turks drove a final nail into the coffin of the Byzantine Empire, capturing Constantinople and using it as a launching point for their assault on Eastern Europe.

persecuted by the Arabs in these parts." There seems little doubt that in the last years of Mamluk rule, life in the City of David changed for the better. With an influx of Marranos and an upsurge of immigrants from Italian vessels, one of Obadiah's disciples could report in 1495 that Jerusalem provided homes for 200 Jewish families. The task of reconstructing Jerusalem's defenses fell to Suleiman, who from 1537 to 1541 had the city walls, gates, and water system rebuilt.

Nowhere was the condition of the Jews more profoundly improved than in the new Turkish capital, Constantinople. In the twelfth century, Benjamin of Tudela portrayed the Jews of Constantinople as isolated and oppressed, though not without a share of the city's general prosperity:

Wealth like that of Constantinople is not to be found in the whole world. Here also are men learned in all the books of the Greeks, and they eat and drink, every man under his vine and his fig-tree. . . .

No Jews live in the city, for they have been placed behind an inlet of the sea. An arm of the sea of Marmora [Sea of Marmara] shuts them in on the one side, and they are unable to go out except by way of the sea, when they want to do business with the inhabitants. In the Jewish quarter are about 2,000 Rabbanite Jews and about 500 Karaites, and a fence divides them. . . . No Jew there is allowed to ride on horseback. The one exception is R. Solomon Hamitsri, who is the king's physician, and through whom the Jews enjoy considerable alleviation of their oppression. For their condition is very low, and there is much hatred against them, which is fostered by the tanners, who throw out their dirty water in the streets before the doors of the Jewish houses and defile the Jews' quarter. . . . So the Greeks hate the Jews, good and bad alike, and subject them to great oppression, and beat them in the streets, and in every way treat them with rigor. Yet the Jews are rich and good, kindly and charitable, and bear their lot with cheerfulness. . . .

As soon as the Turks captured Constanti-nople, they began to repopulate the city by forcibly transferring Muslims, Christians, and Jews from other parts of the empire. Among the Jews were Romaniots (natives of Byzantium and immigrants from Greece) as well as Ashkenazim and Sephardim; but during the 1490s, Sephardic newcomers—perhaps as many as 40,000 of them—assumed prominence. These Spanish and Portuguese refugees received a warm welcome from the Ottoman Sultan Bajazet II (Bayezid, r.1481–1512), who said of Ferdinand, Spain's Catholic monarch, "Can you call such a king wise and intelligent? He is impoverishing his country and enriching my kingdom." By the middle of the sixteenth century, during Su-

The synagogues of Ottoman lands reflected the architecture of the mosque, just as those of Christian Europe reflected the churches of their own time. In this Constantinople synagogue the wall decorations are in Islamic style, as are the richly carved capitals of the pillars of the bimah, the platform from which the Torah is read.

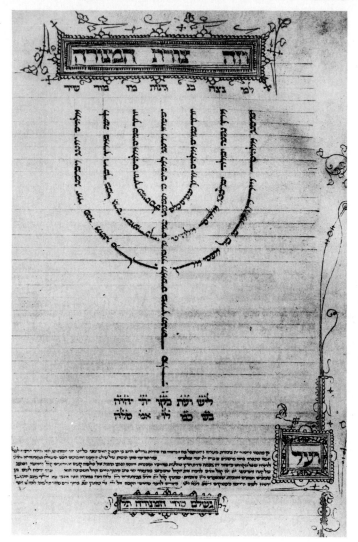

For the kabbalists, every Biblical text, Jewish symbol, and Hebrew letter had a mystical significance that, if properly understood, could hasten the coming of the Messiah. In this fifteenth-century Florentine manuscript, the Hebrew text of Psalm LXVII has been arranged to form a menorah whose seven branches, by a subtle system of numerological equivalences, "add up to" the name of God.

leiman's reign, Constantinople had about 50,000 Jews, organized into some thirty or forty congregations, or *kahalim,* depending on place of origin; each *kahal* was a separate unit, responsible for the spiritual and social welfare of its congregants and collecting taxes from its members for the Turks.

No Jew rose higher at the Turkish court or used his power in ways more beneficial to his own people than Joseph Nasi (Joao Micas, c. 1524–1579), a Portuguese Marrano who left the land of his birth for Antwerp in 1537. The potent allure of Joseph's diplomatic talents and the banking fortune of his family enabled him to mingle freely with European and then with Ottoman nobility. Joseph became the principal adviser to the Ottoman sultanate on European affairs and had the happy task of devising a policy that would augment Turkish power and strengthen the position of the Jews. He also had the good luck (or diplomatic acumen) to choose the winning side in the struggle to succeed Suleiman; the victor, Selim II (r. 1566–1574), rewarded him with the rank of *muterferik* ("gentleman of the imperial retinue"), commercial concessions in Poland, a monopoly on wine imports through the Bosporus, and the titles Duke of Naxos and Count of Andros.

It was apparently at Joseph's urging that Turkey attacked Cyprus, a Venetian possession; and it was no small embarrassment to the Jewish court favorite when Turkey lost the great Battle of Lepanto the following year. This naval encounter, in the course of which the combined forces of Venice, Spain, and the Papal States swamped the Turkish fleet on October 7, 1571, was only a temporary setback for the Turks, who captured Tunis in 1574 and retained control of Cyprus for another three centuries. Nevertheless, Joseph's hand seems not nearly so evident in Turkish affairs after Lepanto. (One further note concerning Lepanto, a site—now called the Gulf of Corinth—that holds a place in literary as well as military history: It was during this epic confrontation of Christendom and Islam that a young Spanish poet, the son of a surgeon, lost the use of his left hand. After the battle he was given the nickname the "Handless One," El Manco de Lepanto, but we know him as Miguel de Cervantes [1547–1616], creator of *Don Quijote de la Mancha* [1605–1615], the great masterpiece of Spanish literature and Western culture's definitive farewell to the chivalric ideal.)

Notable among the specifically Jewish causes that Joseph's family took up was an attempt to organize a boycott of the Adriatic port of Ancona. There the Inquisition, on direct orders from Pope Paul IV, had launched proceedings against a Portuguese Marrano community that earlier popes had sanctioned. The boycott, though a failure, was nonetheless significant as the first attempt at concerted use of economic power by world Jewry. An even more ambitious endeavor was the founding of a new Jewish colony at Tiberias, rights to which Joseph's family secured from Suleiman in 1558 or 1559 in return for a yearly remittance of 1,000 ducats.

The spiritual center of Ottoman Jewry during the sixteenth century was not Constantinople or Jerusalem but a town in the Upper Galilee, Safed. The name does not appear in the Bible, but there was an active Jewish community at Safed in Talmudic times. The conquest of Safed by the Mamluks during the thirteenth century had brought a revival of Jewish settlement; in 1334 the Spanish kabbalist Issac ben Joseph ibn Chelo wrote in a letter from the Holy Land that Safed was "a city peopled by Jews from all parts of the world." By the end of the fifteenth century, there were some 300 Jewish families in Safed; in 1548, according to Turkish tax rolls, there were 716. In 1535, David dei Rossi, a Jewish merchant, wrote to his Italian brethren of this glimpse of the town through trader's eyes:

What shall I tell you about this country, as so

Of Michelangelo's Moses, *in Rome, the Italian artist-historian Giorgio Vasari writes, "With this no other modern work will ever bear comparison (nor, indeed, do the statues of the ancient world)." Vasari notes that the Jews of Rome came on the Sabbath "like flocks of starlings" to visit and adore the work. Another Italian center with a small but influential Jewish community was Venice, storied city of canals, whose hundreds of printers played a vital part in the spread of Renaissance humanism. The painting here is by Antonio Canaletto.*

many people before me have reported its character and greatness in writing and orally? In general I should like to tell you that, just as in Italy, improvements are being made and new settlements founded, while the population is increasing daily. Such is the case here too. He who saw Safed ten years ago, and observes it now, had the impression

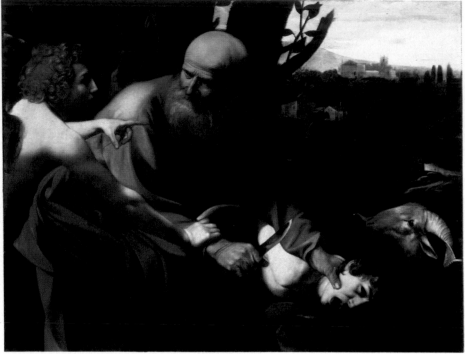

A renewal of interest in the Old Testament during the Italian Renaissance is evident in the art works of the period. ABOVE: *Caravaggio's dramatic Sacrifice of Isaac;* RIGHT: *Jeremiah the Prophet, a sculpture by Donatello;* OPPOSITE PAGE, TOP: *Testament and Death of Moses, painted by Signorelli; and Michelangelo's The Flood.*

soft and so detailed that it seems that Michelangelo must have exchanged his chisel for a brush. . . .

Unquestionably, the Church leaders most favorably inclined toward the Jews of Rome were the Medici popes, Leo X and Clement VII. Leo, whose reign was otherwise distinguished by love of extravagance and display, complete immersion of the papacy in Italian politics, and failure to comprehend the urgency of Luther's Protestant challenge to the authority of Rome, nonetheless won the gratitude of Roman Jewry by abolishing certain discriminatory levies, declining to enforce the badge laws, sanctioning the establishment of a Hebrew printing press in the Eternal City, and allowing the publication, in Venice, of the first complete Babylonian Talmud (1520–1523).

An even greater friend to the Jews was Clement, though in most other respects his reign could not have been less happy. During his eleven-year pontificate, the Lutherans broke decisively with the Roman Church; the army of Holy Roman Emperor Charles V (r. 1519–1556) sacked Rome in 1527 and for seven months held Clement captive; and King Henry VIII (r. 1509–1547) successfully defied papal authority to divorce Catherine of Aragon (1485–1536) and establish the Church of England (1534). It may seem anticlimactic to portray this ill-starred Medici pope as "the favorer of Israel," but his cordial reception of the adventurer David Reubeni (d. 1538?)—one of the most colorful Jewish figures of the Renaissance—remains worthy of mention.

Reubeni, who may have been an Ethiopian Jew, or Falasha, arrived at Venice in 1523, claiming to be the army commander of a Jewish kingdom that descended from Israel's ancient "lost tribes." In February 1524, this short, swarthy man entered Rome on a white horse and headed for the Vatican, where he was received by Cardinal Egidio da Viterbo

(c. 1465–1532), a humanist learned in Hebrew and Greek and well familiar with the kabbalah. Reubeni was received by Pope Clement and interpreted this encounter as an act of reconciliation between the Jews and the ruling Church.

In 1525, Reubeni went to Portugal and was ceremoniously received at the Lisbon court. There his message that the hour of redemption was near inspired the imagination of Diogo Pires (c. 1500–1532), a Marrano then serving as secretary to the king's council. The young courtier circumcised himself, changed his name to Solomon Molcho (from the Hebrew *melekh*, "king"), and then, apparently at Reubeni's urging, fled Portugal for the Ottoman Empire; at Salonika he studied kabbalah, met Joseph Caro, and became more and more convinced that he himself was the Messiah whose coming Reubeni had foretold. In 1530, Molcho went to Rome, where he prophesied both the city's destruction by a flood and the eruption of an earthquake in Portugal, after which the "holy spirit would descend upon the King-Messiah, and he would reign over the great people." Later that same year, in Venice, Molcho again encountered Reubeni, who had in the meantime been forced to leave Portugal, on suspicion of fomenting unrest among the Marranos, and was now attempting to forge a joint Christian-Jewish crusade to reclaim the Holy Land from the Turks. When heavy downpours in Rome and earth tremors in Portugal appeared to confirm Molcho's predictions, Clement VII held lengthy audiences with him, and when the pseudo-Messiah was summoned before the Inquisition, the pope intervened with a writ of immunity.

In 1532, Molcho and Reubeni traveled to Regensburg to call on the Emperor Charles V, who, unimpressed with their scheme for a crusade, had them arrested. This time, with the pope unwilling or unable to protect him, Molcho was tried by the Inquisition at Mantua and burned at the stake in an auto-da-fé;

Reubeni, imprisoned in Spain, probably died there six years later. Meanwhile, Jacob ben Samuel Mantino (d. 1549), a medical practitioner of Spanish descent who had intrigues against Molcho within the Jewish community, entered the service of Pope Paul III (r. 1534–1549) as his personal physician. Paul's pontificate, which saw the settlement (by papal invitation) of Portuguese Marrano refugees at Ancona, marks the end of generally cordial relations between the Renaissance papacy and the Jews.

There probably were not more than 3,000 professing Jews in Rome during the period. The Jewish community of Venice was even smaller, though perhaps no less distinguished. The Venetian Jewish community reflected the great diversity of outlook, opportunity, and political climate among northern and western Italy, the southern part of the Italian peninsula, and the Levant. Jews had originally come to Venice from Germany and the Levant. But when they were expelled from Spain in 1492, many had come to Venice from that country as well. The various elements that made up the Venetian Jewish community each had its own synagogues, its own institutions, its own ceremonies and traditions. There was a very broad diversity—but with a strong underlying unity. As is the whole of Jewish history, the Venetian Jewish community was distinguished by a tradition of self-help, charity and good deeds.

The Banco Rosso in the Jewish ghetto of Venice was not so much a bank as a loan society for the Jewish poor. The Jews of Venice had many institutions of charity and welfare to serve a varied community, with its rich and its poor, its established families and its recent arrivals, its young to be educated and its old to be cared for. The institution that defined Jewish life in Venice from the sixteenth through the eighteenth century was the *ghetto nuovo,* an island (later surrounded by walls and guarded at night by

This portrait of the great German religious reformer Martin Luther is one of several painted by Lucas Cranach, his sixteenth-century contemporary. Cranach was not only a friend of Luther's but also a publicist for the Protestant cause.

patrol boats) in the parish of San Girolamo in the northern sector of the city. This is the place where the word "ghetto" was born; "ghetto," in fact, comes from the Italian *geto vecchio,* meaning "old foundry," and there was once an iron foundry in this place. It was here that in March 1516 a decree was issued that the Jews of Venice could live only in this quarter, surrounded by a wall, closed in for the night by a gate that was locked at sunset.

In the course of history, "ghetto" came to signify the segregation of any people. It came to mean a poverty area from which people

Leo X, a Medici pope, was a true friend to the arts and tolerant toward the Jews, but he was morally and intellectually incapable of meeting the challenge Luther and his followers laid before the Church. Portrait of Leo X by Raphael.

could not escape. The underlying idea of the ghetto is deprivation, isolation, separation, and, in modern times, persecution and even destruction. But there was no atmosphere of deprivation or persecution in the original establishment of the Venetian ghetto, not at the beginning, at least.

The ghetto was always an area of legal separation. Some believe that the establishment of the Venetian ghetto was a protective measure, designed to defend Jews against attack by hostile neighbors. Others point out that for some time before the enactment of the law establishing the area of confinement, Jews had in fact been subjected to many forms of separation: a special tax, a special law preventing Jews from owning land, a requirement to wear special dress—the yellow hat, a yellow badge, later a red hat. In this view, the establishment of the ghetto was simply the ultimate expression of the idea of segregating Jews from the life of the general community.

It is difficult to paint the reality of ghetto life, socially or intellectually, in one single color. Yes, the Jews were separated geographically from their neighbors, but in non-curfew hours there was a great deal of intermingling with non-Jews on the social level. If in time there were periods of repression and persecution, there were also periods of relative tolerance. And if in some places the ghetto had a stunting effect on intellectual life, in others—and especially in the ghetto of Venice—there was a vibrant social and religious life. In its golden days, the ghetto of Venice knew an intensity of artistic and intellectual expression—in poetry, in philosophy, in medicine, and above all in the printing of Hebrew books, including some of the earliest books printed in any language at all.

THE SPREAD OF CULTURE

This is an appropriate point for a few reflections on the history of printing, whose impact on the Renaissance can scarcely be overestimated. The introduction of modern Western printing, with its precision-cast metal type, is traditionally credited to Gutenberg, but a number of printers in the Rhineland appear to have surmounted the technical obstacles almost simultaneously between 1440 and 1450. During the next fifty years, thousands of works were printed. By the end of the century, Italy had 73 printing presses; Venice, which started up its first press in 1469, employed more than 400 printers by the year 1500.

Of all the many Venetian printers, none was more influential than Aldus Manutius (Aldo Manuzio, 1450–1515), who came to Venice in 1490. Manutius's Venetian Academy attracted many Greek scholars exiled from Ottoman lands; these men served between 1494 and 1515 as editors and proofreaders in the production of the famed

Aldine editions of classical Greek texts. (One scholar whom Manutius attracted and befriended was the Dutch humanist Desiderius Erasmus [1466?–1536], who, though never abandoning Roman Catholicism, helped shape the intellectual development of the German Reformation.) Manutius is justly esteemed for his role in the Greek revival; less well known is the fact that Manutius was also a Hebraist who in 1500 published the first printed Hebrew grammar for Christian readers.

The true pioneers of Hebrew printing were two German Jews who, having received permission in 1454 from the Sforza of Milan, settled in Soncino, taking the name of that town for their firm and family. To Soncino belongs the honor of publishing, in 1488, the first complete Hebrew Bible. Equally impressive were the accomplishments of a Christian printer, Daniel Bomberg (d. c. 1550), who as a youth left his native Antwerp for Venice and there published nearly 200 Hebrew books, including the first complete editions of both the Babylonian and the Palestinian Talmuds.

Leone da Modena (Judah Aryeh, 1571–1648), surely the most colorful Jewish figure in Renaissance Venice, also dabbled in the printing trade, overseeing the publication in 1617–1618 of a new edition of the Hebrew Bible. Aptly labeled by one historian as "jack of twenty-six trades, though master of none," Modena was the most celebrated of Venice's Jewish literati, whose ranks also included Simone ben Isaac Simhah Luzzatto (1583–1663), Modena's successor as the community's senior rabbi and the author of *Socrate* (1651), a philosophical dialogue, and the *Discorso circa il stato de gl' hebrei* (1638), a plea for toleration that emphasized the importance of the Jews to the Venetian economy; and Sara Coppio Sullam (1590–1641), a poetess to whom Modena dedicated his Italian adaptation of Solomon Usque's tragedy *Esther*. Modena, among all these luminaries,

Nationalism and Protestantism could be powerful allies. King Henry VIII was proclaimed "Defender of the Faith" by Pope Leo X for writing a tract against Luther in 1521; but thirteen years later he led England out of the papal fold for reasons of royal prerogative and national interest. Portrait of Henry VIII by Hans Holbein.

was the man upon whom the Christian world looked, with some emotional excess, as the apotheosis of Jewish learning.

The revival of Hebrew scholarship and the dissemination of Hebrew books during the Renaissance surely played a part in the rise of German Protestantism, though by no means as large a part as the Church, which regarded the Protestants as Judaizers, tried to make out. The major intellectual conflict in Germany during Martin Luther's formative years was between the Reuchlinists and the anti-Reuchlinists—that is, between those who, like humanist and scholar Johannes Reuchlin, believed that one could read the classic Hebrew texts and still remain a faithful Christian, and those who insisted that Hebrew books must be condemned and destroyed. This "Battle of the Books" began in earnest when a Moravian-born butcher, Johannes Pfefferkorn (1469–1524), abandoned Judaism for Christianity, began writing anti-Jewish tracts, and in 1509, under Dominican sponsorship, won from Holy Roman Emperor Maximilian I (r. 1493–1519) the power to confiscate Jewish books except for the Bible. Asked in 1510 to serve on a commission to determine which books, if any, should be condemned, Reuchlin voted in the Talmud's favor, a decision that pitted Reuchlin and Pfefferkorn (and their respective allies) against each other in a war of pamphlets that kept printers working overtime. Reuchlin was charged with heresy by Jacob Hoogstraaten (1460–1527), a Dominican monk who as professor of theology at the University of Cologne was one of Pfefferkorn's chief supporters. To avoid being tried in the unsympathetic atmosphere of Cologne, Reuchlin in 1513 addressed an appeal to Bonetto de Lattes (Jacob ben Emanual Provenzale), a professing Jew who was not only a rabbi and an astronomer but also personal physician to Pope Leo X. Reuchlin was eventually tried not in hostile Cologne but in nearby Speyer, where he was acquitted in 1514.

Naturally, this bitter dispute took on different meanings from different perspectives. For the Jews, the key battle was won in 1510, when the emperor was persuaded not to have the Talmud burned immediately but instead to return the confiscated books to their rightful owners and to appoint the commission of inquiry on which Reuchlin served. Jews played only a peripheral role in the subsequent controversy, which pivoted on the figures of Reuchlin, Pfefferkorn, and Hoogstraaten and was, accordingly, a conflict between liberal and reactionary elements within the Church. In a wider context, however, the issue was freedom of inquiry versus the authority of the Church of Rome; and in this conflict, the machinations of the Dominicans, the ignorance of the anti-Reuchlinists, the vacillation of both the emperor and

the pope, and the pomp and corruption of Rome provided ready ammunition for the reformers.

An undercurrent of nationalism permeates this dispute and erupts with Luther and his successors. By what right did church officials in Rome control the affairs and consciences of German believers? To a certain extent, we measure the Renaissance papacy by the magnificent works of art and architecture the Medici popes commissioned. But that was not Luther's view. When the Dominican monk Johann Tetzel (1465?–1519) reached the vicinity of Wittenberg in 1517, promising remission of sins for those who donated money for the reconstruction of Saint Peter's Basilica, Luther's righteous anger can only have been exacerbated by the fact that Germans were being asked to pledge their cash for a sumptuous Roman building. Can we justify the crass issuance of indulgences because the fund-raising campaign produced a church planned by Bramante, executed by Michelangelo, and decorated by Raphael?

The precise theological questions on which Luther and his followers differed from the Church of Rome were of little importance to the Jews. But on one question—the traditional Catholic attitude toward the progenitors of Jesus—the Jews of course had a deep personal interest. Luther criticized the traditional Church position in 1523 in his pamphlet *Das Jesus Christus ein geborener Jude sei (That Jesus Christ Was a Born Jew):*

I will therefore show by means of the Bible the causes which induce me to believe that Christ was a Jew born of a virgin. Perhaps I will attract some of the Jews to the Christian faith. For our fools—the popes, bishops, sophists, and monks—the coarse blockheads! have until this time so treated the Jews that to be a good Christian one would have to become a Jew. And if I had been a Jew and had seen such idiots and blockheads ruling and teaching the Christian religion, I would rather have been a sow than a Christian.

The basic elements of Luther's style are not hard to grasp: reliance on the Christian Bible rather than on classical or Church authority; the coarsely polemical language; the unremitting assault on Catholic clergy and theology; the naive belief that he could succeed in converting the Jews where the Church had failed for more than a millennium. And yet, later in this same pamphlet, we encounter a surprisingly sensitive and sympathetic account of Jewish sufferings at the hands of Christian bigots, coupled with a plea for economic and social emancipation:

I would advise and beg everybody to deal kindly with the Jews and to instruct them in the Scriptures; in such a case we could expect them to come over to us. If, however, we use brute force and slander them, saying that they need the blood of Christians to get rid of their stench and I know not what other nonsense of that kind, and treat them like dogs, what good can we expect of them? Finally, how can we expect them to improve if we forbid them to work among us and to have social intercourse with us, and so force them into usury? If we wish to make them better, we must deal with them not according to the law of the pope, but according to the law of Christian charity. We must receive them kindly and allow them to compete with us in earning a livelihood, so that they may have a good reason to be with us and among us and an opportunity to witness Christian life and doctrine; and if some remain obstinate, what of it? Not every one of us is a good Christian.

Luther's popular pamphlet was reprinted nine times in the twelve months following its first appearance. Nineteen years later, in 1542, he published another essay on the "Jewish question." This pamphlet, *Gegen die Juden und ihre Lügen (Against the Jews and Their Lies),* which went through two editions during the four remaining years of his life, was as different from its predecessor in tone as in title:

What then shall we Christians do with this damned, rejected race of Jews? Since they live among us and we know about their lying and blasphemy and cursing, we cannot tolerate them if we do not wish to share in their lies, curses, and blasphemy. . . .

First, their synagogues . . . should be set on fire, and whatever does not burn up should be covered or spread over with dirt so that no one may ever be able to see a cinder or stone of it. . . .

Secondly, their homes should likewise be broken down and destroyed. For they perpetrate the same things there that they do in their synagogues. For this reason they ought to be put under one roof or in a stable, like gypsies, in order that they may realize that they are not masters in our land, as they boast, but miserable captives.

Thirdly, they should be deprived of their prayer books and Talmuds in which such idolatry, lies, cursing, and blasphemy are taught.

Fourthly, their rabbis must be forbidden under threat of death to teach any more.

Fifthly, passport and traveling privileges should be absolutely forbidden to the Jews. For they have no business in the rural districts since they are not nobles, nor officials, nor merchants, nor the like. Let them stay at home. . . .

Sixthly, they ought to be stopped from usury. All their cash and valuables of silver and gold ought to be taken from them. For this reason, as said before, everything that they possess they stole and robbed from us through their usury, for they have no other means of support. . . .

During the second half of the sixteenth century, the Catholic and Protestant nations of Europe formed two armed camps, the Catholic led by Philip II of Spain (here in a portrait by Titian).

Seventhly, let the young and strong Jews and Jewesses be given the flail, the ax, the hoe, the spade, the distaff, and spindle, and let them earn their bread by the sweat of their noses as is enjoined upon Adam's children. . . .

To sum up, dear princes and nobles who have Jews in your domains, if this advice of mine does not suit you, then find a better one so that you and we may all be free of this insufferable devilish burden—the Jews.

It is remarkable that this barely coherent ranting, more vituperative and inflammatory than any papal pronouncement on the Jews, should have come from the same religious reformer who in 1523 had written:

The Jews are the blood relatives, the cousins and brothers of our Lord; if his flesh and blood could be boasted of, the Jews belong to Jesus Christ much more than we do. Hence I beg my dear Papists to call me a Jew, when they are tired of calling me a heretic.

We err, however, if we do not seek the primary explanation for Luther's anti-Semitism. Why, after all, should this man of anguish and courage, one of the crucial figures of European history, have turned to Jew-hatred in his old age? We might say that anti-Semitism so permeated the fabric of Christian society that even the most enlightened thinkers of the sixteenth century could not loosen its hold on their deepest feelings. The gifted humanist Erasmus wrote, "If it is the part of a good Christian to detest the Jews, then we are all good Christians." Should we then be surprised when the far less cosmopolitan Luther casts off his youthful tolerance to embrace a medieval demonology?

Know, O adored Christ, and make no mistake, that aside from the Devil, you have no enemy more venomous, more desperate, more bitter, than a true Jew who truly seeks to be a Jew.

We have met this demonology before, in the writings of Rodulfus Glaber:

. . . the envious devil again began to pass on to the worshippers of the true faith the poison of his iniquity through the race of the Jews who were accustomed to him.

This deeply malignant association—so much more potent than any denunciations of usury or any merely historical assertion of Jewish complicity in the death of Jesus—seems, indeed, to have been part of the German folk heritage. We even detect it in a much later era, when anti-Semitism has graduated from the theological to the "scientific."

It was in Germany during Luther's own lifetime that the Jews suffered the most immediate consequences of the Lutheran Reformation. Even when his attitude toward the Jews was at its most sympathetic, Luther had recognized no ecclesiastical duty to protect them, and the Protestant rebellion excluded the Jews of many German principalities from papal protection. As in other periods of social upheaval in Europe, a rash of blood libels, charges of "host desecration," and attacks on moneylending indicated that Jews had become scapegoats for the dislocating effects of social, economic, and demographic change. Here we must note, however, the tireless efforts of Joseph ben Gershom of Rosheim (c. 1478–1554), an Alsatian-born Jew who, as *shtadlan*, represented the interests of German Jewry before Christian dignitaries and legislative bodies. Not only did Joseph intercede with local authorities whenever an anti-Jewish outbreak threatened, but he also convened a meeting of rabbis and other Jewish notables to establish a ten-point code formally abjuring the commercial abuses that Christians most frequently complained about and regulating financial relations between Jews and Christians. After this code was approved by the assembly, Joseph appeared before the Reichstag (imperial diet) at Augsburg in 1530 to announce the accord:

I and my comrades, authorized by the Jews, promise and pledge ourselves to observe these resolutions, if only the rulers and princes, the officials of the provinces and cities in the Holy Roman Empire, on their part, will do all that is possible to grant us peace in all our domiciles, without disturbing us with decrees about expulsion: if they will secure our freedom of movement and trade without hindrance, and will not fabricate accusations with a view to oppressing us. Because we, too, are human beings, created by the Almighty, to live on earth with you.

If the Reformation era found the Jews of Germany trapped between the Catholic and Protestant contenders, what of Italian Jewry, still under papal protection and control?

Elizabeth I of England (portrayed by an anonymous English artist) was the leader of the Protestant nations of Europe. The scattering of the Spanish Armada in 1588 not only secured independence for the Protestant Netherlands—but established a new haven for Jewish settlement.

The reaction of the Church to Martin Luther's Protestant rebellion was disastrous for the Jews. The Church was resolved to stamp out every heresy, and Jews were regarded as a threat no less than Protestants. Ironically, Jews were regarded as the allies of the Protestant Reformation. And so, in 1553, the papacy endorsed the burning of the Talmud.

The papal assault on the Jews of Italy—the Jews of Rome were ordered into a ghetto and expelled from all other places under papal control except the port of Ancona—was only one aspect of the larger war on heresy that historians call the Catholic Counter-Reformation. With one weapon of the Counter-Reformation many of Jewish ancestry were all too familiar—the Inquisition. But we should not overlook the broader canvas of the reform movement within the Church, spearheaded by such learned prelates as Cardinal Francisco Ximenes (Jimenez) de Cisneros (1437–1517). Cardinal Cisneros, sometime confessor to the Spanish Queen Isabella and inquisitor general of Castile and León, enjoys more enduring renown for having initiated and supported the creation of the Complutensian Polyglot Bible (1513–1517), in which Biblical texts in Hebrew and Aramaic, edited with the aid of *conversos*, appear side by side with the Greek and Latin versions. But the pivotal agency of the Counter-Reformation was undoubtedly the Society of Jesus—the Jesuits—founded by the Spanish soldier and churchman Saint Ignatius of Loyola (Iñigo de Oñez y Loyola, 1491–1556).

The Jesuits' later reputation for political intrigue, often at the expense of national kings and clergy, should not blind us to the fact that for nearly two centuries after its founding in 1534, the Society of Jesus was a leader in European education, establishing hundreds of colleges and seminaries, while carrying the Christian gospel to India, Japan, China, Africa, and the New World. The fact is that, demographically speaking, the Counter-Reformation was a marked success. By one estimate, the proportion of Protestants in the European population declined from 40 percent to 20 percent between 1570 and 1620; in Italy, Austria, Poland, and France, the Protestant tide was rolled back. Even today, in Europe, after centuries of papal decline, Roman Catholics outnumber Protestants by a ratio of 3:2. Across the world, also, Roman Catholicism claims a majority of Christians, overwhelmingly so in the Spanish-speaking countries.

We can see the monarchs and princes of sixteenth-century Europe choosing sides, decreeing which variety of Christian belief—Roman Catholic or one of the Protestant persuasions—would receive official sanction and which would be stripped of its blessing. Indeed, the sixteenth and seventeenth centuries witnessed a succession of religious wars pitting Catholic and Protestant countries and principalities against each other. The resources that each ruler could bring to such a conflict depended, of course, on commercial as much as on ideological factors. Spain, with its holdings in the New World, appeared to enjoy a special advantage. But even nations that could not, as Spain did, exploit the mineral wealth of the Americas, could profit by trade and by plundering Spanish commerce. This, in large measure, was the secret of Britain's prosperity in this period.

The dynamism of the Renaissance passed to the nations along the Atlantic Coast. The opening of shipping routes to the Orient and the New World had made Catholic Spain the most powerful kingdom of Europe. Possessing vast territories in the New World, Spain and Portugal monopolized the Atlantic trade routes.

In 1556, as part of a royal inheritance, the Spanish crown came into possession of the Netherlands, one of the most thoroughly Protestant regions of Europe. In Spain, for sixty years since the expulsion of the Jews, Spanish rulers had waged a blood campaign to root out all vestiges of Jewish and Islamic worship among their subjects. The Spanish Inquisition had tortured and burned at the stake thousands suspected of deviating, however slightly, from strict Catholic orthodoxy. Now, with the Netherlands under Spanish rule, the Spanish Inquisition would deal with the Dutch.

The Netherlands rose in revolt. Protestant England and its queen, Elizabeth I (r. 1558–1603), came to their aid. The battle lines were drawn: Elizabeth and the Protestant lands on one side, the grim and zealous monarch of Spain, Philip II (r. 1556–98), and the Catholics on the other.

Almost from the beginning, the war was not confined to the Netherlands home ground. Spanish ships attacked British slavers, and the English adventurer Sir Francis Drake (1540?–1596), acting on the queen's commission, plundered Spanish vessels and outposts in the West Indies and South America. All-out war became inevitable once Queen Elizabeth, in 1585, dispatched English soldiers to the Low Countries. As the Spanish navy readied for battle, a raid on Cádiz harbor in 1587 by the marauding Drake was no more than a temporary setback.

Spain's attack, when it came, was massive —a fleet of greater proportions than the world had ever seen. It was called the Catholic Armada. The English, under Drake, sailed out to meet it. When the two fleets met, the lighter and swifter ships of the English quickly outmaneuvered the Armada and broke up its formation.

The defeat of the Spanish Armada did not end the struggle between Spain and the Protestants of Europe, but it was a crucial turning point. The Atlantic was no longer a Spanish sea. The Protestant Low Countries achieved their independence, and with it, the right they had so boldly proclaimed when they joined in rebellion:

Where it concerns matters of religion, Holland and Zeeland shall conduct themselves as they think proper, provided that every individual remains free in his religion and that no man shall be molested or questioned on the subject of divine worship.

By the time the independence of the Protestant Netherlands (then called the United Provinces) was formally recognized in the Peace of Westphalia (1648), Amsterdam was already one of the world's great commercial centers.

Amsterdam, once little more than a minor port on the North Sea, welcomed refugees from religious intolerance all over Europe. Protestant merchants came from Flanders, Huguenots, from France, Jews from Spain and Portugal. The city grew into the trade capital of Northern Europe. Spices, textiles, goods of all sorts, crowded the docks of Amsterdam. Its ships went forth in search of trade routes everywhere. The Dutch flag was raised over lands in the distant Orient, in Africa, and in the New World. Its merchants gathered fortunes.

The city of Amsterdam has long had a special relationship with the Jews. Since the end of the sixteenth century, when Jews first came there from Spain and Portugal, they and other groups had found an atmosphere of religious tolerance and political security. Amsterdam has always had a tradition of respect for diversity, for individuality, for the right of people to think and do as they please. And, therefore, this city evokes a special intimacy and affection in Jewish hearts.

This tradition goes back very far. In 1590, Jews fleeing the Inquisition found the Netherlands to be a natural shelter and refuge for them. Three and a half centuries later, in 1941, when the Nazis began to apply their policies of persecution to the Jews of Amsterdam, practically the whole non-Jewish population of the city organized a protest—a strike paralyzing all services—in a dramatic demonstration of solidarity with their Jewish fellow citizens. It is difficult to think of any other community in Europe which so regards the Jews as a component of its own historic experience. This is the special link between the Jews and Amsterdam.

In the seventeenth century most of the world's Jews lived in Eastern Europe and in the Ottoman Empire. But in the tolerant Netherlands and in other Western centers such as Hamburg and (later) London, the Jews, though few in number, were well into the mainstream of economic life. It was a period of florescence, of dynamic expansion in trade, in finance, in exploration, in manufacturing, in communication. It was good to be a Jew and to be alive in Amsterdam in those days. The factors that had excluded Jews from pursuits involving agriculture and land-owning had caused them to specialize in banking and finance, and in the world of international commerce the Jews had certain advantages. They had a common language, and they had a network of trust and confidence, of kinship and affinity, with other Jewish bankers and merchants in the various other countries of the Jewish dispersion.

So here they were in Amsterdam—a Jewish community, part of a thriving society, only 10,000 in number by the year 1700 but still the largest Jewish community in Western Europe. They traded in sugar and tobacco and diamonds; they were active in banking and manufacturing and printing. And because of the atmosphere of relative religious freedom and political security, they were becoming less and less differentiated from their neighbors, more and more similar to them in dress and in speech, in habits of thought and conduct. They were really developing a pattern that was to typify so many Jewish communities in the next century or two. They lived freely in the general life of society, and yet they maintained their own traditions and kept their Jewish sanctuary intact. They were faithful to their own solidarities, but they did not cut themselves off from neighboring society. They were seeking—and very often found—a point of balance between their identity as Jews and their full participation in the flourishing life around them.

The interaction of the Jews with the societies in which they lived nearly always comprised two elements. There was the direct influence and experience of Jews who participated, to the extent that they were allowed, in the local economy and society. This was the direct human influence. But there was also a cultural influence, that of the Bible and of the monotheistic tradition that had such a large part in shaping Western civilization.

These two elements, Jewish life and Jewish thought, were conspicuously represented in the artistic imagination of the great painter Rembrandt van Rijn (1606–1669), who lived in Amsterdam from 1639 to 1660 in a house, surprisingly enough, in the very heart of the Jewish quarter of Amsterdam. The street is called Jodenbreestraat, The Broad Jewish Street, to this very day. It was there that Rembrandt found Jewish neighbors who would model for the masterpieces he painted on Biblical themes. He had inherited a love of the Biblical literature from his mother.

Exactly why he chose to live in the very heart of the Jewish quarter is a matter of conjecture. What is quite certain is that he had a deep, intimate human interest in the simple folk around him and that his mind was especially dominated by Biblical themes. Thus both the Book and the people of the Book are represented in Rembrandt's masterpieces. Whether consciously or intuitively, he seems to have understood that both the Jews and the Jewish legacy are a part of the common heritage of Western civilization.

One of the most sumptuous depictions of Jewish life in Amsterdam was painted not by Rembrandt but by Emanuel de Witte (1617?–1692)—the interior of the Spanish and Portuguese Synagogue, created around 1680. When this very impressive synagogue was dedicated in 1675, there was an orchestra and a choir. We do not expect to hear about music at Jewish religious ceremonies, so this reflected the taste, culture, and temperament of the Spanish and Portuguese Jews who established this community and founded this synagogue. They had been Marranos, Jews who in Spain and Portugal had accepted the outer forms of Christianity but maintained an inner fidelity to the Jewish faith and the Jewish tradition and secretly practiced that faith and followed that tradition. Here in Amsterdam they no longer had to be Marranos. They did not have to be underground Jews. Here they could practice their faith proudly and openly. Something of that pride and that openness is reflected in the dimensions, the structure, and the beauty of this building.

In their prayers they adopted the ritual of

the Sephardim. The Jews of Spain, expelled in 1492, had become scattered across all the countries on the rim of the Mediterranean Sea. They had settled in southern Italy and Greece; they had gone farther east, toward the Adriatic and the Balkans, to Turkey and Bulgaria; they had spread themselves across the whole of the North African littoral. These Sephardim represented one of the two main streams of Jewish practice and tradition. In Amsterdam they were joined by Jews who came from the other great stream of Jewish tradition and ritual—Jews who came from Poland and Lithuania in order to escape the poverty and violence of Eastern Europe in the sixteenth and seventeenth centuries.

The differences between Sephardi and Ashkenazi Jews belong much more to outer form than to inner conduct. There really is no theological difference, as there is between Protestantism and Catholicism in Christianity. Sephardi and Ashkenazi Jews are faithful to the same Torah and celebrate the same festivals, but they give expression to their fidelity in different ways. They each have their own way of pronouncing Hebrew in the synagogue. The Sephardi Hebrew pronunciation belongs to the phonetic context of the Arabic, the Oriental, and the Mediterranean worlds, while Ashkenazi Hebrew has the phonetic cadence of the European languages, especially German. Sephardim and Ashkenazim both have their own non-Hebrew Jewish language written in Hebrew characters. For the Sephardim it is Ladino, which is for all practical purposes a form of Spanish; for the Ashkenazim it is Yiddish, which has a structure and vocabulary based much more on Germanic form. Both have their own rabbinical tradition and chief rabbinate, with distinctive forms of dress. Israel today has a Sephardi chief rabbinate. There are also differences in the ritual melodies and in parts of the prayer book.

In the seventeenth century, if anyone wanted to express diversity, Amsterdam was the appropriate place in which to do it. Amsterdam by that time had its own independent tradition of respect for diversity and dissent. One of the few threads that run consistently through the whole of Jewish history is this insistence on dissent and on diversity. It has often been said that wherever you have two Jews together, you are likely to hear three opinions. There is a popular jest about two Jews who were stranded for many decades on a desert island. By the time they were rescued, they had built three magnificent synagogues, one for each of them to pray in, and a third which both refused, on principle, to attend.

In the more serious context of intellectual history in the seventeenth century, we come across this tendency for individualism and dissent in the life of one of the great giants in European intellectual history, the philosopher Baruch Spinoza (1632–1677), a Jew of Amsterdam. Spinoza, who departed from traditional theology, had been a member of the Sephardi congregation long before the Spanish and Portuguese Synagogue was built. He was excluded from that congregation and excommunicated from the Jewish community because of what was believed to be his revolt against Jewish orthodoxy. Today, when we recall the sobriety and integrity of the man, who earned his living as a lens grinder and seems to have sought little more than a life of quiet—and sometimes lonely—contemplation, the writ of excommunication issued against him by the Sephardi elders on July 27, 1656, has a harsh, almost brutal tone:

Cursed be he by day, and cursed be he by night; cursed be he when he lies down, and cursed be he when he rises up; cursed be he when he goes out, and cursed be he when he comes in. The Lord will not pardon him; the anger and wrath of the Lord will rage against this man, and bring him all the curses which are written in the Book of the Law, and the

Lord will destroy his name from under the Heavens, and the Lord will separate him to his injury from all the tribes of Israel with all the curses of the firmament, which are written in the Book of the Law. . . .

We order that nobody should communicate with him orally or in writing, or show him any favor, or stay with him under the same roof, . . . or read anything composed or written by him.

Spinoza was not a nonreligious Jew, still less an antireligious Jew. Historians of philosophy have even called him a "God-intoxicated man." He believed that scientists and philosophers should be free to pursue their inquiries and speculations about nature wherever their conclusions led them, without any rigid prior commitment to religious dogma. He thought that the real essence and the real value of religion lay in its ethical and human content, in the pursuit of justice and truth and compassion.

Why was this "God-intoxicated man" excommunicated by the Jews, mistrusted by Christians and denounced by some as an "atheist" both during his lifetime and after? Certainly his pantheism—his total identification of the reality of God with the reality of the universe—played a pivotal part in this, for a God that is wholly identifiable with the universe is a God that may be admired and worshiped but can never hear or respond to personal prayer. For Spinoza, God *is* everything: "Whatever is, is in God, and nothing can either be or be conceived without God." But this God has no plan, no purpose, acting "from the laws of His own nature only." The result, for Spinoza, is a thoroughgoing determinism: "In nature there is nothing contingent, but all things are determined from the necessity of the divine nature to exist and act in a certain manner." Few men have viewed the vicissitudes of life and the limitless variety and mutability of the universe from so lofty a philosophical plane.

Spinoza's masterwork is commonly called the *Ethics* (1674), but only the full title conveys the true flavor of his thought: *Ethics Demonstrated with Geometrical Order.* Not only does Spinoza's argument in this work proceed proposition by proposition, as in a geometry text, but even the ethical truths he elucidates impress him by their mathematical precision:

I do not presume that I have found the best philosophy. I know that I understand the true philosophy. If you ask in what way I know it, I answer: In the same way as you know that the three angles of a triangle are equal to two right angles.

Such pretensions to precision were very much in tune with the rationalism of Spinoza's great contemporaries Descartes and Newton. And insofar as Spinoza sought to apply scientific method to the problems of faith, we can point to Saadia Gaon and Maimonides as kindred Jewish spirits. But there was, at least in his own time and perhaps even now, a scarcely bridgeable gap between Spinoza's geometric ethics and the ethics of the Talmud, that distinctively Jewish amalgam of law and legend, insight and tradition.

It is doubtful if his attempts to reconcile faith and reason would have got him into such serious trouble today. The seventeenth century was an age when the intellectual life of Europe in general was occupied by the confrontation between the ancient truths and the new potentiality, and probably in modern times the effort to bring them into harmony would not have resulted in Spinoza's excommunication.

This argument has never really ceased. Spinoza's views were unpopular at the time. But his challenge was destined to shape the course not only of modern Jewish religious thought but of modern religious thought in Western civilization as a whole.

The Spinoza affair remains one of the less happy episodes of Jewish intellectual history. Two other events that involved Dutch Jewry during the mid-1650s, around the time of Spinoza's excommunication, had a far more positive outcome.

The first was the landing in New Amsterdam in 1654 of not quite two dozen Sephardim—the first Jewish settlers on the North American mainland and the pioneers of what would in time become the world's largest and most prosperous Jewish community. We might mention that the arrival of these Dutch Jewish refugees in the New Netherland colony was part of a larger dispersion that saw Dutch Jews trade and settle in coastal Brazil (until they were ousted by the Portuguese), Curaçao, and various Oriental outposts. (But we need not dwell on the New World now. We shall have ample opportunity to speak of American Jewry in Chapter 8.)

The second important development in which Dutch Jews had a hand was the return of their coreligionists to England, from which all Jews had been expelled in 1290. Only a handful of Jews had lived in England during the next two centuries, and the small Marrano community that grew up during the sixteenth century was disgraced by the arrest and execution in 1594 of Roderigo Lopez on charges of plotting to poison the queen. Lopez, a Jew who was Elizabeth's court physician, was probably innocent of the charges, but *was* an intriguer, and his loyalty to the British crown was rightly suspect. When, two years later, William Shakespeare (1564–1616) wrote *The Merchant of Venice*, the Lopez scandal and the wave of anti-Jewish feeling it had engendered remained fresh in the mind of his audience. Shakespeare's Shylock, though humanized and given understandable motives for his bitterness toward Christians, is still very much the stereotypical Jewish moneylender, cold, cruel, and unrelenting:

The son of a Portuguese Marrano, the seventeenth-century philosopher Baruch Spinoza has been called a "God-intoxicated man." Unorthodox in his own day, his conceptions of God, nature, and necessity significantly influenced later Christian and Jewish thinkers.

Antonio: *I pray you, think you question with*
the Jew:
You may as well go ahead upon the beach
And bid the main flood bate his usual height;
You may as well use question with the wolf
Why he hath made the ewe bleat for the lamb;
You may as well forbid the mountain pines
To wag their high tops and to make no noise,
When they are fretten with the gusts of heaven;
You may as well do anything most hard,
As seek to soften that—than which what's
harder?—
His Jewish heart. . . .

By 1609, with James I (r. 1603–1625) on the British throne, London's Marrano community had disappeared. But at midcentury, under the Commonwealth, with the Puritan Oliver Cromwell (1599–1658) as Lord Protector, the climate for renewed Jewish settlement was far more propitious. Marranos had already begun to trickle into London when the Dutch Jewish leader Manasseh ben Israel (1604–1657), who was born a Marrano on Madeira, addressed his famous petition to the British leader for free exercise of the Jewish religion. Manasseh, whose face is immortalized in a Rembrandt etching, came to England in 1655 and remained there for two years, on a pension from Cromwell. Manasseh's petition was not formally granted, but from 1656 onward, Jews were allowed to settle in England and establish their synagogues. British Jewry would grow steadily in wealth and numbers, but concentrated in London, Manchester, Glasgow, Leeds, and Dublin (at that time, of course, under English rule). In the nineteenth and twentieth centuries, English Jews would play a central part in the settlement of Palestine and the rebirth of Zionism.

Until the seventeenth century the Mediterranean region was the central arena of Jewish history. With the eclipse of Spanish Jewry and the beginnings of emancipation in Western Europe, Jewish scholarship and folk tradition find their home in the East. In the middle of the eighteenth century East Europe had a million and a half Jews of which the largest community was in Poland. At the end of the eighteenth century Poland was subjugated by Russia and lost its independence. A million Jews passed from Polish rule to that of Catherine II, Empress of Russia. Harsh residential restrictions compelled the Jews to establish the pales of settlement which, like the ghettoes in Christian Europe, had a dual consequence. On one hand, they cut the Jews off from the main currents of society and culture; on the other hand, they stimulated the creation of an autonomous Jewish life nourished from Jewish sources alone. Within a single century Russian Jewry would grow into the largest single community known to Jewish history until that time.

Jan Vermeer's Young Woman Reading a Letter *(1666) betrays a distinctly modern sensibility, fascinated not with mythological tales nor with religious figures but with the shape and texture of everyday life. Few painters have dealt so analytically with the effects of light on color—an achievement that has its counterpart in the science of optics, developed around this time by Isaac Newton and many Dutch experimenters.*

E VEN AS the Jews of Amsterdam were paving the way for Jewish settlement in the Dutch and British colonial empires, the Jewish population balance within continental Europe was shifting from west to east. The fourteenth century, so traumatic for the nations of Western Europe, saw the distinctive emergence of national monarchies in Hungary, Poland, Lithuania, and, still farther eastward, in the principality of Moscow, the forerunner of modern Russia. With the rise of these monarchies came a period of relative political stability, economic prosperity, and cultural integration, as symbolized by the founding of the universities of Prague, Cracow, Vienna, and Pécs between 1348 and 1367. The demographic origin of this political, economic, and cultural transformation lay in German and Flemish colonizing, which, especially from the twelfth century onward, provided the manpower to drain swamps and clear forests for settlement and cultivation. In the year 1100, the population of Eastern Europe was probably not more than 10 million; by 1625, according to one estimate, Eastern Europeans numbered at least 30 million, surpassing for the first time the aggregate population of Europe's Mediterranean lands.

Jews were not immune to these large-scale demographic movements. Jews in all likeli-

---

The Altneuschul ("Old-New Synagogue") of Prague, built around 1270, survives both as a museum and as a place of prayer. The double-naved, vaulted interior, depicted in the woodcut, is characteristic of medieval synagogue architecture in Central Europe; the exterior (in the photograph) is unusually impressive, indicating a community that felt secure in its surroundings. But the remarkable culture of East European Jewry was to be ravaged in the Holocaust of World War II.

8·
Search for Deliverance

JEWS IN EAST EUROPE: CREATIVITY AND OPPRESSION

hood entered Hungary from the southeast after the collapse of Khazaria around 965. Jews must also have been among Poland's twelfth-century German colonizers: excavations in Poland have unearthed coins from this period with Hebrew inscriptions. This suggests that at least some Polish Jews must have enjoyed considerable wealth and influence. Another general upsurge of German immigration came after the Mongols overran Poland in 1240-1241. No doubt many Germans and Jews at this time crossed the border into Poland because there was no centralized authority to stop them. But the Jews also came by invitation: in 1264 the Polish King Boleslav V issued a charter protecting the Jews and guaranteeing their right to take part in moneylending and commerce. This charter was ratified and then extended by Casimir III ("Casimir the Great," 1333–1370), a formidable administrator who befriended the peasantry as well as the German and Jewish settlers. According to legend, Casimir had a Jewish mistress and their daughters were raised as Jews.

Nor was Poland the only major center of Jewish settlement east of the Elbe. The first documentary evidence of a Jewish presence in Prague dates from about 970; before the end of the eleventh century a Jewish community had been established, drawing on immigrants from both East and West.

In the city of Prague in Bohemia, caravans were assembled to carry manufactured goods to Russia. Other caravans returning from the East unloaded their cargo of Russian grain, lumber, and cattle for reshipment to the West. Here for centuries Jews mingled with Christians in the marketplaces. In the thirteenth century they built the Altneuschul, the "Old-New Synagogue." It alone among the synagogues of medieval Europe survives to this day, a reminder of the antiquity of Jewish settlement in the land.

The world of the Ashkenazim was unlike that of the Spanish Jews in many ways. In Spain, Jews had felt that they were Spanish as much as they were Jewish. But elsewhere in Europe, constant tension between Jews and Christians from the tenth century onward had closed the Jews within their own society. As much as possible, the Ashkenazi community sought to be self-sufficient, a world apart. The Jewish quarter within a city was a town within a town. Jews had their own internal government, their own courts, their own schools and guilds. They cared for one another in times of hardship, trying not to depend upon the Christian world around them. And although over the years they were influenced by the dress, the speech, and the customs of their Christian neighbors, at heart they remained fiercely loyal to their Jewishness and resistant to any change in their way of life.

In the late fifteenth century, large numbers of German Jews arrived in Poland. In many senses, Poland was still a frontier. Its farming system was primitive and feudal. The Polish nobles realized that greater profits could be had if the lands produced more efficiently. The nobles turned to the Jews.

We do hereby lease to the worthy Master Abraham, son of Samuel, our estates, villages, and towns, and the monetary payments that come from the tax on grain, beehives, fishponds, lakes, and places of beaver hunting, on fields, on meadows, on forests, and on threshing floors.

We also give him the authority to judge and sentence all our subjects, to punish by money fines or by sentence of death those who are guilty or who disobey.

The Jews who leased the lands from the nobles were called "rendars," and they enlisted other Jews to help them administer these vast domains. Goods that were produced were turned over to Jewish merchants for sale. All the Jews benefited. In this new land of opportunity, they became innkeepers, traders, artisans, and financial

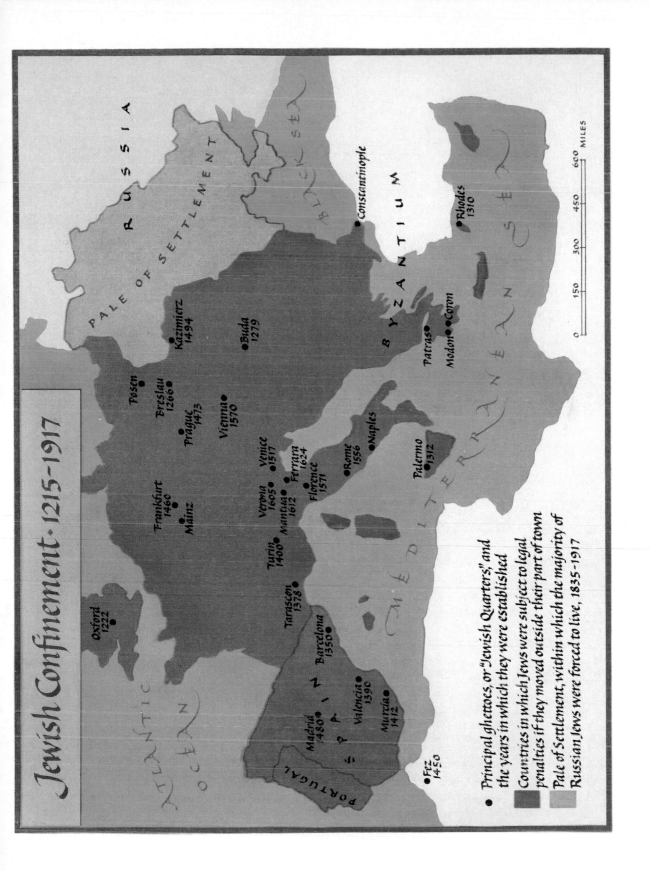

Jewish Confinement · 1215–1917

- Principal ghettoes, or "Jewish Quarters," and the years in which they were established

Countries in which Jews were subject to legal penalties if they moved outside their part of town

Pale of Settlement, within which the majority of Russian Jews were forced to live, 1835–1917

MILES
0   150   300   450   600

RUSSIA

PALE OF SETTLEMENT

BLACK SEA

BYZANTIUM

MEDITERRANEAN SEA

ATLANTIC OCEAN

SPAIN

PORTUGAL

Oxford 1222

Frankfurt 1460

Mainz

Posen

Breslau 1266

Prague 1473

Vienna 1570

Kazimierz 1494

Buda 1279

Turin 1400

Verona 1605

Venice 1517

Mantua 1612

Ferrara 1624

Florence 1571

Rome 1556

Naples

Palermo 1312

Tarascon 1378

Barcelona 1350

Madrid 1480

Valencia 1390

Murcia 1412

Fez 1450

Constantinople

Patras

Modon

Coron

Rhodes 1310

By the time Bernardo Bellotto (1720–1780) painted this street scene of Warsaw, Poland had already passed its peak of prosperity and political power. Warsaw became capital of the Polish Kingdom in 1595, but a small number of Jews had been living there since the late fourteenth century.

agents. The Jewish community of Poland grew to be the largest in the world. There were an estimated 25,000 Jews in Poland and Lithuania by the end of the fifteenth century. Within 150 years, their numbers may have increased to 500,000.

This people who had come from Germany found in Poland a land on a crossroads between Europe and the Orient. From its culture they relearned elements of an Eastern heritage and created a blending of East and West that was uniquely theirs.

It is with a sort of painful foreboding that we look back on the period of greatest prosperity for the Polish Jews. In 1569, Poland annexed the Ukraine. Huge regions of wilderness were brought under Polish rule. Rendars and other Jews were sent in to colonize these territories. The Ukrainians were members of the Eastern Orthodox Church, their language and culture distinct from that of the Polish rulers. They hated the Poles with their Roman Catholic priests and their Jewish rendars.

Conditions were certainly ripe for rebellion in 1647, when a Ukrainian officer named Bogdan Chmielnicki (1595–1657), born to the petty aristocracy, fled across the Dnieper River to Zaporozh'ye, a Cossack stronghold, after losing a personal quarrel with a Polish nobleman. Chmielnicki found a ready audience among the Cossacks for his message of hatred against Poles and Jews. Moreover, he secured the support of the Tatar khan of Crimea and managed to rouse the peasantry to rebel against their masters. "What the peasant earns, the noble spends and the Jew profits by"—so goes an old Polish proverb, one indication among many that Chmielnicki did not have to dig very deeply to find the wellsprings of anti-Jewish feeling.

The first wave of violence, in the springtime of 1648, destroyed the Jewish communities east of the Dnieper. Thousands of Jewish refugees fled across the river to the western towns, where the Cossacks and peasants pursued them. The first large-scale massacre of which we have full documentary evidence took place at Nemirov (Niemirow, now within the Ukrainian S.S.R.). This massacre, not different in kind from the Crusader massacres of 1096—how little some things had changed in five and a half centuries!—was only the first surge of what would become a two-year tidal wave of bloodshed, destroying, if the chroniclers are correct, some 300 Polish Jewish communities and claiming at least 100,000 Jewish lives. Added to this toll of misery was the plight of the homeless.

Subsequent invasions by Russians and Swedes brought a new wave of massacres, and the task of housing the homeless, feeding the orphans, and fulfilling Jewish tax obligations to the Polish authorities represented an enormous drain on the organs of Jewish self-government. Some Polish Jews sought refuge in the West, others in mysticism and messianic expectations.

Throughout the world of Judaism there was shock. Shock at the fate of the Polish victims. Shock at the recurring pattern of violence to which Jews everywhere were subject. The turmoil and violence of the times seemed proof that the End of Days was near. Jewish tradition had promised redemption at the End of Days, but it had also promised a time when the Messiah would come to re-

The eighteenth-century London that Canaletto saw, though a modern city of brick and stone (most of Old London's wooden structures were destroyed in the Great Fire of 1666), is a far cry from today's commercial and industrial metropolis.

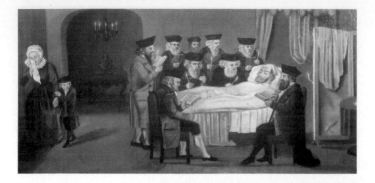

Life and death among the Ashkenazim. ABOVE LEFT: prayers at the deathbed; ABOVE RIGHT: the body is ceremonially washed and prepared for burial; and the casket is lowered into the grave. Participation in funeral rituals was regarded as a religious obligation within the Jewish community, and burial societies customarily included the community's most prestigious members.

store the world to holiness and redeem the nation.

In 1665, when the massacres in Poland were almost ending, Shabbetai Zevi (1626–1676), a Turkish Jew, proclaimed that he was the Messiah. Scholars have differed in their assessment of Shabbetai Zevi and the Shabbatean movement. Some have regarded him as merely a charlatan, a fraud. Others, presuming that he was mentally deranged, grant him at least a sincere belief in his own messianic pretensions. He may have proclaimed himself the Messiah as early as 1648,

when news of the Polish massacres reached his native Smyrna. In 1663, when the eccentric and ascetic Shabbetai was living in Jerusalem, he attracted the notice of the rabbi and kabbalist who would become his most important disciple, the young scholar Nathan of Gaza (c. 1643–1680). Two years later, when Nathan had begun to style himself a prophet and had become convinced through a vision of Shabbetai's messianic purpose, he publicly proclaimed it, along with his master, at Gaza on May 31, 1665. Thereafter, in a series of fervent epistles, Nathan, like a seventeenth-century Saint Paul, broadcast the messianic message throughout the diaspora.

There had been many messianic pretenders in the past, but never before had one man united the Jewish people of all lands in a movement so inspired with enthusiasm and hope. It is not to the person of Shabbetai Zevi that we must look for an explanation of this outpouring of emotion. Most Jews had never seen him and had little direct knowledge of him. Rather, we must look to the Jewish people themselves and see the movement as poignant testimony to their deep longing for an end to suffering, an end to 1,600 years of exile.

In September 1665, the pseudo-Messiah returned triumphantly to Smyrna, whose rabbis had banished him more than a decade earlier. From Smyrna, in a long letter that would eventually circulate throughout the diaspora, Nathan prophesied the glad tidings:

And now I shall disclose the course of events. A year and a few months from today, he [Shabbetai] will take the dominion from the Turkish king without war, for by [the power of] the hymns and praises which he shall utter, all nations shall submit to his rule. He will take the Turkish king along to the countries which he will conquer, and all the kings shall be tributary unto him, but only the Turkish king will be his servant. . . .

On the strength of these promises, Jews throughout the diaspora—in Central and Eastern Europe, of course, but also in London and Amsterdam, Italy and Macedonia, Morocco and Egypt—began to purify themselves for the day of redemption. The Yiddish memoirist Glueckel of Hameln (1645–1724), recalling those days, tells a story that is not at all untypical:

Many sold their houses and lands and all their possessions, for any day they hoped to be redeemed. My good father-in-law left his home in Hameln [near Hanover, in what is now the Federal Republic of Germany], abandoned his house and lands and all his goodly furniture, and moved to Hildesheim. He sent on to us in Hamburg two enormous casks packed with linens and with peas, beans, dried meats, shredded prunes and like stuff, every manner of food that would keep. For the old man expected to sail any moment from Hamburg to the Holy Land. . . . For three years the casks stood ready and all this while my father-in-law awaited the signal to depart. But the Most High pleased otherwise.

Many chose not to wait. As Shabbetai readied himself for the journey from Smyrna to Constantinople, the Turkish capital, Jews began streaming toward Palestine, joyously taking part in what they believed was the long-promised "ingathering of the exiles." But as the fateful year 1666 began, Shabbetai's plans went awry. We can hardly blame the Turkish officials for perceiving in the Shabbatean movement the threat of insurrection; thus, it comes as no surprise that Shabbetai was intercepted in the Sea of Marmara, brought ashore in chains, and taken to the capital as a Turkish prisoner. What is surprising is that the pseudo-Messiah was not immediately put to death. Instead, he was confined to a cell, but allowed to receive visitors, who departed his presence full of stories of the new miracles that Shabbetai had performed there. For the Shabbateans, it seems, even the Messiah's imprisonment became part of the grand design.

Finally, the bubble burst! In September 1666, Shabbetai was hauled before the Turkish court and, in the presence of the Sultan's physician, Mustapha Hayatizadé, an apostate Jew, he was compelled to choose: Islam or death. On September 15, 1666, Shabbetai's choice was confirmed. Without excessive soul-searching he chose Islam! He took a Muslim name, Aziz Mehmed Effendi. He took a Turkish title *Kapiči* Bashi ("Keeper of

This engraving produced by Thomas Coenen in 1669 is probably the only authentic portrait of Shabbetai Zevi, the false Messiah.

the Palace Gates"). He accepted a royal pension of 150 piasters a day. The choice was clear.

Some Jews, including many of the pseudo-Messiah's most devout followers, likewise embraced the religion of Allah. Others, though retaining their Jewish identity, clung desperately to the belief that Shabbetai's apparent apostasy was yet one more mystery to be revealed.

But in reality the miracle had failed, there was nothing left but despair. In Poland, in the wake of spiritual ruin, there was now spiritual desolation.

Out of this bleak physical and spiritual landscape arose a Jewish religious revival that would change the face of Judaism as no sectarian movement had since Roman times. That movement was Hasidism—literally, "pietism"—and its father was Israel ben Eliezer (c. 1700–1760), better known as the Ba'al

Shem Tov ("Master of the Good Name"), or anagrammatically to his followers as the Besht. The Besht edited no texts, wrote no tracts, compiled no manuals. We know little about his life other than that which generations of Hasidic storytellers have passed down to us.

Hasidic tradition has it that the Besht was born in Ckop, a small town of Podolia, a region then part of southeastern Poland and today within the Ukrainian S.S.R. After bearing the full force of the Chmielnicki horrors, Podolia fell under Ottoman rule in 1672; the Polish crown did not reestablish control over Podolia until 1699, around the time of Israel ben Eliezer's birth. Orphaned and impoverished, the Ba'al Shem Tov supported himself and, later, his family through a succession of odd jobs, including those of synagogue watchman, clay digger, and innkeeper. The legends emphasize the young man's love of nature and of solitary contemplation, and tradition has it that while in his twenties he went off into the Carpathian Mountains to meditate on the ways of God and man. On his thirty-sixth birthday, the Hasidim say, the Besht made known his true vocation as a healer and teacher.

Unlike the rabbis of his day, he believed that even a simple, unlearned man could approach God directly through prayer and worship. In coming closer to God, a man could through himself bring divine influence into the world. "Cleaving to God" it was called— and it was a joyous, ecstatic experience. The paths to it were many: through prayer, through the keeping of any commandment, even through so simple an action as the tying of one's shoelaces. God was everywhere, and everywhere to be found.

There is some controversy among scholars over the origins of these ideas. Some recent writers have pointed to the influence of Polish peasant ways on the Besht's thinking. Nevertheless, there is a substantial body of scholarship that holds the teachings of the

Old photographs and drawings are all that remain of Poland's unique wooden synagogues, all of which were burned down by the Nazis during World War II. Shown here are, **ABOVE LEFT**: the fortified synagogue of Zholkva, built about 1695; **ABOVE RIGHT**: the interior of the wooden synagogue at Zabludow, probably dating from the seventeenth century; **RIGHT**: the interior of the Old Synagogue of Kazimierz (Cracow), constructed around 1400; and, **BELOW**: the wooden synagogue at Przedborz (c. 1760).

Ba'al Shem Tov to be well rooted in purely Jewish traditions. Israel ben Eliezer was not, after all, an ignorant peasant. He counted among his friends and disciples Meir ben Zevi Hirsch Margolioth (d. 1790). Would the son of a famous rabbinic family, a man who would later become preeminent as an exponent of Talmud and kabbalah, lightly have championed the Hasidic cause? Would he have embraced Hasidism if he believed that the Besht's teachings were alien to or ignorant of the fundamentals of Jewish learning? As for the idea of "cleaving to God"—*devekut* in Hebrew—the idea is at least as ancient as Deuteronomy:

For if ye shall diligently keep all these commandments which I command you, to do them, to love the Lord your God, to walk in all His ways, and to cleave unto him. . . .
(Deuteronomy 11:22)

The secret of the Besht's power resides not in an originality of ideas but in the earthiness and intensity with which he applied them, and in his ability to bridge the gap between the heights of religious ecstasy and the realities of village life. The insistence of the Hasidim on the celebration of God was, in its own time, a healthy antidote to a culture that had come to equate commitment to Judaism with the arduous study of religious texts. It reminds us of the wellsprings of the Jewish experience in an *oral* tradition—even though, by our own century, the Hasidic tales would all be transcribed and codified, and the Hasidic outlook fully analyzed by a philosopher as formidable as Martin Buber.

Hasidism is not merely a specific way of looking at God and man; its theological differences are subsidiary to its gift to Jewish cultural history. Hasidism is a special, enchanting world, rich with stories, homilies, and endless wonders about the rabbinical courts and dynasties that are the heart and center of the Hasidic vision. The Hasidic rabbis, revered for their learning and piety, were given unconditional devotion by their disciples. The positive side of this folklore lies in the intensity and purity of its faith. The obverse side of the coin is the obsequious worship of charisma, which seems to run counter to the traditional scepticism of the Jews in all ages to claims of divine authority in human beings.

The Ba'al Shem Tov had many followers, but he also had many detractors. Today we call them *Mitnagdim*, which in Hebrew literally means "opponents." These traditionalists saw the Hasidic movement with its growing emphasis on *zaddikim* (the charismatic leaders who reigned over their disciples as a king over his court), as a threat to their own authority. They swiftly condemned the religious enthusiasts. It is said that a scholar once asked the Ba'al Shem Tov, "What of the rabbis who call your teachings false?" The Ba'al Shem Tov replied, "Once, in a house, there was a wedding festival. The musicians sat in a corner and played upon their instruments, the guests danced to the music and were merry, and the house was filled with joy. But a deaf man passed outside the house; he looked in through the window and saw people whirling about the room, leaping and throwing their arms. 'See how they fling themselves about,' he cried. 'It is a house filled with madmen!' For he could not hear the music to which they danced."

While in Eastern Europe Jews were turning to Hasidism, in the West, Judaism was to find a different direction. In the Netherlands, in England, in Germany, and in France—where Jews had been allowed to settle during the seventeenth century, despite an expulsion order that remained on the books—the early eighteenth century saw unprecedented growth in trade and commerce, and with it a new attitude toward the Jews. In 1712 the following item appeared in *The Spectator*, a respected English periodical:

The Jews are so disseminated through all the

trading parts of the world that they are become the instruments by which the most distant nations converse with one another. They are like the pegs and nails in a great building, which though they are but little valued in themselves, are absolutely necessary to keep the whole frame together.

Symptomatic of the rising fortunes of London Jewry was the opening, 1701, of the Spanish and Portuguese Synagogue in Bevis Marks, now a historic landmark. Twelve Jewish financiers—the "Jew brokers"—were admitted to the Royal Exchange during this period, and Jews in due course entered the upper echelons of Lloyd's of London and the East India Company. In the cultural sphere, the Jewish influence in London may be one reason why the composer George Frederick Handel (Georg Friedrich Handel, 1685–1759) so often turned to Old Testament subjects—*Esther, Deborah, Saul, Israel in Egypt, Judas Maccabeus*—for his operas and oratorios. But we should not exaggerate the security of Jewish life in England. Though surely tolerated, Jews remained an uneasy presence in London society, as a second look at *The Spectator*'s reference to "pegs and nails . . . but

Partly by custom and partly as a result of restrictions imposed upon them, the Ashkenazim evolved their own distinctive style of dress. Characteristic of the men's costumes were caftans and fur hats. Decorated lace caps, forehead bands, and the plastron, or brüsttüch, the biblike trimming of a dress, were typical of Ashkenazi women.

little valued in themselves" might lead one to suspect. In 1753, for example, the government introduced in Parliament the Jewish Naturalization Act, or "Jew Bill," allowing foreign-born Jews access to the same privileges of citizenship as were already available to their English-born children:

Be it therefore enacted by the King's most excellent Majesty, by and with the Advice and consent of the Lords Spiritual and Temporal, and Commons, in this present Parliament assembled, and by the Authority of the same, That Persons professing the Jewish Religion may, upon Application for that Purpose, be naturalized by Parliament, without receiving the Sacrament of the Lord's Supper. . . .

This right, granted in 1753, was withdrawn

Jews of Vienna Marching to Meet Nathan of Gaza, 1666. "Many sold their houses and lands and all their possessions, for any day they hoped to be redeemed. . . ." Quotation from the Jewish memoirist Glueckel of Hamelu (1645–1724).

a year later because of the outcry from Christian merchants. Not until 1890—nearly a century and a half later—would emancipation be complete.

In the German states, meanwhile, rulers turned to Jewish merchants for assistance, often putting the finances of state in the hands of their Jewish advisers. It was from these early *Hofjuden,* or "Court Jews," that there rose the great families of European Jewry—the Oppenheimers, the Wertheimers, and the Rothschilds.

Wealth, influence, prestige—the rewards of the court were manifold for these Jews. They lived in elegant surroundings, rode in carriages with large retinues, and gave parties that even Christian nobles would attend.

But if in manners and fashion the Court Jews followed the German aristocracy, they remained Jews in both spirit and intellect. And when, as some did, a Court Jew exercised the dual role of *Hofjude* and *Shtadlan,* he could intervene—while he still enjoyed court favor—to ameliorate the persecution of his people. Nevertheless, the Court Jews were only cases of privilege. Although the Jews of eighteenth-century Germany suffered fewer massacres and expulsions than their predecessors, they were still constrained by many forms of legal harassment. Sumptuary laws, or *Kleiderordnung,* still prescribed what clothes Jews could wear, which streets Jews could walk on (and at what times), how many Jews could attend a wedding party, and which foods their state or town would allow them to eat. In 1726 the Viennese court decreed that only the eldest son of a Jewish family might legally marry; the other sons were not entitled to produce legitimate offspring. In 1750 the Prussian monarch Frederick II ("Frederick the Great," r. 1740–86)

The life of the Ba'al Shem Tov is shrouded in legend, but there is no doubt that the movement he fathered—Hasidism—revitalized Judaism and Jewish culture in Eastern Europe. Here, a portrait of the Hasidic leader by one of his followers.

issued a charter classifying Jews into several groups. Among the privileged classes defined by this charter, an unrestricted number of "extraordinary" Jews could not pass on their privileges to the next generation, while a much smaller number of "ordinary" Jews were allowed to bequeath their rank to only one male heir. No Jews were permitted to enter farming, brewing, innkeeping, and most professions; trade in local agricultural products was also forbidden. As for Jewish family life, the charter declared an overriding state interest:

In order that in the future all fraud, cheating and secret and forbidden increase of the number of families may be more carefully avoided, no Jew shall be allowed to marry, nor will he receive permission to settle in further numbers, nor will he be believed, until a careful investigation has been made by the War and Domains offices.

This from the monarch whom most historians have portrayed as the epitome of the enlightened despot, a prolific writer who patronized the Bach family and Voltaire. How long could the men of the Enlightenment ignore the religious bigotry in their midst?

Knowledge once thought proper to God alone now seemed within the grasp of mankind. Science had revolutionized the thinking of a generation, with startling discoveries

Under their hetman Bogdan Chmielnicki, Cossacks and Ukrainians rebelled against their oppressive Polish masters in 1648. The uprising unleashed a reign of terror against the Jews, who had profited from their service to the Polish state as rendars (leaseholders), innkeepers, traders, artisans, and financial agents.

A key figure of the German Enlightenment and of the Jewish Haskalah, Moses Mendelssohn, here in a portrait by Johann Christoph Frisch, came to symbolize for Christian Europeans what the Jew, if educated and emancipated, could accomplish.

He is really a Jew . . . a man who without any guidance has achieved a great strength in languages, in mathematics, in philosophy, in poetry. I regard him as a future honor to this nation.

Mendelssohn, born in Dessau and the son of a poor Torah scribe, was not entirely self-taught. As a boy, he pursued traditional Jewish studies with the brilliant young rabbi David ben Naphtali Hirsch Fraenkel (1707–62), who introduced his protégé to the works of Maimonides. When Fraenkel was appointed chief rabbi of Berlin in 1743, his stu-

Rembrandt's famous etching of Menasseh ben Israel dates from 1636, by which time the thirty-two-year-old scholar had already founded the first Hebrew printing press in Amsterdam and written a highly regarded Biblical commentary. His petition to Cromwell and mission to England were still nearly two decades away.

in physics, in chemistry, and in mathematics. The Enlightenment philosophers—Voltaire, Rousseau, Locke, Hume—excited and optimistic, turned to examine human society with the reasoned techniques of science. They called for an end to all social oppression, an end to religious intolerance.

In 1754, in Germany, a play was published that created a storm of controversy. The play, *Die Juden (The Jews)*, was written by a Christian, Gotthold Ephraim Lessing (1729–1781), whose purpose was to show his fellow Christians that a Jew could be wise sophisticated —in a word, enlightened.

The public was skeptical. Most Christians could not imagine such a man coming from the isolated and traditional world of the German Jews. When accused of having conceived the impossible, a cultivated Jew, Lessing pointed to a young man he had just met, Moses Mendelssohn (1729–1786).

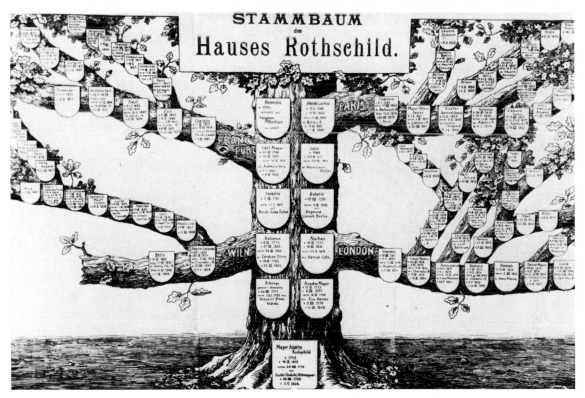

The Rothschilds emerged from among the Hofjuden to become the best-known and most powerful banking family of nineteenth-century Europe. This Rothschild family tree, drawn up in 1901, shows paterfamilias Mayer Rothschild and his wife, Gudula Schnapper, at the roots; their sons and daughters on the trunk; and the main Paris, London, Vienna, and Frankfurt branches.

dent, then only fourteen, went with him. In Berlin, Mendelssohn eked out a bare living as a tutor, copyist, and bookkeeper; years of poverty and malnutrition left their scars in the form of delicate health and a humped back, presumably caused by rickets. Nevertheless, what Berlin's "privileged" Jews could not offer Mendelssohn in material support they made up for in German books and assistance in the mastering of modern languages, Latin, and metaphysics. In this hub of the Enlightenment, Mendelssohn in time became one of Germany's foremost thinkers. His acceptance as an equal by enlightened Europeans was without precedent, and it indicated a path that other Jews might follow.

Adopt the mores and constitution of the country in which you find yourself, but be steadfast in upholding the religion of your fathers, too. Bear both burdens as well as you can.

Mendelssohn argued that only by opening their minds to non-Jewish knowledge could Jews leave the isolation of the ghetto. It was the beginning of the Jewish Enlightenment—the Haskalah. Those who embraced Haskalah believed that Western education was the way to a full and equal partnership with the Christians of Europe. As we approach the eighteenth century we find the holes in the ghetto walls becoming larger and larger. The walls were destined to crumble, at least in the West, during the three spectacular decades between the French Revolution and the fall of Napoleon in 1815.

CONCLUSION

For centuries the experience of the Jews had been one of separation. Separation had tried and preserved them. It was the source of their vitality. They had recently given birth to the Hasidic movement, which seemed to offer a way of spiritual fulfillment within exile. To give up their particular identity by merging it with the lives of the society around them seemed a frightening idea. After all, the Enlightenment principles of freedom and equality were still only principles, and Christian Europe carried with it a dark heritage of resentment toward the Jews. It was not until the end of the eighteenth century that these ideas were expressed in the politics of nations:

We hold these truths to be self-evident, that all men are created equal, that they are endowed by their Creator with certain unalienable Rights, that among these are Life, Liberty and the pursuit of Happiness.

The appetite for freedom that moved the American colonists in their Declaration of Independence now took hold in Europe. In revolutionary France, a land from which Jews had for centuries been officially excluded, the National Assembly issued in 1789 its Declaration of the Rights of Man and of the Citizen:

I. Men are born, and always continue, free and equal in respect of their rights. . . .

II. The end of all political associations is the preservation of the natural and imprescriptible rights of man; and these rights are liberty, property, security, and resistance of oppression. . . .

IV. Political liberty consists in the power of doing whatever does not injure another. . . .

X. No man ought to be molested on account of his opinions, nor even on account of his *religious* opinions, provided his avowal of them does not disturb the public order established by the law. . . .

Two years later, the National Assembly removed all doubt that Jews were citizens of France and therefore entitled to enjoy the full rights of French citizenship:

The National Assembly, considering that the conditions requisite to be a French citizen, and to become an active citizen, are fixed by the constitution, and that every man who, being duly qualified, takes the civic oath, and engages to fulfill all the duties prescribed by the constitution, has a right to all the advantages it insures;

Annuls all adjournments, restrictions, and exceptions, contained in the preceding decrees, affecting individuals of the Jewish persuasion, who shall take the civic oath. . . .

There was a sense of the world on the threshold of a new age. The central political vision of the late eighteenth century was of a state in which religious differences would count for little, in which citizens would be equal before the law.

Somehow, ethical and moral traditions that had been born thousands of years before, and visions of universal peace and social justice that had been voiced by the Hebrew prophets, had survived to be taken up again with renewed spirit and enthusiasm. It seemed that at last a time had come when the Jewish people could join in fellowship with all others to work for the common good of humankind.

The nineteenth century would show how exaggerated these hopes had been.

Especially at times when access to the broader European culture was denied them, Jews devoted their artistic energies to the creation of religious ornaments. *ABOVE LEFT*: a gilded brass votive tablet (shivviti), inscribed in Danzig in 1804; *ABOVE RIGHT*: silver headpieces (rimmonim) for the Torah scrolls, cast in Mantua, Italy, about 1600; *BELOW LEFT*: a silk brocade Torah Ark curtain, embroidered in the early 1750s, probably in Frankfurt; and, *BELOW, RIGHT*: an Ashkenazic Torah case.

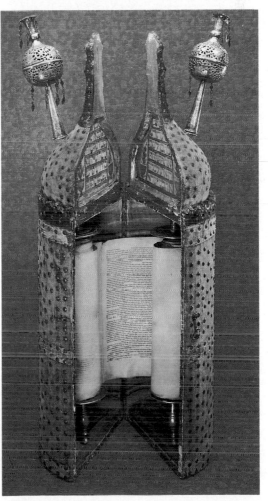

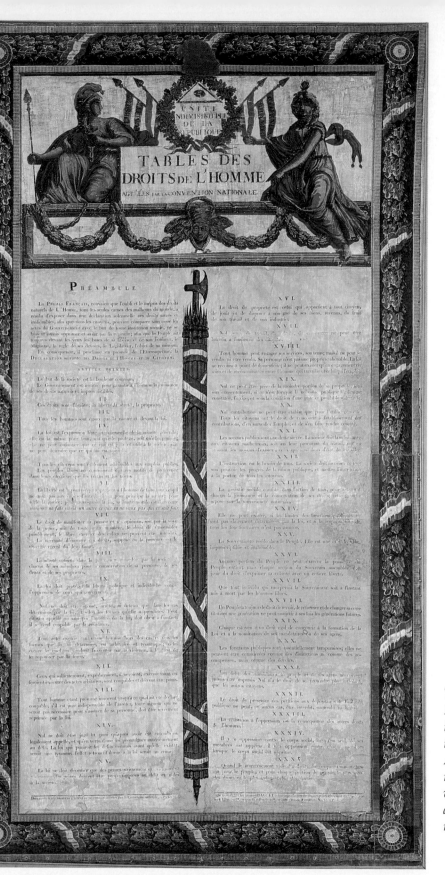

The Declaration of the Rights of Man and of the Citizen, adopted by the French National Assembly in 1789, replaced loyalty to king with loyalty to country as the citizen's primary responsibility.

9.
Roads
from
the Ghetto

Tᴴᴇ ᴇʀᴀ in Europe from 1789 through 1848 has often been called an "age of revolution," most obviously because of its frequent political upheavals: in France in 1789, in Greece in 1821, in Poland, Belgium, again in France in 1830, and in Austria-Hungary, Germany, Italy, and yet again in France in 1848. Broadening our gaze to the whole of the nineteenth century and to the beginnings of our own, we can see in the soil of 1848 the seeds of the Russian Revolution of 1917, a cataclysm whose consequences have been momentous for the life of our generation. It was in 1848 that two young German intellectuals, Karl Marx (1818–1883) and Friedrich Engels (1820–1895), issued their challenge to the European bourgeoisie:

A specter is haunting Europe—the specter of communism.

The *Communist Manifesto*, published just before the Parisian outbreak in 1848, specifically mentions the revolutionary ferment in France, Switzerland, Poland, and Germany, but it confines itself to no nation or continent:

The communists everywhere support every revolutionary movement against the existing social and political order of things. . . . The proletarians have nothing to lose but their chains. They have a world to win.

We err, however, if we restrict our consideration of this revolutionary century only to *political* revolutions. Equally important—and equally revolutionary—was the transformation of the means of production. The first phase of this *industrial* revolution, lasting

In the nineteenth century, Jews looked to learning—especially to secular learning—as a path from oppression to emancipation.

roughly from the late eighteenth century to the middle of the nineteenth, has its leader in Great Britain and its symbols in the coal mine, the ironworks, the cotton mill, and the railroad. The second phase, beginning especially after the end of the American Civil War and the completion of German unification, would be led by Germany and the United States. The keys to this second phase are the development of special steels, followed by the harnessing of electricity and the rise of the petrochemical industry. Among its symbols, still with us today, are the electric light, the motor car, the airplane, and the oil well.

Intimately linked with this industrial transformation was a *demographic* revolution that saw the population of Europe increase dramatically by 85 million between 1800 and 1850. (European population growth had been no more than 80 million during the two preceding centuries.) In the British Isles, the population expanded from about 10 million in 1750 to 28 million in 1850, a rise of 180 percent. By 1900 there were some 42 million people living on British and Irish soil, and 390 million people in Europe as a whole. Never before or since has Europe held so large a share of the world's inhabitants.

In addition to these political, industrial, and demographic revolutions, there was a no less explosive revolution of *nationalism*—a dramatic change in the way the average person defined his loyalty and identity. Not by accident did the leaders of the French Revolution, in their statement of democratic principles, address the question of the rights of man *and of the citizen:*

III. The nation is essentially the source of all sovereignty; nor can any individual, or any body of men, be entitled to any authority which is not expressly derived from it.

The revolutionaries had toppled the monarchy and aristocracy, undermined the privileges of the clergy, abolished regional and class distinctions. France was now one nation, bound together by uniform laws and institutions. The old loyalty—loyalty to the king—was as dead as the king himself soon would be. In its place, the revolutionaries enshrined loyalty to country, to the fatherland, to *la patrie.* (Hence, from the common Greek root, the English word *patriotism.*) Any Frenchman, whatever his region, religion, or former status, would be a *citoyen*, and what, after all, was any citizen but a creature of the state?

For the Jews of Western Europe, the revolutionary nineteenth century presented a vast opportunity—but also an immediate dilemma. What, after all, was a Jew? Was he still an alien in diaspora, dwelling amid strangers only until, with the advent of the Messiah, he could return to the land of Israel, his true and eternal home? Or was he fully a citizen of a modern European state, indistinguishable from his French, German, Dutch, or British compatriots save for a few dietary peculiarities and affiliation with a synagogue instead of a church? Was Judaism, in short, to be a nationality or a religion? In the late eighteenth century, when autonomous Jewish communal institutions still functioned in France and Germany, it was plain that if the Jews wished to come to terms with the modern state, and its relentless claims to state sovereignty, they would have to get their loyalties clear.

The presumption, common among West European and American Jews by the early nineteenth century, that full participation in the life of a modern state could be gained only at the cost of the Jews' own nationalistic aspirations can be traced back to the Edict of Toleration issued in January 1782 by the Holy Roman Emperor Joseph II (r. 1765–1790). This enlightened despot, hoping to make the Jews of his Austrian realm "more useful to the state," repealed the badge laws and the onerous Leibzoll (literally, "body tax"), a special levy that Jews had to pay when passing through or stopping in a jurisdiction that

Liberty Leading the People, painted in 1830 by Eugène Delacroix. Three times within six decades —in 1789, 1830 and 1848—French governments were overthrown by popular uprisings.

customarily banned them. He also opened up avenues for Jewish educational and financial advancement. On the other hand, Joseph also made the Jews liable for state military service, required them to adopt German-style personal and family names, barred the use of Yiddish and Hebrew in communal and commercial record-keeping, and eradicated the last vestiges of rabbinic juridical autonomy. These policies—beneficial to a limited number of "tolerated" Jews but disruptive to the traditional fabric of Jewish life—were the two sides of the same coin. Emancipation meant assimilation. The price was one that several generations of European Jews seemed fully prepared to pay.

The next step in the balancing of this equation comes with Napoleon Bonaparte (1769–1821), one of the very few dictators on whom Jews look back without anger. The story has often been told how, born to an impover-

ished Corsican family and educated in French military schools, the young Bonaparte rose through the ranks of the French revolutionary army, seized power in 1799, proclaimed himself Napoleon I, Emperor of the French, in 1804, and within six years controlled, directly or indirectly, Spain, the Netherlands, Switzerland, western Germany, northeastern Italy, the Kingdom of Naples, and the Grand Duchy of Warsaw. What is less well known is how pivotal a part he played in defining the Jewish role in modern European society through his policies and conquests. "Peoples of Italy, the French army comes to break your chains," pro-

At the Battle of Wagram (1809), depicted here by an unknown artist, Napoleon led the French forces to a smashing triumph over Austria.

claimed Bonaparte in 1796, at the outset of his brilliant Italian campaign. For much of Italy, the French victory would mean an end to regional divisions and aristocratic privileges. But for the Jews, the coming of the French army had a more immediate meaning —an end to the Inquisition, the dismantling of the ghettoes. Everywhere Napoleon went, Italian Jews hailed him as their savior; and when Bonaparte entered Ancona, Jewish soldiers, citizens of France, led the march into the ghetto, tearing off the yellow badges of the residents and offering them the tricolor rosette, symbol of the revolution.

Napoleon regarded himself not as the architect of a greater French empire but as a true liberator who, by destroying the old regimes, would lay bare the patterns of nationhood that centuries of war and political division had scrambled.

One of my grandest ideas was *l'agglomeration:* the concentration of people geographically united, but separated by revolutions and political action. There are, scattered over Europe, 30 million Frenchmen, 15 million Spaniards, 15 million Italians, and 30 million Germans. My intention was to make each of these peoples into a separate national state.

And what of the Jews? What nation had been more dispersed; what nation was more scattered over the face of Europe? Sentiments such as these—as well as more practical political considerations—probably underlay the proclamation, generally attributed to Napoleon, which was issued on April 20, 1799, the first day of Passover, while the French army was still in the midst of its Palestine campaign:

Rightful Heirs of Palestine!

The great nation [i.e., France] which does not trade in men and countries as did those who sold your ancestors unto all peoples (Joel 4:6) hereby calls on you not indeed to conquer your patrimony, nay, only to take over that which has been conquered and, with that nation's warranty and support, to maintain it against all comers. . . . Hasten! Now is the moment which may not return for thousands of years, to claim the restoration of your rights among the population of the universe which has been shamefully withheld from you for thousands of years. . . .

This proclamation has been called by one prominent historian the symbol of "Europe's acknowledgment of Jewish rights in Palestine." Perhaps so. But the proclamation was stillborn. Although the document purports to issue from "General Headquarters, Jerusalem"—surely the appropriate place to sound the call for a messianic rising—the French army never reached Jerusalem. Napoleon must have been confident that once Acre fell, nothing could keep the French from taking the Holy City. But the British held Acre, and Napoleon's army, weakened by plague, retreated to Egypt. As for the proclamation itself, the text was suppressed by Bonaparte and not recovered until the late 1930s.

With the idea of a Jewish state now dropped from Napoleon's program, the French leader still faced the problem of how to define the status of an emancipated Jewry. It was for this purpose that the emperor convened the Sanhedrin, a Jewish assembly of seventy-one members, two thirds of them rabbis, the remainder laymen, that met in Paris during February March 1807. To the Sanhedrin he submitted twelve groups of questions, among them the following:

In the eyes of Jews, are Frenchmen con-

In this piece of Napoleonic propaganda, the emperor extends a magnanimous hand to the Jewish people, portrayed as a submissive Jewess, as rabbis give their obsequious thanks. He holds a copy of the new statutes governing French Jewry, while her arm rests on the Ten Commandments.

The mechanization of textile making was a main thrust of the first phase of the industrial revolution, lasting roughly from the late eighteenth century through the middle of the nineteenth.

sidered as their brethren? Or are they considered as strangers?

Do Jews born in France, and treated by the laws as French citizens, consider France their country? Are they bound to defend it? Are they bound to obey the laws and to conform to the dispositions of the civil code?

We err if we regard this Parisian Sanhedrin as a deliberative body on a par with the Great Sanhedrin of Roman times. In reality, the French Sanhedrin was a rabbinic rubber-stamp to decisions taken by the Assembly of Jewish Notables, a convocation of more than 100 Jewish leaders that met continuously from July 26, 1806, to April 6, 1807. It would be an exaggeration to say that the fruits of the assembly's deliberations were foreordained, but surely the delegates understood what kinds of answers the emperor wanted and would give them to him.

As to the question of whether Jews considered France their country and felt bound to defend it, the assembly was both effusive and unequivocal:

The love of country is in the heart of Jews a sentiment so natural, so powerful, and so consonant to their religious opinions, that a French Jew considers himself in England, as among strangers, although he may be among Jews; and the case is the same with English Jews in France.

To such a pitch is this sentiment carried among them, that during the last war, French Jews have been seen fighting desperately against other Jews, the subjects of countries then at war with France.

The events of the next few years gave French Jewry a lesson in the pitfalls of putting their faith in princes. On March 17, 1808, Napoleon signed an edict that became known as the "Infamous Decree," imposing discriminatory restrictions on Jewish money-lending and on the movement of Jews within France. These restrictive laws were to remain in effect for a period of ten years—by which time, as it happened, the Emperor had met disaster in Russia and defeat at Leipzig and Waterloo. In France the Jews would remain full citizens, but in Rome, Venice, Mainz, and Frankfurt the ghettoes, abolished by Napoleon, were being restored.

EMANCIPATION AND ASSIMILATION

It is the year 1815. At the Congress of Vienna, convened to fashion the new international order, there is a Jewish delegation. The great Austro-Hungarian statesman and diplomat Metternich enjoys the company of Jews. He welcomes them, especially his friend the Baron Salomon Rothschild. At this time Europe finds it increasingly difficult to reconcile its own vision of expanding freedom with the traditionally grotesque, rigorous, suspicious, defensive attitude to what were, after all, a few small, innocuous Jewish communities. What happens to the Jews now might be described as the second exodus: not from the Sinai wilderness into the Promised Land, but from the stunted, squalid world of the ghetto into a different world whose dominant themes are emancipation, liberalism, creativity, and aesthetic refinement. This transition was a problem for Jews everywhere, but especially so in Germany, where anti-Jewish attitudes were still widespread, even at the highest intellectual levels.

Germany in 1820 was home to an estimated 223,000 Jews, scarcely one percent of the total population. These Jews had, by and large, been loyal Germans during the Napoleonic Wars, and German Jews had died fighting French Jews in the climactic battles of Leipzig and Waterloo. Prussian Jewry received its emancipation on March 11, 1812, but although this edict removed many economic disabilities, it did not allow professing Jews the right to hold government office or to take an advanced degree. Thus the Jews were barred from taking professional advan-

The founder of political Zionism, Theodor Herzl (1860–1904), is shown with his mother, Jeanette, in this photograph taken in Vienna in 1902.

tage of the new learning they had begun to master in conformity with the example of Moses Mendelssohn.

An especially poignant illustration of this dilemma is the career of the poet and essayist Heinrich Heine (1797–1856). Heine was a lifelong outsider. Born in Düsseldorf, he was educated first in a Jewish school, then in a Catholic *lycée*, and grew up in a region of Germany which the French had conquered and where Napoleon was regarded with admiration. Neither his Jewishness nor his Francophilia made Heine's entry into German society any easier. Nor did his political liberalism in an era of reaction, or his internationalism in an age of nationalist agitation:

And what is the great task of our day? It is emancipation. Not simply the emancipation of the Irish, the Greeks, Frankfurt Jews, West Indian blacks, and all such oppressed peoples, but the emancipation of the whole world, and especially of Europe, which has now come of age, and is tearing itself loose from the apron-strings of the privileged classes.

Heine converted to Lutheranism in 1825. He made no attempt to justify his baptism as a matter of principle. He knew, and the world knew, that he had embraced Christianity only so that he could receive his doctorate and pursue a career as an academic or civil servant. His baptismal certificate, he explained, was his ticket of admission to European culture.

After his baptism, Heine wrote to his friend Moses Moser (1796–1838), "If I could have made a living by stealing silver spoons without going to prison, I would have never been christened." But the fact is that, even

In 1848 the fiery whirlwind of revolutionary liberalism swept across Europe, inflaming not only Paris, as shown here, but also the great capitals of Germany, Italy, and Austria-Hungary.

after his conversion, Heine was still blocked from any university or government appointment. Toward the end of his life, still searching for his true identity, he told another friend, "I make no secret of my Judaism, to which I have not returned, because I never left it."

Other Jews, denied full citizenship, tended to blame not the state that cheated them of their rights but themselves or their religion. Thus was born during the German Enlightenment the phenomenon of the "self-hating Jew," the Jew who has so internalized the beliefs of Christian society (including its anti-Semitic undertones) as to find himself at war with his own ancestral heritage. For an extreme case of this, we may look to the father of communism, Karl Marx. Marx's formal ties to Judaism were tenuous: his father, a lawyer, had converted to Christianity to advance his career in 1817, the year before Karl was born, and had all eight of his children baptized in 1824. Nevertheless, there is reason to believe that Marx's psychic bonds to

Judaism ran very deep. His grandfather and his great uncle on his father's side were rabbis, as was his mother's father. Marx, who after leaving Germany spent his last thirty years in London, lived for six of those years at the house of a Jewish lace dealer. Moreover, his daughter Eleanor regarded herself as Jewish even after her father had made his loathing of Judaism abundantly clear to the world. What Marx did in his writings was to dwell upon the stereotype of the money-grubbing Jew, associating Judaism (*Judentum* in German, a word that had the secondary meaning "commerce") with all the bourgeois traits he most despised:

What is the worldly basis of Judaism? Practical necessity, selfishness. What is the worldly culture of the Jew? Commerce. What is his worldly God? Money.

We recognize therefore in Judaism a generally present anti-social element which has been raised to its present peak by historical development, in which the Jews eagerly assisted. . . . *In its final meaning the emancipation of the Jews is the emancipation of humanity from Judaism.*

Let us, however, give the last word on this subject not to the choleric Marx but to another German Jewish socialist, Moses Hess (1812–1875). Hess's early Jewish education was provided by his Orthodox grandfather, but by his early twenties he had become convinced that the Jewish mission in history was over. Not until the late 1850s, when he came to appreciate the power and progressive character of Italian nationalism, did he begin to formulate an understanding of what Jewish nationalism could accomplish:

A thought, which I believed to be forever buried in my heart, has been revived in me anew. It is the thought of my nationality, which is inseparably connected with my ancestral heritage and the memories of the Holy Land, the Eternal City, the birthplace of the belief in the divine unity of life, as well as the hope in the future brotherhood of men.

Ferdinand I of Austria-Hungary, depicted on this Jewish wall plaque, was an inept ruler who surrendered his power to Metternich long before the 1848 uprising drove him to abdicate.

Decades later, Hess's return to Judaism, and his early Zionist stirrings, would strike a responsive chord in the father of political Zionism, Theodor Herzl. "What an exalted noble spirit!" wrote Herzl in his diary in 1901 after reading Hess's *Rome and Jerusalem* (1862). "Everything that we have tried is already in his book."

UNDER THE CZARS

By the middle of the nineteenth century there are 4,750,000 Jews alive in the world, 72 percent of them in Eastern Europe, 14 percent in Western Europe, 1.5 percent in America. So Jewish history is now a part of European history.

In that European history, 1848 stands out as a landmark. The winds of revolutionary liberalism swept from France across Germany, Austria, and Italy. Now the Jews had a choice. They need not necessarily live the warm, intimate, but strangled life of the ghetto and shtetl; they could climb to individual glory in an expanding age. A Jew could leave his Jewishness behind and, like

Benjamin Disraeli, become prime minister of England. Jews by the hundreds of thousands could now flock into what had previously been the closed, reserved domains of parliaments and universities. A new heaven and a new earth!

This, at least, was the pattern in Western Europe. If the price of emancipation was assimilation—abandonment of formal ties to Judaism, or, more commonly, acting like a Jew in one's own home but like a modern secular European everywhere else—this was a price that many Jews were willing to pay.

In Eastern Europe, under the domination of the Russian czars, the situation was different. In these lands, still backward by Western European standards, liberalism and secularism were not well established and the legacy of anti-Semitism was more brutal. There were, in fact, persecutions and pogroms so full of blood and anguish, of misery and humiliation, that hundreds of thousands of Jews uprooted themselves and left, most of them for the expanding horizons of the new American world, and some for pioneering villages in the Land of Israel.

Nor was it only a question of being unable, through exclusion, to join the new enlightenment. Many Jews of czarist Russia and other Jews of Eastern Europe did not want to join it. In their squalid shtetls and ghettoes they were impoverished, drab, without external dignity. But they knew who they were and who they were not. Their lives might be poor and full of humiliations, but in their own memory and consciousness, they were the descendants of kings and prophets, and they enriched their lives with the images and symbols of an ancient faith. For them and for many Jews elsewhere, the desire to be like others took collective and not individual form. Not to be like others as men within society, but to be like others as a nation, within the emerging concert of nation-states. This was their dream, to which the Western European Herzl would give definitive expression. He would send into the waves of history the revolutionary idea of a Jewish state, secure in its land and legacy, leaving Europe behind. This dream had a special appeal to the Jews of Russia.

To understand the situation of the Jews of Russia, we must first understand the broader pattern of Russian history. From the kernel of Muscovy, which freed itself from Mongol domination in 1480, the land of the czars expanded eastward across the Urals and into Siberia, southeastward along the Volga, northward across the Novgorod Territory, northwestward into the Baltic region, and westward into Lithuania and Poland—all within the span of three centuries. Territorial aggrandizement was the policy of the czars from the moment that Ivan III Vasilievich, the Grand Duke of Moscow (r. 1462-1505), began calling himself "Sovereign of All Russia." The Soviet Union has merely inherited the consequences of the expansion.

What began as a landlocked principality, wholly isolated from the main currents of European civilization, is now a world superpower and a great trading nation, with ports on seven seas—the Baltic, Barents, White, Bering, Caspian, and Black seas, and the Sea of Japan. The lands controlled by the principality of Moscow probably comprised no more than 7 million people in 1500 and 10 million a century later. By 1800, 30 million people were living within the Russian Empire; by 1850, 70 million; by 1982, in the Soviet Union (excluding satellite nations), more than 268 million. Territorially, the gains have been even more astonishing: today, Moscow is the capital of a country that encompasses more than 8.6 million square miles (22.4 million sq km) and covers approximately one-sixth of the world's inhabited land area. Virtually all this territory constitutes the legacy of the czars to their Soviet successors.

But the Soviets have received a second legacy from the czars—that of anti-Semitism. From the earliest phase of recorded Russian

history, Jews were not tolerated within the principality of Moscow. In 1504, near the close of the reign of Ivan III, members of a sect accused of Judaizing in Novgorod and Moscow were burned at the stake. When, in 1550, the Polish King Sigmund II Augustus (r. 1548–1572) urged Ivan IV Vasilievich (1530–1584) to allow several Jewish merchants to enter Moscow, the czar—aptly known to history as "Ivan the Terrible"—bitterly rejected the proposal. Typical of czarist attitudes was that of the Czarina Elizabeth Petrovna (r. 1741–1762), who in 1742 sought to expel all Jews from her domain. Informed of the economic hardships Russian merchants would suffer if the Jews were forced out, she answered, "I do not want any benefit from the enemies of Christ."

It was during the reign of Catherine that Russia's "Jewish problem" became agoniz-

Although Jews and other Russians might sometimes mingle in the open marketplace, they lived mainly apart. As Chaim Weizmann later recalled, the peasants and the Jews "were strangers to each other's ways of thought, to each other's dreams, religions, festivals, even languages. . . ."

ingly acute. More than a million Jews were living in Poland in 1772 when Russia, having already reduced the Polish kingdom to the status of a client state, began to annex huge chunks of Polish territory. Russia was not the sole beneficiary of the three "partitions" of Poland, in 1772, 1793, and 1795; Prussia and Austria also gained from the demise of Poland.

The overwhelming bulk of Polish Jewry, close to a million Jews, came under the rule of the czars. Although they were a minority of the Polish population, these Jews were far from an inconspicuous minority. There were Jewish craftsmen, tradesmen, tax collectors, and professionals. Jews made up a majority of the population in certain cities, sometimes to the extent of 70 percent or more. For the most part they lived as middlemen, caught between the landed aristocrats and the seething peasantry.

From the first, the Russian rulers discriminated blatantly between their new Jewish and non-Jewish citizens. In 1772, the year of the first partition, Catherine issued a decree permitting all non-Jews in the new territories to exercise their former rights within the entire Russian Empire; the Jews, on the other hand, could retain their rights only as long as they continued to live in their communities of residence before partition. A 1791 decree, also during the reign of Catherine, confirmed this policy, although it also allowed the Jews to settle in two provinces east of the Dnieper River and in certain sparsely populated territories captured from Turkey.

This policy of confinement within the larger ghetto of Russian Poland and a few satellite regions took a more definite shape during the reign of Czar Alexander I (Aleksandr Petrovich, r. 1801–1825). His Statutes Concerning the Organization of the Jews, promulgated in December 1804, begin from the premise that the Jews, long isolated and ignorant, are a parasitic element in a society that, at least since Peter the Great, has prided itself on its progressivism. Those who drew up the charter saw the solution of the Jewish problem in that favorite Enlightenment panacea—education.

The czar laid out before the Jews of Russia a path not very different from the one Mendelssohn had envisioned for German Jewry:

Adopt the mores and constitution of the country in which you find yourself, but be steadfast in upholding the religion of your fathers, too.

Of course, this strategy for survival is as old as Jeremiah:

Seek the peace of the city whither I have caused you to be carried away captives, and pray unto the Lord for it; for in the peace thereof shall ye have peace.

(Jeremiah 29:7)

Or as a leader of the *maskilim*—the "enlightened ones" of nineteenth-century Russia—put it, with unconscious irony: "Be a Jew in your tent and a man abroad." The kernel of Jewish identity would not be lost, but like the rough stone of a smooth-skinned fruit, it would be well hidden from public view.

As for Mendelssohn and, later, the writers of the Russian Haskalah, the key to emancipation, as expressed in the Statutes of 1804, was language. Yiddish, with its roots in medieval Germany, would have to be abandoned if the Jews were to enter the modern age. The Russian, Polish and German languages were to be the passports to emancipation. Force was not necessary to solve the Jewish problem: so went the verdict of the Committee for the Amelioration of the Jews, whose deliberations led to the 1804 Statutes. Instead, the committee proposed "to lead the Jews to self-improvement by opening to them the roads that will lead them to happiness." In practice, this meant more subtle forms of coercion. From 1807—the year in which Napoleon posed his questions to a Sanhedrin of French Jewry—no Jewish public document would be valid within the Russian Empire unless written in one of the three accepted languages. Nor, from 1808 and thereafter, could any Jew unlettered in Russian, Polish, or German hold a position on a municipal council. From 1812, no Jew who did not know Russian, Polish, or German could be appointed to a communal position or even to the rabbinate.

If in the Germany of Heine's time baptism was the ticket of admission to European culture, in Russia that ticket was, more often than not, the Russian language. This question of language, which also involved the question of whether children should attend modern, Russian-language schools or antiquated *shuls* where most instruction was in Yiddish, became a litmus test of Jewish identity. By and large, "enlightened" Jews accepted and even encouraged the czarist program for the abandonment of Yiddish. Typical of such opinion was a manifesto by O. Rabinowich, founder in 1860 of the first Russian Jewish weekly, *Razsvet (Dawn)*:

We in Russia . . . instead of learning the glorious Russian language, persist in speaking our corrupted jargon (i.e., Yiddish), that grates on the ears and distorts. . . . It is our obligation to cast off these old rags, a heritage of the dark Middle Ages. . . . We believe the time has come for the Russian language to become the Jew's guide on the road to enlightenment and to the widening of their spiritual and material sphere of activity. . . .

For decades this controversy raged. The outcome was startling. A government census in 1897 revealed that of all Jews living within the Pale of Settlement, 96.7 percent still spoke Yiddish as their mother tongue and less than 1.3 percent spoke Russian as their first language. The fact is that no Jewish writer in Russian came close to equaling the achievements of the great Russian authors. In Hebrew (which celebrated a renewed vitality in part as a reaction against Yiddish by those who did not want to embrace Russian), the record of accomplishment was brilliant: we can point to the great poet, essayist, and translator Hayyim Nahman Bialik (1873–1934), born in Volhynia, now part of the Ukrainian S.S.R.; and to the father of modern Hebrew, Eliezer ben-Yehuda (1858–1922), a writer and lexicographer of Lithuanian birth. No less impressive, however, are the attainments of those writers who explored and enriched their mother tongue, Yiddish. Among these was Mendele Mocher Seforim ("Mendele the Bookseller"), born in Byelorussia as Shalom Jacob Abramowitz (1836–1917) and a

Empress Catherine the Great (r. 1762–1796), as portrayed in 1793 by Jean Baptiste Lampi. It was during Catherine's reign that, by sharing in the dismemberment of Poland, Russia became overlord of the world's largest Jewish community.

master of both Yiddish and Hebrew; the popular short-story writer and humorist Shalom Aleichem, born as Salomon Rabinovich (1859–1916) near Kiev and creator of the Tevye tales, which later authors adapted for *Fiddler on the Roof*; and Isaac Bashevis Singer (b. 1904), writer of novels and short stories, who was born in Poland and went to the United States in 1935.

In our own time, of course, the battle for Yiddish seems virtually over. The Holocaust and the hostility of the Soviet leaders have dealt crippling blows to Yiddish language and culture. Hebrew, not Yiddish, is the language of the State of Israel; English, not Yiddish, is almost universal among the world's largest Jewish community, that of the United

Writer and lexicographer Eliezer ben-Yehuda (1858–1922), the father of modern Hebrew.

States (although Yiddish has enriched English with such words as *schmaltz, schlock, schlep, nosh,* and *chutzpah*). In the U.S.S.R., according to official Soviet statistics, more than 80 percent of all Jews now speak Russian as their primary language. Despite these indications that Yiddish is in decline, let us give the last loving and hopeful word to Bashevis Singer, winner of the Nobel Prize for Literature in 1978:

The high honor bestowed upon me . . . is also a recognition of the Yiddish language—a language of exile, without a land, without frontiers, not supported by any government, a language which possesses no words for weapons, ammunition, military exercises, war tactics; a language that was despised by both gentiles and emancipated Jews.

The truth is that what the great religions preached, the Yiddish-speaking people of the ghettos practiced day in and day out.

They were the people of the book in the truest sense of the word. . . .

There are some who call Yiddish a dead language, but . . . Yiddish has not said its last word. It contains treasures that have not been revealed to the eyes of the world. It was the tongue of martyrs and saints, of dreamers and cabalists—rich in humor and memories that mankind may never forget. In a figurative way, Yiddish is the wise and humble language of us all, the idiom of the frightened and hopeful humanity.

Whatever attractions the carrot of emancipation may have held for the Jews of Russia, the stick of compulsion posed much harder and more painful choices. When Alexander I died in 1825, his younger brother Nicolai Pavlovich (1796–1855) ascended the throne as Nicholas I. As Emperor of Russia, Nicholas showed great aptitude for aggression and repression, the former against the Persians and Turks, the latter against the Poles, the Hungarians, the Jews, and the Russian people. In his edict of April 1835, Nicholas, a man of genuine anti-Jewish feeling, plainly delineated the areas of Jewish settlement and spelled out the penalty for venturing "beyond the pale": loss of Russian citizenship and permanent exile. As in the 1804 Statutes, Jews were divided into classes, or estates, and threatened with prosecution for vagrancy—no minor matter—if they failed to identify themselves accordingly.

Worse than these regulations, which did little more than codify existing practice and make it more rigid, was an 1827 law requiring the general conscription of Jewish adult males, who were obligated to fulfill twenty-five years of military service. Not, of course, that every man served. There were exemptions, the conditions of which, like the conditions of military service, were intended to disrupt the fabric of Jewish society. For each recruitment, for example, a sum of money could be substituted; in other words, a rich man was able to buy his sons' way out, while the poor were snatched up by the draft.

And there were other inequities. Jewish youths who enrolled in general (i.e., non-Jewish) schools were exempt from service. Also exempt were Jews who served Gentiles as apprentices. Because the entire Jewish community was responsible for the fulfillment of draft quotas and would suffer a penalty if the quotas were not met, it fell to the leaders, who were often rabbis, to decide who could stay and who had to go to the army. In the most notorious cases, kidnappers—the Yiddish word is *khapers*—were hired to do the unpleasant work, sometimes seizing boys as young as eight or nine.

The most heartrending cases were those of the "cantonists"—Jewish children drafted legally between the ages of twelve and eighteen and sent to barracks (cantonments) far from their families and then brutalized and neglected. If they survived—and many of the 40,000 cantonists did not—they could look forward to a full twenty-five years of service in the regular army, since the years served before age eighteen did not count against their obligation.

The ordeal of the cantonists and some other Jewish hardships ended in 1856 with the abolition of the special system of Jewish conscription by Nicholas's successor, Emperor Alexander II (1818–1881). Alexander's twenty-six-year reign, which began in 1855, led Russia at least part of the way from feudal obligation and imperial fiat to a system of rights, laws, and popular representation. So Russia too was on the verge of modern statehood. Alexander freed the serfs in 1861, and by that act not only allocated to the peasantry half the lands in Russia but also made the peasants subjects of the state rather than subjects of their masters. This new class of citizens needed legal protection, which the former lords could no longer provide; thus Alexander took steps to establish a local court system, with open jury trials and professionally trained judges. A system of provincial

The reign of Emperor Alexander II, beginning in 1855, led Russia at least part of the way from feudal obligation and imperial fiat to a system of rights and popular representation. Here, Alexander in the cap and cloak of the Horse Guards.

and district councils, or *zemstvos*, was introduced by imperial edict in 1864. Concomitantly, restrictions on foreign travel and on the universities were eased, and press censorship was relaxed.

Ideas flourished—sometimes, as Alexander found to his dismay, ideas hostile to his rule. The arts also flourished. This is the period when Russia's great creative geniuses of the nineteenth century reached their pinnacles of achievement. Fyodor Dostoyevsky (1821–1881), imprisoned and nearly executed for socialist activities during the reign of Nicholas I, published his masterful psychological novel *Crime and Punishment* in 1866, *The Possessed* (a portrait of Russian revolutionists) in 1871, and *The Brothers Karamazov* in 1880. Count Leo Tolstoy (1828–1910) completed his greatest novels, *War and Peace* and *Anna Karenina*, in 1869 and 1877, respectively. Another masterpiece of this period, anticipating *The Possessed* in its concern with nihilism and other socially disruptive currents, is *Fathers and Sons,* published in 1862 by Ivan Turgenev (1818–1883). In music, also, there was a great creative outburst. The mature works of Petr Ilich Tchaikovsky (1840–1893) and Aleksandr Borodin (1833–1897), as well as that quintessentially Russian opera *Boris Godunov* by Modest Moussorgsky (1839–1881)—these too belong to the remarkable reign of Alexander II.

Jews saw no reason to stay outside the excitement of the times. Judah Leib Gordon (1831–1892), the leading poet of Haskalah, urged his brethren to plunge wholeheartedly into these new and exhilarating movements:

Awake, my people! How long will you slumber?
The night has passed, the sun shines bright. . . .
This land of Eden now opens its gates to you,
Her sons now call you "brother"?
How long will you dwell amongst them as a guest,
And why do you now affront them?

Good poets do not always make true prophets, and history has been particularly unkind to the *maskilim.* Gordon wrote his optimistic poem "Awake My People!" in 1863, when Russia was still in its first flush of freedom. How could he have foreseen the cruel laws, pogroms, and institutionalized anti-Semitism that awaited the Jews during their next 120 years of rule by czars and Soviets? In any event, Gordon's illusions of the early 1860s soon shriveled away. By the 1870s he had seen firsthand the excesses of assimilationism among the young, the ineptitude and isolation of the Russian liberals, and the increasingly heavy hand of the secret police.

FROM THE BIRTH OF ZIONISM TO THE BALFOUR DECLARATION

The cataclysm that fell upon Russian Jewry in the 1880s and 1890s has often been identified as the period of Zionism's birth. In fact, the roots of the Jewish national idea lie much deeper in the soil of history. Jewish religious life was illuminated by the memories of an ancient glory when Hebrew kings reigned and prophets preached and Jewish priests walked and prayed in Solomon's temple. The images of an age of freedom, past but not forgotten, had never been obliterated from the Jewish mind. The greater the gloom and adversity of Jewish life, the more intense became the recollection of an ancestral pride. The daily prayers perpetuated those memories in majestic language. Jews never ceased to brood on their early literature, not only in a spirit of religious ecstasy but also in search of distinctive national roots. The hope of renewal was an organic part of the memory: "I will bring your seed from the east and gather you from the west. I will say to the north 'give up' and to the south 'keep not back.' Bring my sons from far and my daughters from the ends of the earth."

The effect of these myriad repetitions day by day over the centuries was to infuse Jewish life with a peculiar nostalgia, strong enough to prevent any sentiment of finality or permanence in any other land. But it was not only a matter of prayer and hope. The physical link was never broken. A thin but crucial line of continuity had been maintained by small Jewish communities and academies in Jerusalem, Safed, Jaffa, and Hebron. Palestine never became the birthplace of any other nation. Every one of its conquerors had his original home elsewhere. Thus the idea of Palestine as the Jewish land had never been obscured or superseded. The notion that they were a special people charged with a distinctive destiny was one of the motives that drove Jews to develop a talent for corporate existence in whatever environment and jurisdiction they found themselves. Another motive was, of course, the reluctance of Gentile societies to enfranchise them. Thus Jews were driven inward

advis
(1877
admi
Chur
not i
meml
that h
Jewes
1882).
but sl
revolt
death
of he
Peters
allege
Semit
perial

onto themselves both by their own will and by the absence of a viable alternative. This concept of nationhood converged in the nineteenth century with the movements of national emancipation in Europe. A continent in which Italians, Poles, Irish, Serbs, Greeks, and others were raising their flags in revolt against long-established servitudes was one in which the idea of renewing Jewish national independence did not seem eccentric or incongruous.

But the Jews had for so long cherished the idea of renewed independence as a dream that there was a prospect of perpetual sublimation. The habit of praying for the restoration of Zion had lived together with the habit of not doing anything to fulfill the prayer. Within a single generation the prayer had become a concrete political prospect thanks to a movement led first by Theodor Herzl and shortly afterward by Chaim Weizmann. Herzl (1860–1904), the founder of political

Scenes during the Russo-Turkish War, 1877–1878. At number 1, Emperor Alexander II reviews his Jewish troops. 2. An execution by firing squad. 3. A temporary synagogue for the Day of Atonement. At number 4, a bridge over the Danube.

Zionism, was born in what is now Budapest, took a law degree at the University of Vienna, and held an assignment as a newspaper correspondent in Paris at the key stage of his career. The preeminent leader of practical political Zionism and, later, the first president of the State of Israel, Chaim Weizmann (1874–1952), though born in a Russian shtetl, pursued his university studies in Germany and Switzerland and was established as a chemist in Manchester before he came to the forefront of the Zionist movement.

Herzl and Weizmann did not work in a vacuum. Jewish settlement in the Land of Israel preceded the development of political Zionism and then ran parallel with it. It re

Wherever they colonized, Europeans brought with them not only their technology but also their culture, customs, and outlook.

ship of Jews with their environment was not always free from tensions and uncertainties, but over the years and decades it would develop an intimacy and a sense of rootedness that Jews had never known in any other diaspora community.

In 1880 there were only 230,000 Jews in the United States. Fifty years later their numbers were between 4.5 million and 5 million. Clearly the impulse that creates such a vast migration must be very strong. The Jews of Eastern Europe were being both pushed and pulled. They were being repelled from Europe by the dark, bleak hostility that often erupted into the violent bloodshed of the pogroms. And they were also being pulled, attracted to America by the force of a utopian vision. In the shtetls and ghettoes of Eastern Europe there was no chance at all that today's misery would ever be transcended by tomorrow's hope. But westward, look, the land was bright! In America there would be freedom, opportunity, perhaps even some

degree of prosperity, and, above all else, dignity.

And so the great trek began. Countless ships unloaded their bearded passengers, with their dark-clad women and their numerous pale children, in New York harbor, from which they would go forth, to build new shtetls on the Lower East Side of New York and in similar areas of Chicago, Philadelphia, Boston, Pittsburgh, and the cities of the American Midwest. It was not just the transfer of a mass of individuals from one continent to another. It was the weaving of a whole new thread into the tapestry of American civilization, a new color and a new taste.

Above everything else there was an air of romance and chivalry: America, the redeemer of humanity from servitude!—"your huddled masses yearning to breathe free." The Jews of Eastern Europe had a simple, uncomplicated, innocent vision of America. They had never heard of George Washington or Thomas Jefferson, of the Constitution or Bill of Rights. They were even somewhat alienated from the 230,000 original American Jews: those who had come to New Amsterdam from Recife in Brazil in the 1600s; those who during the revolutionary period had settled in Newport, in Charleston, in Savannah; the solid, established German Jews who had been there from the time of the Napoleonic Wars, the heads of great banking houses, people with grand names like Speyer, Loeb, Kuhn, Warburg, Schiff, Lehman.

The original American Jews were trying hard to be indistinguishable from their American environment. The Eastern European immigrants, on the other hand, had no choice but to defend their right to be different. Their speech was Yiddish; their faith was the traditional Orthodox Judaism of the Russian and Polish ghetto and shtetl. Everything about them—their synagogues, their schools, their delicatessens, their dress, their speech—was different. The original American Jews looked at them with a mixture of apprehension, embarrassment, but, after all, solidarity. In the last resort, they would be held responsible. They had a common fate.

It was not all Utopia for the newcomers. There was much poverty and hardship, and an unremitting burden of toil. There was also an undercurrent of resentment at the snobberies of established America. There were some rivalries with immigrant groups of Christian descent, from Italy, Ireland, Scandinavia, and Poland. The Congress of the United States continually considered, and sometimes even adopted, legislation restricting the entry of what were called "unskilled immigrants." Sometimes, in years of recession, unemployment, and approaching war, American Jews would be reminded by outbursts of opposition that anxiety is always at the root of the Jewish condition. But by and large, it was a triumphant saga, with a conclusion of credit for both sides: for the Jews, who poured their love and hope into America, and for America, which received them and co-opted their vitality as part of its own strength.

NAVIGATORS, TRADERS, PILGRIMS, AND PEDDLERS

The emergence of the United States as a world power, and of the Jews as central actors on the American scene, belongs to a larger story of European expansion in which the Jews played an important part. Today, the sun has set on the great colonial empires: scarcely more than a few territories in South America and the Caribbean remain under European control. The European empires in Africa have been entirely dismantled. The interaction of the Old World and the New is sometimes portrayed as a story of greedy Europeans denuding distant territories of minerals and manpower. There is more than a grain of truth in this picture. Many Europeans were looking for quick riches—gold,

A portrait of Admiral Christopher Columbus by Ridolfo Ghirlandajo (1483–1561) of Florence. Whether Columbus was a Marrano is one of the tantalizing questions of Jewish history.

silver, tin, furs, slaves, new trade routes, even guano. But there is also a deep sense in which, just as Alexander the Great founded dozens of Alexandrias to spread Hellenic civilization throughout the known world, the European conquerors and settlers were transplanting their own developed culture to each frontier outpost.

The European imprint in the New World is first of all evident in the names of the colonial regions: New Spain, New France, and—one of the many English names that survive—New England. From the American Indians the European settlers learned to grow corn, tobacco, and potatoes, but the cultivation methods and crops such as wheat, rice, sugar, yams, bananas, for which Europeans acted as agents of diffusion, proved of even more durable significance. It was this European-borne agricultural revolution, more than anything else, that permitted the Americas to increase in population from about 14 million in 1500—declining by 1600 to less than 12 million, under the immediate impact of European conquest and disease—to more than 650 million in 1984. The latter total exceeds the population of the entire world at the close of the seventeenth century.

Europeans brought the wheel, the horse, and cattle to the New World. But just as important as these technological developments were two essential features of the European cultural heritage—language and religion. There are today more people who speak English in North America than there are in England, more who speak Portuguese in Brazil than in Portugal, and more who speak Spanish in Latin America than in Spain. Nor can we overlook the millions who speak French in Quebec, Haiti, and other former and present French possessions. With this linguistic patrimony came a powerful literary and religious heritage. And this brings us to perhaps the most pervasive of all European exports, Christianity.

The Christianization of the New World was not haphazard. Jesuit missionaries were among the earliest explorers of French North America, and in the Spanish colonial empire, Roman Catholic missionaries followed hard on the heels of the conquistadores, and often helped to safeguard the remaining Indians from exploitation by the Spanish secular authorities. Before 1500, Christianity had been almost entirely a phenomenon of Europe and the Near East, its spread limited by difficult transportation and the power of the Ottoman Turks, who presided over an Islamic empire. Today, the population of the New World is overwhelmingly Christian and, in Latin America, predominantly Roman Catholic.

The Jews, who in the Muslim lands had figured prominently in the development of astronomy—the key to the science of navigation—played no small role in the initial penetration of the New World. Maps exe-

cuted by Jews and Marranos were employed by Portuguese, Spanish, and Italian mariners during the early period of exploration. The first treatise in Arabic on the astrolabe—a device used for calculating the position of heavenly bodies, and thus the position of a ship relative to the stars in the sky—was written by a Jew known as Mashallah of Basra around the year 800. And when the Portuguese explorer Vasco da Gama set sail from Lisbon for India via the Cape of Good Hope in 1497, his ships were outfitted with astrolabes newly perfected by the Jewish astronomer Abraham ben Samuel Zacuto.

Whether Christopher Columbus was of Marrano origin is still hotly debated by historians, but we have the Admiral's testimony to the effect that at least one man of Jewish birth accompanied him on his epochal voyage to America. That man was a *converso*, Luis de Torres, who because of his talent for languages—though not, regrettably, for Amerindian dialects—was among the first ashore when the Admiral landed at Cuba on November 2, 1492:

The Admiral [i.e., Columbus] decided upon sending two Spaniards, one named Rodrigo de Jerez, who lived in Ayamonte, and the other Luis de Torres, who had served in the household of the Adelantado of Murcia, and had been a Jew, knowing Hebrew, Chaldee, and even some Arabic. With these men he sent two Indians. . . . He gave them strings of beads with which to buy food if they should be in need, and ordered them to return in six days. . . . Their instructions were to ask for the king of that land . . . to inquire after his health and establish friendship. . . .

The drama and charm of this scene are abated only slightly by the fact that no one in the party, least of all the learned Torres, could converse with the Arawaks they encountered, nor did the landing party find any valuable spices or gold. Torres and his companions were nonetheless treated hospita-

bly, for the Arawaks believed, in the words of Columbus's diary, that the Europeans "came from heaven." Jerez and Torres "met with many people on the road going home, men and women with a half-burnt weed in their hands, being the herbs they are accustomed to smoke." Torres could thus be claimed not only as the first man of Jewish birth to set foot in the New World but also as one of the two European codiscoverers of tobacco, the "half-burnt weed" to which the Arawaks were so addicted. Knowing a good opportunity when he saw it, Torres settled on the island, became a land baron and slave owner, and lived out his life on a royal pension from Spain's Catholic sovereigns.

No professing Jew sailed with Columbus under the Spanish flag in 1492 or with Vasco da Gama under the Portuguese flag in 1497 for one simple reason: During this decade the practice of Judaism was banned by both nations. No professing Jew could settle in any of the lands claimed by Spain or Portugal—a prohibition that, if defied by Jews or "Judaizing" Christians, the Inquisition stood ready to enforce. Eventually there would be sizable

When the first Jews to settle permanently on the North American mainland landed at New Amsterdam in 1654, the small Dutch trading outpost must have looked very much like this.

Jewish communities on the South American continent—in 1980, Argentina had an estimated 242,000 Jews, Brazil 110,000, and Uruguay 40,000—but these settlements had not developed until well into the nineteenth century, when those nations had freed themselves from Spanish colonial rule and the Inquisition had ceased its work. Nor could Jews settle freely in New France, for Jews had been barred from the mother country for several centuries. England, too, was officially closed to Jewish settlement during the first two decades of the seventeenth century, when the Jamestown and Plymouth colonies were established.

The fact is that during the early 1600s there was only one great seafaring nation under whose flag Jews could travel and trade freely, the Netherlands. It was under Dutch auspices, in the time of Spinoza and Manasseh ben Israel, that Jews would settle, in small numbers, in the West Indies (especially Curaçao), South Africa (at Cape Town), India, Ceylon (now Sri Lanka), Mauritius, Borneo (now part of Indonesia), and Formosa (Taiwan).

Of all the Dutch Jewish settlements, ultimately the most important were those of Brazil—not because of their success but because of their failure. In 1630 the Dutch occupied several harbors in northeastern Brazil and pledged themselves to respect the liberty of persons of all nationalities and religions. To these Dutch colonies came not only Jewish traders and settlers from Amsterdam, via the West India Company, but also Portuguese *conversos* who wished to practice Judaism openly, without fear of persecution. By the end of the 1630s, Jews in Brazil were actively involved in the export-import business, in slave trading and slave owning, and in sugar cultivation. By 1645, there were about 1,500 Jews in Dutch Brazil—perhaps half its European population—when the Portuguese effort to recapture the colony intensified. Within five years, because of war deaths and emigration, the Jewish population had dwindled to 650. In 1654, with the collapse of Dutch resistance and the triumph of Portugal, an expulsion decree was issued: All Jews would have to leave Brazil by April. Many of the Dutch Jews returned to Amsterdam, but a significant number settled in the other small Dutch colonies of the Americas. Among these was a North American port town that was destined to remain a Dutch possession only ten years longer—the city of New Amsterdam, soon to become New York.

The twenty-three Sephardim who landed at New York harbor in early September 1654 were not the first Jews on the North American mainland, but they did establish the first permanent Jewish community there. Just how permanent this community would be was in doubt from the very beginning. Since 1647 the director-general of the New Amsterdam colony had been Peter Stuyvesant (c.

1610–1672). Autocratic and intolerant, Stuyvesant was so disliked by the New Netherland colonists that, when a British fleet arrived in 1664, they chose to surrender to English rule rather than rally round the director-general and the West India Company that he represented. Stuyvesant, who had lost his leg in a battle with the Portuguese papists in the Caribbean, had brooked no dissenters in his colony, and he was certainly not about to extend any welcome to the Jews, who had arrived short of funds, unable even to pay the captain of the *Saint Catherine* for their passage. On September 22, 1654, Stuyvesant wrote to his superiors in Amsterdam, asking them to allow him to expel the Jews:

. . . The Jews who have arrived would nearly all like to remain here, but learning that they (with their customary usury and deceitful trading with the Christians) were very repugnant to the inferior magistrates . . . [and] also fearing that owing to their present indigence they might become a charge in the coming winter, we have, for the benefit of this weak and newly developing place and the land in general, deemed it useful to require them in a friendly way to depart; praying also most seriously in this connection, for ourselves as also for the general community of your worships, that the deceitful race,—such hateful enemies and blasphemers of the name of Christ,—be not allowed further to infect and trouble this new colony. . . .

The grudging reply to this vicious communication from Stuyvesant came in a letter dated April 26, 1655, after the Jews of Amsterdam had addressed their own petition to the company on behalf of their brethren in the New World:

We would have liked to effectuate and fulfill your wishes and request that the new territories should no more be allowed to be infected by people of the Jewish nation, for we foresee therefrom the same difficulties which you fear, but after having further weighed and considered the matter, we observe that this would be somewhat unreasonable and unfair, especially because of the considerable loss sustained by this nation, with others, in the taking of Brazil, as also because of the large amount of capital which they still have invested in the shares of this company. Therefore after many deliberations we have finally decided . . . that these people may travel and trade to and in New Netherland and live and remain there, provided the poor among them shall not become a burden to the company or the community, but be supported by their own nation. You will now govern yourself accordingly.

Stuyvesant did not give up without a fight. Would the Jews be allowed to trade freely throughout the colony? Would they be permitted to participate in the defense of the colony? Could they own land? Could they operate a wholesale or retail business? At each turn Stuyvesant said no; but on each of these points the Jews of New Netherland, led by the merchant and landowner Asser Levy

(d. 1681) and aided by the Jews of Amsterdam, fought and won. The Jews of the colony were doubly fortunate. Jewish rights were an accomplished fact by the time that King Charles II awarded "all the land from the west side of the Connecticutte River to the East Side of De La Ware Bay" to his brother, the Duke of York and future King James II (r. 1685–1688). The English agreed to abide by Dutch rights of property and inheritance and to preserve liberty of conscience, but these might have been empty promises as far as the Jews were concerned had it not been for the efforts during the 1650s of Manasseh ben Israel, who had persuaded Oliver Cromwell to readmit Jews into England.

A landmark in the history of American toleration (even if subsequent actions by white settlers rarely lived up to this ideal) was the meeting at Shackamaxon in which the Quaker William Penn, founder of Pennsylvania, exchanged vows of peace with the Leni-Lenape Indians.

By the late 1650s, the Marranos of London had received a pledge of protection for their religious services, a pledge that was reaffirmed by the Crown in 1664. From that point on, Jews were free to settle in England—or any of the English colonies—without fear of expulsion. As the British extended their control over North America, Jewish horizons in the New World likewise expanded. By 1763, not only had the French Empire in what would become the United States collapsed, but Canada also had been opened to Jewish settlement by the British military victory. We now know that Jews were living in Halifax, Nova Scotia, during the 1750s, but the first permanent Canadian Jewish settlement dates from the very end of the decade, in the vicinity of Montreal.

Montreal, of course, remains an important city of Jewish settlement, but if we survey the contemporary pattern of urban Jewish life in North America, some striking divergences appear. Of course, the name of New York remains preeminent: with a Jewish population of nearly 2 million in 1981, it has long been at the core of the American Jewish experience. Philadelphia, the nation's third-leading Jewish population center in our own time, had Jewish settlers well before the great English Quaker, William Penn, founded the colony of Pennsylvania in 1682; it also has had its share of illustrious Jewish families. On the other hand, the second-, fourth-, and fifth-leading centers of American urban Jewish life—Los Angeles, Chicago, and Miami—were quite slow to develop, both as havens for Jews and within the larger American context. In fact, as the eighteenth century began, Los Angeles and Miami were part of territories still ruled by Catholic Spain, and Illinois was inhabited only by Indians and a few trappers and traders of New France.

Apart from New York and Philadelphia, the major centers of Jewish life in the Thirteen Colonies were Savannah, Charleston, and Newport. Jews first arrived in the Geor-

The Touro Synagogue of Newport, Rhode Island, now a national historic site.

gia seaport in 1733, on a ship that had been chartered by London's Sephardi synagogue. Not surprisingly, records of the Georgia colony mention a Dr. Samuel Nunes, who helped to halt an epidemic; but there are also records of Jewish landowners, cultivators of wine grapes and silkworms. A congregation was organized in 1735. Both Sephardim and Ashkenazim were present by this time, and it took the better part of two years before they could reconcile their personal and religious differences—and a *mikveh*, or ritual bath, was opened in 1738. The first synagogue in Savannah was built in 1820; the present Gothic edifice was dedicated in 1878.

Charleston's splendid temple, in Greek Revival style, dates from 1840, but the city's Jewish community is much older. Jews began arriving in Charleston in the late seventeenth century, not long after the port city was founded; it soon became a haven not only for Jews but also for Huguenots fleeing persecution in France. To Charleston in December 1773 came a young English Jew named Francis Salvador (1747–1776), who, having lost most of his inheritance, bought 7,000 acres of land in South Carolina and became a plantation owner and slaveholder. As tensions with Britain mounted, and the Revolution came closer, Salvador readily allied himself with the patriots, and in 1774–1776 he served in the Revolutionary Provincial Congress of South Carolina. When South Carolina proclaimed its sovereignty in 1776, Salvador became the first Jew to hold state office—perhaps the first Jew in modern history to participate in a secular representative body. But it is not for this distinction alone that Salvador is commemorated in a plaque still displayed in Charleston's City Hall. Rather, it is because, while serving with patriot forces after the British forces attacked Charleston, Salvador was shot and scalped in an Indian ambush in August 1776, thus becoming the first known Jew to die in the cause of American independence.

The first Jews arrived in Newport from Barbados in 1677, nearly four decades after the Rhode Island colony had been founded by Roger Williams (1603?–1683) as a haven for religious dissenters. There is something quite fitting in this association, for Williams was a true champion of religious liberty and social justice. The two questions on which he broke with the Massachusetts Bay Colony, where he had accepted a pastorate in 1631, were whether the colonial government had the right to impose a uniform creed and worship on the colonists and whether the colonial authorities had the right to seize Indian lands without fair compensation.

In 1763, Newport's Congregation Yeshuat Israel moved into the small Georgian temple now known as the Touro Synagogue—the oldest synagogue in the United States, officially designated since 1946 as a national historic site. The Touro Synagogue is named for the philanthropist Judah Touro, a native of Newport, who left a generous bequest for the synagogue's upkeep. The structure is similar to the Sephardic synagogues of London and Amsterdam, but there is one striking architectural feature that has aroused much speculation. Beneath the reading desk is an opening to an unfinished underground pas-

Thomas Jefferson, a leading champion of religious liberty, wrote in 1820 that he was "happy in the restoration of the Jews to their social rights."

sageway that leads out toward the street. This may be no more than a storage space (like the Cairo *genizah*), but the prevailing local tradition holds that these Jews of the New World, still carrying with them the scars and memories of Marrano persecution, had begun to build a tunnel in case they ever needed to escape.

During the American Revolution, Newport was occupied by the British from 1776 to 1779, and the Jewish population—like the merchant class in general—was scattered.

After the British left Newport in 1780, however, the synagogue building was used as a meeting place by the General Assembly of the State of Rhode Island. The Assembly continued to hold its sessions there until 1784, as did the state Supreme Court. When General George Washington (1732–1799) visited the city in 1781, the town meeting was held there, too.

Nine years later, Washington—who by this time held the office of President of the United States, the Constitution having been drawn up in 1787 and ratified in 1788—paid another visit to the Newport congregation, prompting the exchange of good wishes upon which rests the congregation's most enduring fame. While in Newport, Washington received an address from Moses Seixas (1744–1809), then president of the Jewish community and an organizer of the Bank of Rhode Island. After complimenting Washington with the assertion that "the same Spirit who rested in the bosom of the greatly beloved Daniel, enabling him to preside over provinces of the Babylonish Empire, rests, and ever will rest, upon you," Seixas went on to say:

Deprived as we heretofore have been of the invaluable rights of free citizens, we now (with a deep sense of gratitude to the Almighty Dispenser of all Events) behold a Government erected by the majesty of the people, a Government which gives to bigotry no sanction, to persecution no assistance; but generously affording to all liberty of conscience and immunities of citizenship, deeming everyone, of whatever nation, tongue, or language, equal parts of the great Governmental machine.

Washington's reply, echoing and expanding upon Seixas's original phrasing, endures as an indelible statement of the most fundamental tenets of American democracy:

All possess alike liberty of conscience and immunities of citizenship. It is now no more

that toleration is spoken of, as if it was by the indulgence of one class of people, that another enjoyed the exercise of their inherent natural rights. For happily the government of the United States, which gives to bigotry no sanction, to persecution no assistance, requires only that they who live under its protection should demean themselves as good citizens, in giving it on all occasions their effectual support. . . .

May the children of the Stock of Abraham, who dwell in this land, continue to merit and enjoy the good will of the other inhabitants, while every one shall sit in safety under his own vine and fig-tree, and there shall be none to make him afraid.

The quotation from the Hebrew prophets (Micah 4:4) is not an isolated instance. The founders of the American republic were steeped in the ideas and cadences of the Hebrew Bible, and the very first English colonists, the Puritans, had modeled their society on the theocracy of Israel in Biblical times. Not surprisingly, the early Americans strongly identified with the Biblical theme of revolt against Pharaoh and of Exodus to the Promised Land. Benjamin Franklin (1706–1790) proposed that the seal of the United States show the Israelites crossing the Red Sea, with Pharaoh's chariots in vain pursuit. Thomas Jefferson (1743–1826) suggested that "Rebellion to tyrants is obedience to God" serve as the motto of the new nation. This was, in essence, the message of the prophets, Nathan's warning to David. It is also the message that pervades the Declaration of Independence:

We hold these truths to be self-evident, that all men are created equal, that they are endowed by their Creator with certain unalienable Rights, that among these are Life, Liberty and the pursuit of Happiness. That to secure these rights, Governments are instituted among Men, deriving their just powers from the consent of the governed. That whenever any Form of Government becomes destructive of these ends, it is the Right of the People to alter or to abolish it. . . .

The intent of the Founders was not merely to justify America's desire to free itself from the clutches of George III. Rather, they wished to signify that America was a new kind of nation—a nation that, unlike those of the past, was in a perpetual state of evolution, constantly measuring itself according to its own evolving values and reshaping itself to realize those values.

In the vast task of nation building, of realizing this extravagant American promise, the Jews, though a small minority of the population, played a surprisingly varied and effective role. There were only about 2,500 Jews in the Thirteen Colonies at the time of the American Revolution, and yet we find Jews at Bunker Hill and Valley Forge and Savannah, fighting the British, provisioning American troops, tending the wounded. For centuries, Jews as bankers and moneylenders had helped European princes fight their wars. Now, in a war against European domination, a prominent Jew, Hayyim Salomon (1740–1785) of Philadelphia, would raise funds to support the French troops fighting on the Americans' behalf, and would lend money without charge to members of the Continental Congress. Salomon later would do battle against a Pennsylvania law requiring officeholders to take an oath on the New Testament—a reminder that although the national commitment to liberty of conscience was clear, many state and local laws still embodied the belief, held by some Americans, then and now, that the United States was and ought to remain an exclusively "Christian country."

From the beginning of the nineteenth century to the eve of the Civil War, the Jewish presence in the United States expanded from 10,000 to well over 100,000, as the total population grew from over 5 million to more than 31 million. Most of the Jewish population increase comprised German-speaking immigrants, especially after the abortive European revolution of 1848 and the hard years that followed. Documents record the activities of Jewish doctors, lawyers, butchers, frontiersmen, and slave owners as well as a few abolitionist crusaders. Overwhelmingly, however, most of the immigrants went into trade, most often as itinerant peddlers with packs on their backs.

From these humble but hardworking beginnings came the families of the "merchant princes" later in the century. The Gimbel Brothers department store chain was founded by the sons of Adam Gimbel (1817–1896), who had come to America from Bavaria as a teenager and peddled dry goods along the Mississippi before opening his first store in Indiana in 1842. The Macy's and Abraham & Straus chains trace their origins to the sons of Lazarus Straus (1809–1898), a German-Jewish immigrant who made his living as a crockery importer. Another German Jew, Levi Strauss (1829–1902), arrived in New York in 1848 and immediately headed westward, as did thousands of other Jews, to the Gold Rush boom in California, where he found a ready market for the hardy blue denim pants that still bear his name—Levi's.

Generally speaking, the most prominent American Jews during this period were those whose families had lived in America since prerevolutionary times. Probably the most influential and surely the most colorful of these figures was Mordecai Manuel Noah (1785–1851), a merchant's son whose checkered career recalls that of Leo da Modena, except that Noah was no scholar. As editor of New York's *National Advocate*, Noah was drawn into Democratic party politics, and he soon became a pillar of Tammany Hall. He was at various times also a playwright; a judge; a Whig; an early supporter of the Native American (Know-Nothing) party, whose agitation against immigrants and Roman Catholics set the tone for American politics at mid-century; a vehement antiabolitionist; and something of a Utopian visionary who unsuccessfully sought to establish a Jewish colony, which he called Ararat, on a tract of land on an island in the Niagara River. When this plan fell through, Noah turned toward Zion as a possible Jewish homeland.

Surely more typical of American Jewry during the late eighteenth and early nineteenth centuries was the Gratz family, whose paterfamilias, the trader Michael Gratz (1740–1811), came from London to Philadelphia in 1754. Members of the Gratz family, having supported the patriot cause in the Revolutionary War, went on to become prominent in banking, insurance, and railroads; supplied funds for the exploration of the American West; and founded Philadelphia's Gratz College, the first Jewish teacher-training institution in the United States. Of all the good works performed by the Gratzes, none changed more lives than those of Rebecca Gratz (1781–1869). A woman of beauty and intelligence who moved in accomplished literary circles, Rebecca served as secretary of the Female Association for Relief of Women and Children in Reduced Circumstances, as an organizer of the Philadelphia Orphan Society, and as founder of the Hebrew Sunday School Society, which opened the first Jewish Sunday school in the United States. This woman, who turned down an offer of marriage from a socially prominent Christian whom she loved, is also reputed to have been the model for the character Rebecca in Sir Walter Scott's historical novel *Ivanhoe* (1820).

During this period, we see a pattern beginning to emerge. On the one hand, the Jewish community grows as America grows, strengthened by a steady flow of immigrants. These Jewish newcomers, chiefly from Germany and often sympathetic to the Reform movement in Judaism, as well as the established Jewish families, accumulate wealth and power, and use their prosperity to create strong Jewish institutions—temples, schools, benevolent societies, and charitable funds. On the other hand, as the newcomers fan out from their cities of disembarkation, especially New York, we see a pattern of assimilation and intermarriage, as well as nonmarriage, which will ultimately place a cap on Jewish population growth. In fact, a huge upsurge of immigration from Russia and Eastern Europe between 1880 and 1920 would vastly increase the size of the American Jewish community, but the underlying social pattern holds to the present day.

THE TRANSFORMATION OF AMERICA

Unquestionably, the turning point in American history is the Civil War, and like the more prolonged struggle of reconquest waged by the Christian kingdoms against Muslim Spain, the American conflict found Jews on both sides. It is estimated that about 7,000 Jews served with the Union armies, the highest-ranking officer being Frederick Knefler (1833–1901), the first Jew to hold the rank of brevet major general. On the Confederate side, probably only 3,000 Jews fought, but prominent in the Southern cause was Judah Philip Benjamin (1811–1884), not only as the first professing Jew to serve in the United States Senate (where, representing Louisiana, he passionately championed the secessionists) but also as secretary of war and then secretary of state in Jefferson Davis's Confederate cabinet. As for the moral issue raised by the war—the question of slavery—most Jews, even the most influential religious leaders, kept silent.

The Civil War is noteworthy in Jewish history for one other reason: It produced the single most anti-Semitic act ever taken by a high United States government official. In December 1862, Major General Ulysses S. Grant, seeking to halt cotton speculation within the Department of the Tennessee (comprising portions of Mississippi, Kentucky, and Tennessee then under the control of the Union) and blaming Jews for the entire illicit traffic, issued General Orders No. 11:

The Jews, as a class violating every regulation of trade . . . are hereby expelled from the department within twenty-four hours from the receipt of this order. . . .

This draconian order of expulsion, reminiscent of the treatment of Jews in medieval Europe, was promptly rescinded by President Abraham Lincoln.

The Union victory in 1865 determined that the United States would henceforward be "one nation, indivisible" (as the Pledge of Allegiance, adopted in 1892, phrased it), that slavery no longer had a place in the fabric of American life, and that the dominant economic power in America, at least for the next hundred years, would rest with the industrial North rather than the agricultural South. In fact, the war dealt the southern states an economic blow from which they had barely begun to recover by the 1940s. In the North, on the other hand, the Reconstruction era ushered in a great business boom, and it was this period of prosperity that enabled many German Jews to make the leap from peddling to owning their own small shop and then, perhaps, to managing a chain of commercial concerns. The settlement of the frontier, the provisioning of a rising population, the building of railroads and great cities—there were fortunes to be made in all of these, although for Jews the fortunes were mainly to

The Civil War found Jews on both sides of the conflict. **BELOW, LEFT:** *a portrait of President Lincoln, who earned the gratitude of Jews throughout the United States by rescinding General Grant's order expelling all Jews from the Department of the Tennessee; and a portrait of Judah P. Benjamin, who served the Confederacy in several high-ranking positions.*

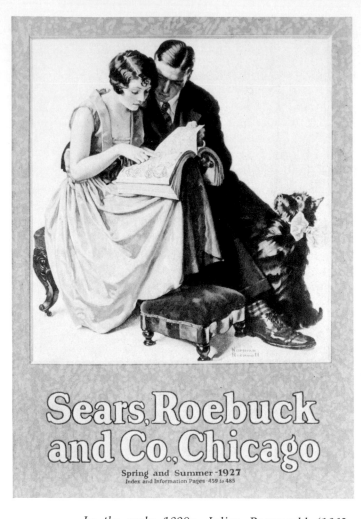

Sears, Roebuck and Co., Chicago

Spring and Summer · 1927
Index and Information Pages · 459 to 485

In the early 1890s, Julius Rosenwald (1862–1932), the son of German-Jewish immigrants, bought a quarter interest in the small mail-order firm of Sears, Roebuck for less than $40,000. By the 1920s, the Sears catalog was a familiar fixture in tens of millions of American homes.

be found in commerce and finance rather than in industry.

Apart from the Civil War and the northern business boom, there were major demographic forces transforming America. Between 1840 and 1930, the astonishing total of 37 million immigrants arrived at America's shores! Some of these newcomers, notably the Chinese, were brought in under contract as laborers. But most of the successive waves of migrants—Irish, Germans, Italians, Rus-

sians, Poles, Jews, Hispanics, and many others—came of their own volition, in search of political freedom, physical security, or (most commonly) economic opportunity. We can see that the events that triggered Jewish emigration from Russia, Russian Poland, and Romania were political—a wave of pogroms and persecutions—but the underlying cause, overpopulation, was the same as elsewhere in Europe, and it was exacerbated in the Jewish case by the newly tightened restrictions on areas of settlement within the Russian Empire. Between 1880 and 1925, no less than 2 million Jews came to the United States. And yet the Jewish population of Eastern Europe may have increased, or at least held steady, during the same period.

The overwhelming majority of immigrants from the late 1880s onward sailed into New York harbor, where the first figure to greet

Levi's—the blue denim pants with the copper rivets—first became a part of the American scene when a Bavarian-born dry-goods merchant, Levi Strauss (1829–1902), began selling the trademark overalls in California during the Gold Rush.

them was that of the majestic Statue of Liberty, holding aloft her torch of freedom, the broken chains of slavery at her feet. In 1883, the year in which the cornerstone of the Statue of Liberty was laid on Bedloe's Island (now called Liberty Island), an American Jewish poet named Emma Lazarus (1849–1887), who had already published translations of Heine and Halevi as well as her own *Songs of a Semite*, wrote a sonnet called "The New Colossus." Twenty years later, her tribute to the spirit of Liberty was engraved on a plaque and permanently affixed to the pedestal of the statue. The plaque was too small to be read by the shiploads of newcomers, and in truth, very few of the immigrants, if shown the letters, could have understood the words. Nevertheless, the concluding lines of "The New Colossus" hold a message that virtually all of them would intuitively have understood:

"Keep, ancient lands, your storied pomp!" Cries she

Born in Bohemia, Isaac Mayer Wise (1819–1900) came to New York in 1846 and later settled in Cincinnati. There he pioneered in the establishment of Reform Judaism in the United States.

Lillian Wald (1867–1940), the daughter of German-Jewish immigrants, founded the Henry Street Settlement in New York City, developed the city's first visiting nurse service, and campaigned successfully for the establishment of the United States Children's Bureau.

With silent lips. "Give me your tired, your poor,
Your huddled masses yearning to breathe free,
The wretched refuse of your teeming shore.
Send these, the homeless, tempest-tossed to me.
I lift my lamp beside the golden door!"

Let us briefly look at the American immigrant experience through the eyes of Jews who made the arduous and dislocating passage by steerage from the ghettoes and shtetls of Eastern Europe to the teeming tenements of New York's Lower East Side. First came the "tempest-tossed passage" from Europe to America, during which, as the philosopher Morris Raphael Cohen (1880–1947) recalled, the passengers were "huddled together . . . like cattle."

We could not eat the food of the ship, since it was not kosher. We only asked for hot

Scenes from life on the Lower East Side. ABOVE: a crowded tenement apartment; RIGHT: an open market on Hester Street; OPPOSITE PAGE: a pushcart peddler of used clothing; and a dilapidated schoolroom for boys.

water into which my mother used to put a little brandy and sugar to give it a taste.

Another voice paints a more Dantesque picture:

On board the ship we became utterly dejected. We were all herded together in a dark, filthy compartment. . . . Wooden bunks had been put up in two tiers. . . . Seasickness broke out among us. Hundreds of people had vomiting fits, throwing up even their mother's milk.

This same witness points out that all the immigrants were making an oceanic passage for the first time; many had never before left dry land. And as most people taking their first transoceanic voyage by ship or air can attest, imagination is even a more potent and terrifying force than any physical hardships endured. This is precisely the point made by Cohen in his memoir:

My imagination was preoccupied with the terrors of ships colliding, especially when the fog horn blew its plaintive note. . . . One morning we saw a ship passing at what seemed to me a considerable distance, but our neighbor said that we were lucky, that at night we escaped a crash by only a hair's breadth.

Next we follow the hungry, ill-clothed, disoriented immigrants off the ship, down the gangplank, onto the Customs Wharf, and into the unfathomable Ellis Island immigration hall, through which some 20 million newcomers passed between 1892 and 1947. They are herded from line to line, from interpreter to interpreter, from doctor to doctor, from official to official, questioned about their health, their family background, their political views, and their economic prospects, and often given a new "American" name by an immigration officer too tired or too harried or too ignorant to make out the strange-sounding names that the immigrants brought with them. To a certain extent, the rough treatment of the immigrants was the product of overstrain: as one historian has noted, although the quota of immigrants to be handled in a single day might be 5,000, that did not prevent 15,000 newcomers from descending upon the Ellis Island facilities. To the immigrants themselves, however, the experience was a nightmare:

We were met by interpreters, given entry cards, and taken to dormitories. After lunch, we were taken to a big hall for a lecture. They kept us three days because they had to look over the papers; they ask you all kinds of questions. It's an awful place; it's so morbid, it's like a dungeon. This one cries and this one faints and this one pulls their hair. It's such an awful place, you cannot describe it. During the day, we went in the yard and that was worse yet. Some children had to go back; they wouldn't let them into the United States. And some committed suicide.

The immigrant experience would certainly have been even more traumatic were it not for the work of the Hebrew Immigrant Aid Society (HIAS), which stationed interpreters and advisers at Ellis Island to greet the newcomers, offered practical advice for getting through immigration and surviving in the new land, helped the new arrivals to find lodging and work, and protested disgraceful conditions in steerage. HIAS was only one of many charitable agencies that were funded and organized mainly by established American Jews of German origin. This was fully in keeping with the Jewish tradition of self-help and strong communal allegiance, but there was also a strong cultural factor at work here: the "uptowners"—English-speaking, German in origin, Reform in religious affiliation, assimilated, acculturated—found these "downtowners"—Yiddish-speaking, Eastern European in origin, Orthodox or irreligious (or, worse still, Socialist), culturally about as "un-American" as they could be—both a burden and an embarrassment.

By the turn of the century, virtually every city in the United States had its "uptown" and "downtown." Of course, the most famous of them all was New York's Lower East Side, where by 1915 it is estimated that 350,000 Jews lived in an area about 2 miles (5 km) square, flanked by Irish and Italian sections. Despite idealization in subsequent nostalgia, the neighborhood was actually nothing but a Jewish slum. It was specifically Jewish because the concentration of Jews was so intense as to make possible a complete array of supporting services—synagogues, Jewish schools, kosher butchers, Jewish bookstores, Yiddish newspapers—clustered in the same section, creating what one writer has called a "voluntary ghetto." And, of course, it was a slum for all the obvious reasons: cramped, dirty, unhealthy, ill-lit, with tenement apartments meant for two or three people housing eight to ten. Such overcrowding could scarcely be seen in New York City today; only photographs, or perhaps a visit to some overburdened Third World city, could adequately convey what life was like at such close quarters.

Many of the immigrants found work in the "needle trades," in the notorious sweatshops that churned out ready-made clothing from dawn past midnight, paying wages of less than 40 cents an hour. These wage earners were the lucky ones, for those paid at piece rates might earn as little as 6 cents an hour over the course of an 80-hour workweek. Here is one sweatshop, by no means the worst, as described in 1890 by the Danish-American social reformer Jacob Riis, author of *How the Other Half Lives:*

Five men and a woman, two young girls, not fifteen, and a boy, who says, unasked, that he is fifteen, and lies in saying it, are at the machines sewing "knee-pants." . . . The faces, hands, and arms to the elbows of everyone in the room are black with the color of the cloth on which they are working. . . . They are "learners," all of them, says the woman, who proves to be the wife of the boss, and have "come over" only a few weeks ago. They turn out 120 dozen "knee-pants" a week. They work no longer than to nine o'clock at night, from daybreak.

Conditions as deplorable as this were ripe for labor organizers, and in 1900 the International Ladies' Garment Workers' Union was formed. The shirtwaist makers went on strike in 1909, in what was billed as the "Uprising of the 20,000." In 1910 the "great revolt," a strike by New York City cloakmakers, brought the first labor settlement in the garment industry, planned with the aid of three figures who were among the leaders of American Jewry: Jacob Schiff (1847–1920), a financier and philanthropist who contributed generously to almost every major Jewish welfare agency; Louis Marshall (1856–1929), prominent both as a lawyer and as a Republican, who would take the initiative in the fight against renascent anti-Semitism in the 1920s; and Louis Dembitz Brandeis (1856–1941), renowned as the "people's attorney" because of his frequent participation in public cases, who was destined to become, in 1916, the first Jewish justice of the United States Supreme Court. The 1910 settlement, providing for a maximum workweek of 54 hours and the payment of overtime rates, was an important victory, to be sure, but conditions in the garment industry did not truly become the public scandal they deserved to be until the Triangle Shirtwaist Company fire of 1911, in which 146 garment workers, most of them young Italian and Jewish girls, perished in flames.

It has been said that the Lower East Side was a great place—to come from. And, in fact, from the ghetto of the Lower East Side

The badge decreed by the Nazis for the Jews of France.

11·
Out of
the Ashes

MORE JEWISH history was made from 1933 to 1949 than in any other epoch of which we have memory or record. After all these years, it is hard to recapture the crowded intensity of those times: the rise of Hitler to power in Germany in 1933, the first inauguration of Franklin Delano Roosevelt . . . and then, like claps of deafening thunder, one after the other . . . the persecution of the Jews in Germany, the burning of their books and synagogues, the first hideous concentration camps, the Nazi German invasion of Austria, the betrayal of Czechoslovakia at Munich, the British repression of the Jews in Palestine, the smash of German tanks into Poland, the outbreak of world war, the bombings and the deportations, the German invasion of Russia, the entrance of the United States into the war, what was to have been the "Final Solution" of the "Jewish problem" through mass annihilation, and the landing of the Allies in Normandy. In close succession we saw the collapse and defeat of the Axis powers; the establishment of the United Nations; the international debates on the future of Palestine; the declaration of Israel's independence; and the Arab-Israeli War of 1948–1949.

Within a single decade the whole international system had been totally destroyed. Fifty million people had lost their lives. A new dimension had been added to the human memory, and the exploration of it will never end.

The years covered by this chapter, which are horrifyingly unique because of the Holocaust, marked a general crisis of civilization. At the center of this crisis stood the unique ordeal of the Jews. From the darkest depths of man's divided nature there sprang at the throat of the Jewish people the most violent hatred that had ever convulsed the life and spirit of mankind. The agony follows us, it

The crematorium of the concentration camp at Dachau—a monument to man's inhumanity.

will never let us go . . . the 6 million Jews, men, women, and children, carried off to the gas chambers, the furnaces, the firing squads, among them one million children asphyxiated in the gas chambers in their mothers' arms, or thrown still alive into the furnaces . . . the obscene places of death and slaughter, scattered over Nazi Europe.

In one of them alone, Auschwitz, 3 million people, nearly all of them Jews, were done to death. In the summer of 1944 alone, 400,000 Hungarian Jews were murdered there. This monstrous outrage was accomplished by Nazi Germany against humanity in the name of an idea—the idea that to destroy the allegedly "inferior" non-Nordic peoples was a

As the Soviet revolutionaries and their sympathizers sought to hold aloft the Red banner of international communism, reactionary movements both in Europe and in the United States nourished themselves on the Communist threat.

noble task. But the Holocaust was enacted in the midst of a Europe ostensibly rational, scientific, and civilized. It was accomplished mostly in the war, but it was independent of the war. It began before, and it would have continued after . . . if victory had not gone to the Allies.

In the hearts of millions of Jews there is a sanctuary in which they carry their grief in intimate solitude. Many events in Jewish history are too terrible to be believed, but nothing in Jewish history is too terrible to have happened. After the war, the Jews rose from the nightmare to find that it had not been a nightmare after all. It had been a reality. The Jews were fearfully depleted in manpower. There would be 27 million, not 14 million, Jews alive today but for the Holocaust. Is it any wonder that Jews have a profound scepticism about the stability of civilization, that they have an obsessive anxiety about their own physical security, that in any appraisal of their destiny they make provision for the worst? And that they *remember?* They remember not only the crimes of the Nazis but also the apathy and neglect of much of the rest of the world—the governments and churches that passed by on the other side, the nations that closed their gates so that refugees from the Holocaust could not enter.

The Holocaust and the world's response to it mark the lowest point in the moral history of mankind. There is a flower in every dustheap, and there are some fragments of partial consolation in the ashes of the Holocaust. There *was* Jewish resistance, desperate, hopeless, but heroic—and not only in the Warsaw Ghetto uprising of April 1943. There were some acts of Christian compassion and of human solidarity. Above everything else, the tyranny *was* defeated in the last resort; it did not win. If Hitler's purpose had been to destroy the name and identity of the Jewish people, that evil design was frustrated. The remnant was gathered in, and the flag of modern Israel gives the ghost of Hitler de-

British Prime Minister Neville Chamberlain and Adolf Hitler reach agreement at Munich in September 1938. The Munich Pact, which Chamberlain said would bring "peace in our time," collapsed a year later when Germany invaded Poland, igniting the fires of World War II.

The Fascist faith in state power and military conquest could not long coexist with the Jewish commitment to unfettered inquiry and democratic ideals. In this photograph, taken in 1938, German Führer Adolf Hitler is shown with his ally Benito Mussolini, premier of Italy.

fiant answer. *Am Yisrael chai* . . . the people of Israel lives.

THE ROOTS OF EUROPEAN TOTALITARIANISM

In seeking to find the roots of European totalitarianism of which the most horrifying result was the Holocaust, we must turn to the political and cultural configuration of Europe after World War I. This "war to end all wars" had done nothing of the kind. During the four-year conflict, an unprecedented total of 65 million men were mobilized, 8.5 million of them were killed, 21.2 million wounded, and 7.8 million taken prisoner or classified as

missing in action. The war decimated an entire generation of Europeans. Moreover, the armed conflict that brought an end to empires in Central Europe, Russia, and Ottoman Turkey, unleashed more tensions than it resolved. There was the rising force of Bolshevism in the U.S.S.R., and the ill-fated and embittering attempt of the Western powers to suppress it in the Soviet Union. There was the still potent force of nationalism, which had reshaped the map of Eastern Europe by the creation of mutually hostile nation-states and of a large refugee population. There was the large and insupportable burden of European debt—not merely the onerous reparations imposed on Germany through the Treaty of Versailles (1919), but also the obli-

gations to Britain and to the United States incurred during the war by the continental powers and by Britain itself to its North American ally. Europe, which before World War I had consistently been a net importer of resources, now faced the task of converting its economies to produce more than they consumed, at a time when European enterprises were facing increasingly severe competition from the United States, Japan, and even some of Europe's overseas colonies. It was still believed that each European power could control its own economic destiny through state planning. This idea had gained currency through the full-scale war mobilization of 1914–1918, which seemed to bear witness to the centralizing force of state power. There was ruinous competition between states for dwindling economic resources. Meanwhile, the idea that a government, acting through propaganda and censorship, should be the arbiter of right thought was growing. There were efforts toward conciliation, expressed in the work of the League of Nations and in a series of limited disarmament agreements; but these movements toward peace were no match for

the accelerating economic and political tensions among the European powers. The nation-state was the only effective actor in the international system, the source of power and the focus of allegiance and pride.

Germany lost its colonial empire as a consequence of the Versailles Treaty, but colonialism was not dead or dying. A small minority of English colonists, buttressed by the power and authority of the mother country, still managed to rule hundreds of millions of subject peoples on the Indian subcontinent and in the Middle East (including Palestine), Asia, Africa, and the Caribbean. The second imperial power, France, ruled Indochina and much of Africa, and also held territories in the Pacific and the Caribbean. Italy also had a significant stake in Africa, and Holland maintained extensive holdings in the East Indies (now Indonesia). In the Pacific, two non-European powers rivaled the Europeans for supremacy. The United States, which during the 1920s had experienced a rollicking postwar boom, held Hawaii and the Philippines; and Japan, then in the midst of a vast industrial expansion, had moved into northeastern China (Man-

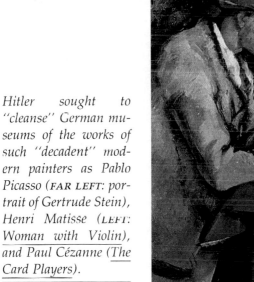

*Hitler sought to "cleanse" German museums of the works of such "decadent" modern painters as Pablo Picasso (**FAR LEFT**: portrait of Gertrude Stein), Henri Matisse (**LEFT**: <u>Woman with Violin</u>), and Paul Cézanne (<u>The Card Players</u>).*

churia) and the Korean Peninsula. In India, in Indochina, in the Philippines—indeed, if one looked below the surface, in almost every colony—the force of nationalism, coupled with the desire of the European settlers to exercise greater autonomy in their political and economic dealings, deepened the sense of instability.

This instability extended to the cultural climate as well. Brilliant writers, painters, composers, and performers sought to rewrite the rules of artistic expression, questioning what had been regarded as time-honored rules of literary and musical form and visual representation. Impressionism, expressionism, cubism, fauvism, serialism, surrealism, Dada, stream of consciousness— such were the watchwords of what, from the late nineteenth century through the early 1930s, marked a period of feverish creativity such as Europe had not seen since the Renaissance. This era, in which manifestoes were often as important as the works of art themselves, was the heyday of a self-conscious avant-garde, intent on fashioning something *new*— something that would upset established val-

ues and shock comfortable bourgeois preconceptions.

Jews played an active role in the artistic ferment of this era. One thinks immediately of the Viennese composer who pioneered twelve-tone music, Arnold Schoenberg (1874–1951), and of his great Austrian precursor, Gustav Mahler (1860–1911), whose elevation to the directorship of the Vienna Court Opera in 1897 could not be secured without his conversion to Catholicism. In literature we see figures as diverse as Franz Kafka (1883–1924), the American expatriate Gertrude Stein (1874–1946), and the Bulgarian-born playwright and novelist Elias Canetti (b. 1905), winner of the Nobel Prize for Literature in 1981. Although not of Jewish birth, the German novelist and essayist Thomas Mann (1875–1955) married a Jewess, was backed by a Jewish publisher, treated Jewish themes positively in several of his major novels—notably the Biblical tetralogy *Joseph and His Brothers* (1933–1944), written during the Hitler era—and in the mid-1930s emerged as a leading opponent of the Nazis, first from within Germany and then from exile. How

Paralleling the growth of anti-Semitism in Europe was the resurgence in the United States of racist groups such as the Ku Klux Klan, shown on a march through Washington in 1926.

fitting, finally, that the hero of the magnificent prose epic *Ulysses* (1922), written by an Irish Catholic, James Joyce (1882–1941), should have as its hero a Dublin Jew, Leopold Bloom. We know from Joyce's biographer Richard Ellman that in creating Bloom as his fictional protagonist, "Joyce recognized implicitly what he often spoke of directly, his affinity for the Jews as a wandering, persecuted people."

But there is more to the choice than personal affinity. Just as the Jews themselves had by this time become central to the shaping of European culture, so the question of the Jews as a part of European society and yet still somehow outside it, was now pivotal. Many artists, Christians as well as Jews,

united in their alienation from the mainstream of middle-class values, must have seen their own predicament in the diaspora Jew. The paradox is that, at the very same time, and especially in Germany, a large number of Jews were "making it" on very middle-class terms, entering commerce as always, but also succeeding in medicine, law, and the other professions in unprecedented numbers.

Even more than in the arts, European Jewish philosophers, social critics, and scientists had been intimately involved in transforming the way in which the modern Western European looked at himself and his world. Karl Marx, a Jew hater though of Jewish origin, had sought to strip away what he regarded as the veneer of bourgeois civility to reveal the mechanics of class antagonism. Sigmund Freud (1856–1939), the Austrian-born founder of psychoanalysis, penetrated the veil of Victorian repression to investigate the basic drives of life, death, and sexuality which he believed underlay all human action. Albert Einstein (1879–1955), a physicist and mathematician of German birth and Swiss training, brought the concept of relativity into public discourse. Even in its narrowest applications, the concept was revolutionary: it trumpeted the limitations of the Newtonian world-view and suggested complexities that few human beings had ever imagined, and none had ever seen. But as the concept of "relativity" seized the public mind, it seemed to herald an age in which everything would be "relative," in which all the traditional verities—political, social, moral, artistic, religious—would vary with the eye of the beholder. Not that Einstein himself believed this; indeed, he was active in Jewish affairs, sympathetic to Zionism, and a man of deep humanitarian feeling. But this did not prevent him from coming to symbolize, in the minds of the bigoted and the ill-informed, a distorted "Jewish science" that, if not curbed, would eat away at the very foundations of European thought.

It is not difficult to see in this neurotic period the seeds of *two* wars. The first is the war with which everyone is familiar: World War II, in which the Axis powers (Nazi Germany, Italy, Japan) engaged the Allies (England and France and the Soviet Union, then the United States) across a global battlefield, at a cost of 30 million civilian lives as well as 20 million military personnel.

The second war, which began earlier than the first and continued until the final capitulation of the Nazis, was what more than one historian has called the "war against the Jews." It was Hitler's attempt through mass persecutions and military conquest to reverse the tide of European civilization and to recast it in an Aryan mold. Hitler's war against the Jews, as we have seen, involved the murder of 6 million innocent human beings. To deprive these Jews of their social and economic status, their political and legal rights, their

The great physicist Albert Einstein arriving in America after fleeing Europe in 1933.

freedom, and ultimately, their lives, required the kind of ruthlessness that could have flourished only in an age of restlessness and frustration.

The Holocaust was not a sudden eruption; it could not have occurred without the deep-rooted tradition of anti-Semitism to which we have pointed in earlier chapters. During the 1920s, we encounter rising anti-Jewish feelings even in the United States, expressed by quotas on admissions to colleges, universities, and medical schools; discrimination, both overt and covert, in employment practices; and the dissemination of crudely anti-Semitic propaganda not only from such expected sources as the Ku Klux Klan, but also by such "respectable" public figures as automobile manufacturer Henry Ford (1863–1947), who used the pages of his *Dearborn Independent* as a vehicle for the publication of the scurrilous *Protocols of the Elders of Zion* and repeated warnings and denunciations of the "Jewish menace."

There was no country in Europe that lacked an anti-Semitic chapter in its history in the period between the two World Wars. In France the Jew haters created the legend

STUDY OF
PRESIDENT ROOSEVELT
FOR PAINTING
BIG THREE AT YALTA
CANVAS SIZE 92"×92"
WITH OUTLINE SKETCH

AD FAMILIAM GENTIVM COMEM CONTENDIT

CHANDOR MARCH 1945. THE WHITE HOUSE WASHINGTON.

During the 1930s, President Franklin D. Roosevelt (depicted in an official portrait by Douglas Chandor) was a target of criticism from right-wing anti-Semites who denounced the New Deal as the "Jew Deal."

of Jewish domination. In terms of power and political influence the Jews of France were always marginal, but the glamour of the Rothschilds and the occasional rise of Jews to political power, such as Léon Blum in the mid-1930s, seemed to lend a pale semblance of credibility to a legend that was intrinsically absurd. The extreme right wing in French politics preached anti-Jewish prejudice without any concealment, and some of its contributions to racist literature evoke the memories of the Dreyfus era. Across the channel the Jews of Britain created a solid, prosperous community with a tidily fashioned network of institutions built in hierar-

chical shape, with a clear demarcation of institutional authority. (Jewish communities tend to take the structural shape of the non-Jewish societies in which they live. American Jewry copies the federal, decentralized pattern of the United States, avoiding clear-cut leadership without a Chief Rabbinate or a universally recognized representation. British Jewry creates a miniature edition of the British structure; there is one Chief Rabbi, a Board of Deputies recognized as a representative spokesman, and even a weekly journal, *The Jewish Chronicle*, which calls itself, with justification, "*The* Organ of British Jewry.")

Even in Britain, idealized by European Jews, including Herzl and Weizmann, as the quintessential tolerant, humane society, the fires of anti-Jewish prejudice occasionally kindled a wave of rancor. The general picture of Jewish life in Britain was one of tranquility. Jews could rise to Cabinet rank, beginning with Herbert Samuel (1870–1963), who was Home Secretary before becoming High Commissioner for Palestine in 1920, and running through a series of distinctions such as those celebrated by Rufus Isaacs, who was Lord Chief Justice, Viceroy of India, and Foreign Secretary. At the outbreak of World War II a Jew, Leslie Belisha, was Secretary of State for War. In law, medicine, and academic life, Jews were more prominent than their restricted numbers seemed to indicate. Even when British policy became hostile to the Zionist enterprise, the Jews of Britain flourished in their communal enterprises and freely and boldly expressed their dissent from their government's Palestine policy. It was, therefore, all the more alarming when,

in the 1930s, a Fascist movement, blackshirted and booted, cast a pall of anxiety over British Jews. It was led by Oswald Mosley, a politician of exceptional arrogance and intellectual superficiality, whose anti-Semitism was a matter of cold, brutal calculation rather than of searing passion as it was with Hitler. All in all, the condition of the Jews in Europe between the wars always fell short of complete security even if its dominant note was optimistic.

The Jews of the United States more than those in Europe had the financial and organizational strength to fight back, and the advent in 1933 of Franklin Roosevelt's New Deal (denounced as the "Jew Deal" by the minority that hated FDR and the Jews with

Some of those activists who opposed American entry into World War II were motivated, like the Radcliffe students shown here, by pacifist ideals, but others did so out of isolationist, pro-German, or anti-Jewish sentiments.

equal vehemence) gave American Jewry the climate of liberalism within which its struggle could be waged with greatest effect. In Eastern Europe, on the other hand, the situation was incalculably worse. In Russia, for example, the Jewish anarchist and pacifist Emma Goldman (1869–1940), initially a supporter of the Revolution, found that the treatment of the Jews had changed more in outward form than in inward content by the 1920s:

It was claimed that the Bolsheviks made no pogroms . . . but that was true only in a certain sense. There were two kinds of pogrom: the loud, violent ones, and the silent ones. Of the two the Zionists considered the former preferable. The violent pogrom might last a day or a week; the Jews are attacked and robbed, sometimes even murdered; and then it is over. But the silent pogroms continued all the time. They consisted of constant discrimination, persecution and hounding. . . . If a Jew and a Gentile happened to be arrested on the same charge, it was certain that the Gentile would go free while the Jew would be sent to prison and sometimes even shot. They were all the time exposed to insult and indignities, not to mention the fact that they were doomed to slow starvation, since all trade had been suppressed. The Jews in the Ukraine were suffering a continuous silent pogrom.

In the embattled Polish state, meanwhile, Jews found themselves caught in the violence between the Poles and their Lithuanian, Ukrainian, and Bolshevik enemies; worse still, they were the victims of a "silent pogrom" that aimed systematically at the elimination of Jews—who made up at least 10 percent of the population—from national economic life. In Romania, where about 800,000 Jews (5 percent of the population) were living in the early 1920s, there were anti-Jewish riots, and the rise of Nazism in Germany inspired the Romanian government to take an explicitly anti-Jewish turn. In Hungary, which had a Jewish population of 473,000 in 1920, the anti-Jewish agitation that customarily accompanied nationalist resurgence was intensified by anti-Bolshevik feeling, for the revolutionary Communist regime that briefly governed Hungary in 1919 was led by a nonobservant Jew, Béla Kun (1886–1939), and had substantial Jewish representation. In none of these lands did the Holocaust begin. But the wholesale slaughter of Jews—most of which, though orchestrated and directed by Germans, took place on Polish soil—could not have gone on without the complicity of large numbers of Eastern Europeans and their leaders.

If anyone had suggested in the early 1930s that Germany was destined to be the author of the Jewish people's most tragic ordeal, no one would have dismissed the prospect more emphatically and indignantly than the Jews of Germany themselves. In 1933 there were 503,000 Jews in Germany, and they lived more intimately with the surrounding culture than had any Jewish community since the era of florescence in Spanish Jewry. Jews were ubiquitous in German culture, commerce, and society, although they represented only one percent of the population. They shone and sparkled in the German firmament. They convinced themselves that they were authentically at home. One hundred thousand of them had served in the German forces in World War I, and 12,000 of them had fallen in battle. The Weimar Republic, established after the war, had abolished all restrictions of law and status, and the Jews reached a position in German life that they had never before dreamed of. A Jew, Walter Rathenau, even became foreign minister after the war. He was assassinated in 1920 by a fanatic motivated, at least in part, by anti-Semitism. A million people attended his lavish state funeral; the Jews of Germany, who should have been frightened by the assassination, were, in fact, gratified by the prestigious funeral, which they interpreted as a ceremonial acknowledgment of Jewish power and pride. Although there was a rich religious and cultural life and a fairly robust Zionist movement, the dominant theme in Jewish life in Germany was assimilation. Jews called themselves Germans of the Mosaic persuasion and ignored the evidence that should have told them that their integration was never complete. Many of them, exuberant in their celebration of their German identity, looked in disdain and embarrassment on the Jewish immigrants from East Europe (the *Ostjuden*), who had to be acknowledged but were shown no real warmth or understanding. Their very appearance seemed to belie the theory that Jews and Germans were indistinguishable. In a few years in the 1930s the Utopian dream of the German Jews would be shattered. It would be followed by a living hell.

There is no single answer to the question why Germany, with its tradition of rationality and its prosperous Jewish community, should have become the arena of the Holocaust. Many have sought the answer in the Versailles Treaty, which humiliated and embittered Germany without impairing its ability to wreak vengeance; in the weakness of

"Behind the enemy the Jew" shrieks this blatant Nazi propaganda poster, depicting a crude Semitic caricature behind the flags of the Allies that faced Germany on the battlefront.

During the first phase of the Holocaust, from 1933 to 1939, the Nazis mounted a campaign of economic discrimination, social ostracism, and personal humiliation that paved the way for the mass deportations and exterminations of the next six years. The photograph shows German soldiers enforcing a boycott of Jewish shops.

the democratic tradition in Germany, the instability of the Weimar Republic, and the cult of state power that had been growing since the nineteenth century. Others look to the traumatic effects of the hyperinflation and depression that climaxed the 1920s; to the psychology of scapegoating, which in the case of Germany meant the isolation of a single malevolent cause (i.e., the Jews), for the nation's wartime and postwar tribulations; or to the demonic personality and undeniable rhetorical gifts of Hitler himself. But, as in Eastern Europe, a major factor in the creation

of opinion was a deep-seated anti-Semitism, which previous chapters have traced from the early Christian era through the Crusades to the seminal figure of Martin Luther.

It is no exaggeration to say that by the end of the nineteenth century, the "Jewish question" had become the central problem of German culture. It was a period in which Germany sought to define its role in Europe and Jews began to penetrate every sphere of German social, economic, and cultural life. In 1881 the great opera composer Richard Wagner (1813–1883), who was at the time putting the finishing touches on his Easter epic *Parsifal*—which, by an odd irony, would be conducted by a Jew, Hermann Levi (1839–1900), at its world premiere at Bayreuth the following year—wrote a blunt letter about the Jews to Bavarian King Ludwig II:

I regard the Jewish race as the born enemy

of pure humanity and everything that is noble in it; it is certain that we Germans will go under before them, and perhaps I am the last German who knows how to stand up as an art-loving man against the Judaism that is already getting control of everything.

In his letter Wagner uses a phrase we have not previously encountered—"the Jewish race." Judaism is the Jewish *religion*, those who are born Jews are the Jewish *people*, Israel today is the Jewish *state*—but what constitutes the Jewish *race*? A thoroughgoing analysis of the development of racial classifications—and, concomitantly, of racism—would point to the impact of colonialism on the growing European awareness of human diversity, and to the inevitable tendency for the European theorists of race to justify in terms of natural or racial superiority ("survival of the fittest") the political and military ascendancy of Europeans over other peoples, especially those of dark complexion. But to understand the labeling of the Jews as a race (a practice now discredited by anthropology), we must return to the main stem of anti-Jewish prejudice, upon which the racial theory is but a late graft.

The intellectual problem for the committed, fervent anti-Semite was how to justify the old prejudices when the Jews themselves, seizing the opportunities that emancipation offered, no longer dressed the old way, spoke the old language, pursued the old avenues of making a living, or even followed their old religion. The answer, as it emerged from the anti-Semitic tracts of the period, was that the Jew might look like a German, dress like a German, speak like a German, even pray like a German, but he was not a *real* German because he was of a different race—which meant, in effect, an inferior race. It followed from this line of reasoning that a Jew who looked, dressed, spoke, or prayed like a German was betraying his own nature, reaching beyond his sta-

Flag-waving Germans celebrate the annexation (anschluss) of Austria in March 1938.

tion, seeking to subvert German culture, or (in the case of intermarriage) polluting German blood.

Did anyone really believe such nonsense? The answer, tragically, is yes. For an example of such virulent thinking, also from 1881, we turn to the German economist and philosopher Karl Eugen Dühring (1833–1921), whose career neatly spans the period from Wagner to Hitler:

A Jewish question would still exist, even if every Jew were to turn his back on his religion and join one of our major churches. Yes, I maintain that in that case, the struggle between us and the Jews would make itself felt as ever more urgent. . . . It is precisely the baptized Jews who infiltrate furthest, unhindered in all sectors of society and political life. . . . Through these portals the racial Jew

[*Racenjude*] who has forsaken his religion can enter unhindered. . . . The diverse admixture of our modern cultures, or in other words the sprinkling of racial-Jewry in the cracks and crevices of our national abode, must inevitably lead to reaction. It is impossible that close contact [between Germans and Jews] will take effect without the concomitant realization that this infusion of Jewish qualities is incompatible with our best impulses.

Not a single Nazi racial theory originated with Hitler. What Hitler did was to turn expounded theory into practice with a relentless consistency, extracting from the doctrine of racial anti-Semitism its murderous implications. Here is Hitler in *Mein Kampf*, at the low point of his political career, after a futile attempt to overthrow the Bavarian government (the "Beer Hall Putsch"):

If at the beginning of [World War I] and during the war twelve or fifteen thousand of the Hebrew corrupters of the people had been held under poison gas, as happened to hundreds of thousands of our very best German workers in the field, the sacrifice of millions at the front would not have been in vain. On the contrary: twelve thousand scoundrels eliminated in time might have saved the lives of a million real Germans, valuable for the future.

And here is the very same man, now Führer of all Germany, uttering his "last testament" in 1945, as his empire crumbles around him:

I demand of all Germans, all National Socialists, men and women, and all the men of the Armed Forces, that they be faithful and obedient unto death to the new government and its president.
Above all I charge the leaders of the nation and those under them to scrupulous observance of the laws of race and to merciless opposition to the universal poisoner of all peoples, international Jewry.

How did Hitler come to formulate these warped racial views? We cannot directly examine the distorting prism of his psyche, but we do know that virulently anti-Semitic materials were abundantly available in the Austria and Germany of his time, and that his beliefs in Teutonic superiority and Jewish vulnerability must have crystallized soon after he came to Vienna as an adolescent in 1906. In this city of Mozart and Beethoven, Freud and Mahler, Schnitzler and Schoenberg, we can imagine the young Adolf, hungry, vulnerable, envious, and seething with rage:

To me Vienna, the city which to so many is the epitome of innocent pleasure, a festive playground for merry-makers, represents, I am sorry to say, merely the living memory of the saddest period of my life.
Even today this city can arouse in me nothing but dismal thoughts. For me the name of this . . . city represents five years of hardship and misery. Five years in which I was forced to earn a living, first as a day laborer, then as a small painter; a truly meager living which never sufficed to appease even my daily hunger.

Decades later, Hitler would have his revenge. In 1938 the Nazis entered Vienna and immediately began harassing, humiliating, exporting, and arresting its Jewish population. Jewish properties were seized, and in one terrible night—*Kristallnacht* ("The Night of Broken Glass"), November 9–10, 1938, also a night of terror for Jews throughout Germany and elsewhere in Austria—more than forty Viennese synagogues were destroyed and there began the massing and shipping of Jews to forced-labor camps (the last transport would leave in September 1942). That November of 1938, the Jewish community of Vienna was formally dissolved. Except for the underground, Jewish Vienna was no more, and the gay city of "innocent pleasure" had died with it.

A typesetting plant, its windows smashed, bears the scars of Kristallnacht, the "Night of Broken Glass" (November 9–10, 1938), an organized onslaught on Jewish homes, shops, and synagogues in Germany and Austria.

EUROPE AND THE HOLOCAUST

When the Nazi horror broke over Europe, the Jewish population on that continent exceeded 8 million. In some countries, including those of Central and Western Europe, Jews were closely integrated into the surrounding cultures. Those who chose to live segregated lives in the service of their ancient faith relied on European traditions of pluralism and tolerance. The majority put their faith and sought their security in the rationalism and scientific progress that had made Europe the hub and center of the civilized world. Jews had given their full devotion to those cultures, and Jewish names glowed brightly in the galleries of literary, scientific, and artistic fame. The picture was darker as one looked farther east. In Poland and Romania a measure of anti-Semitism seemed endemic to the ruling establishments, but the discomfort that this situation inflicted on the Jews gave no premonition of the mass slaughter that would soon engulf them. To believe in the oncoming tragedy would be to believe that Europe would turn its back on itself and make a mockery of all the principles that had inspired its greatness.

This is exactly what happened. Europe became anti-European, obliterating the entire legacy of values by which it had advanced for nearly two centuries.

The Nazi era lasted only twelve years and four months, but the convulsions that it gen-

The Holocaust

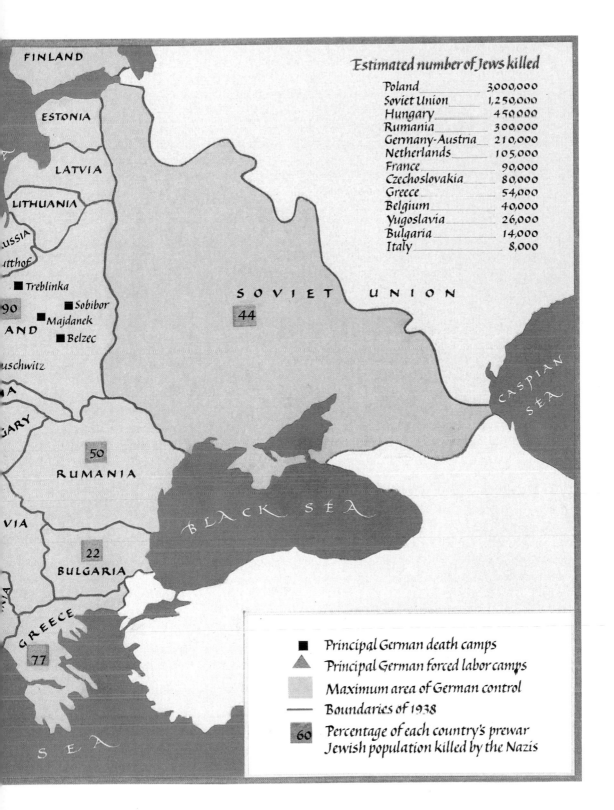

FINLAND

ESTONIA

LATVIA

LITHUANIA

...USSIA

...tthof

■ Treblinka

90

■ Sobibor

■ Majdanek

■ Belzec

...uschwitz

...AND

...A

...GARY

S O V I E T   U N I O N

44

CASPIAN SEA

50

RUMANIA

B L A C K   S E A

...VIA

22

BULGARIA

GREECE

77

SEA

Estimated number of Jews killed

Poland	3,000,000
Soviet Union	1,250,000
Hungary	450,000
Rumania	300,000
Germany-Austria	210,000
Netherlands	105,000
France	90,000
Czechoslovakia	80,000
Greece	54,000
Belgium	40,000
Yugoslavia	26,000
Bulgaria	14,000
Italy	8,000

■ Principal German death camps

▲ Principal German forced labor camps

　Maximum area of German control

— Boundaries of 1938

60 Percentage of each country's prewar Jewish population killed by the Nazis

erated in world history were beyond measurement or compare. In the words of a contemporary historian, "it caused an eruption on this earth more violent and shattering than any previously experienced, raising the German people to heights of power they had not known in more than a millennium, making them at one time the master of Europe, from the Atlantic to the Volga, from the North Cape to the Mediterranean and then plunging them to the depths of destruction and desolation. At the end of the world war which their nation had cold-bloodedly provoked, during which it instituted a reign of terror over the conquered peoples which, in its calculated butchery of human life and the human spirit, they outdid all the savage oppressions of the previous ages." (William L. Shirer, *The Rise and Fall of the Third Reich*)

The martyrdom of the Jews was enacted in three stages. From Hitler's assumption of power in 1933 to the outbreak of war in 1939, the only victims exposed to physical outrage were the Jews of Germany, who numbered 500,000, and the 400,000 Jews of Austria. From 1939 to 1941 nearly all the Jews in continental Europe west of Stalingrad were under Nazi domination, but the satanic idea of a "Final Solution" aiming at the physical liquidation of the Jews was not determined until 1941. From 1941 onward the German Nazis unleashed on millions of Jews the most excruciatingly savage torrent of hatred and violence that has ever convulsed the life and spirit of mankind.

In the first stage, the aim of the Nazis was to impoverish and humiliate German Jews without proceeding to physical extermination. The rubber truncheon and other tortures were reserved for the relatively few who were dragged to the concentration camps, from which they sometimes emerged beaten, crushed in spirit, but still alive.

The fact that these outrages, together with the disenfranchisement of German Jews and the campaign of racial incitement, were ac-

cepted by the world without drastic reaction undoubtedly paved the way to the next stages. A doctrine of race in which pure "Aryans" were contrasted with a verminous, subhuman species of "non-Nordic man" was promulgated across the world. It became the formal religion of Germany. The terrible truth is that German scientists and professors gave their endorsement to this morbidly sadistic heresy. There was talk of "Jewish Einstein corruption." Scientific truths were banished if Jews had taken part in their elucidation. "Science, like every other human product, is racial and conditioned by blood," declared a Nazi professor. When the Nazi propaganda minister Joseph Goebbels ordered a bonfire in which the books of Einstein, Freud, Zola, Thomas Mann, and Heinrich Heine were cast to the flames, he emitted a hysterical scream: "The soul of the German people can again express itself. These flames not only illuminate the final end of our era, they also light up a new age."

Literature was not the only target of Nazi censorship. Music, drama, journalism, radio, and films were "cleansed" of decadence, as represented by Picasso, Matisse, Cézanne. All Jews were expelled from all universities. And in 1935 the racist theme was given legislative expression by the enactment of the Nürnberg Laws. Jews were formally excommunicated from German society, declared "unclean" and unfit for any social contact with Aryans. A Jew was formally defined as someone three of whose grandparents had been Jews. Within a year of the adoption of the Nürnberg Laws, 75,000 Jews had emigrated from Germany and 8,000 had committed suicide. On March 12, 1938, Germany annexed Austria and applied its anti-Semitic legislation to the 400,000 Jews of Austria. Half a million Jews were under German rule, but they were now to become a fraction of the vast Jewish populations that would become the victims of Nazi violence.

Wherever a Nazi army accomplished a

ILS DONNENT LEUR SANG

DONNEZ VOTRE TRAVAIL
pour sauver l'Europe du Bolchevisme

"They give their blood, you give your work to save Europe from Bolshevism" declares this Nazi propaganda poster.

the
tak
lea
tab
I
193
Bu
zer
the
tee
by
to

the
toe
sha
Sel

It v
eve
pai
sno
an
the
lor
hu
to
as
sho
cou
for
on
pu
fou
ask
on
Th
wh
we
two
for
sho
to
cou
ser
dat
ma
aft
a d
the

new conquest, one of the first tasks was to seek out the Jews and to organize their annihilation. Jews were herded into vast death camps, to be shot, burned, or gassed; Jews in Russian towns and villages were taken out into the fields, stripped naked, forced to dig their own graves, and machine-gunned in the thousands; Jewish children were rounded up, put into buses as though for a school picnic, and then gassed or burned in death camps; Jews were sent to "clinics," where their bodies were used for satanic medical experiments before they met their tortured deaths; Jews were flogged, hanged, poisoned, clubbed to death, strangled, electrocuted, submitted to every torment that diseased minds could contrive. Millions of such tragedies played out all over the continent of Europe have left their scarred memories on the blood-stained pages of human history.

INSTITUTIONS AND TECHNIQUES OF THE HOLOCAUST

The concentration camp at Dachau, near Munich in southern Germany, was established very soon after Hitler came to power. It therefore became the training ground and the pilot plant, the prototype for the concentration camps that were to arise elsewhere.

From the concentration camps and ghettoes, Jewish prisoners were loaded into freight cars (LEFT) and shipped to Auschwitz or to one of a half-dozen other death camps. More than 3 million prisoners lost their lives at Auschwitz. OPPOSITE PAGE: the hollowed eyes and emaciated bodies of these concentration camp victims shocked the Allied troops and Jewish rescue workers who liberated them in 1945. And yet, these were the lucky few—the few who survived. BELOW: the camp at Dachau, where at least 40,000 people died, more than 80 percent of them Jews. Today, part of the camp serves as a memorial and museum.

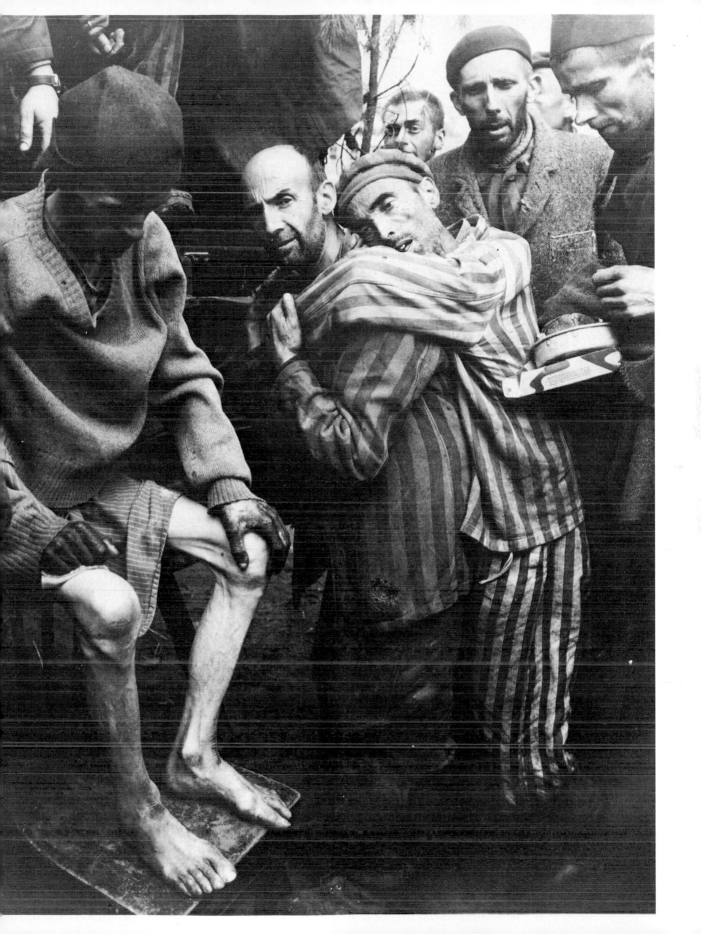

ashes of cremated Jews were used as fertilizer, as chemical raw materials, even as part of a flourishing side business in which urns packed with what purported to be the ashes of the deceased (but which in reality were filled at random from the ash heap) were sent to grieving relatives and friends. Nor could any enterprise be complete without the banquet at which the eager workers were congratulated for a job well done. Such, at least, is the impression conveyed by the deposition of Kurt Gerstein, who was German supervisor of sanitation at the Belzec death camp:

Then, in our honor, a banquet was held. . . . Obersturmbannführer Professor Doctor Pfannestiel, Professor of Hygiene at the University of Marburg/Lahn, made a speech: "Your work is a great work and a very useful and very necessary duty." To me, he spoke of the establishment [Treblinka] as "a kindness and a humanitarian thing." To all present, he said, "When one sees the bodies of the Jews, one understands the greatness of your work!"

At the business of death, the Nazis and their collaborators were astonishingly efficient—so efficient, in fact, that during the last stages of World War II, with the Allies on the attack and the Russian front going badly, the Nazis committed themselves to launching the "Final Solution" (Endlösung), the ultimate phase of their war against the Jews, even at the expense of their global war effort. It is estimated that of 3.3 million Jews in Poland in 1942, on the eve of the Final Solution, fully 3 million, or about 90 percent, were exterminated. Similar percentages hold for the Baltic countries and for Austria and Hungary; but even in the occupied Netherlands, where Jewish roots ran deep and the population was by and large sympathetic to the plight of the Jews, fully 75 percent of all Jews were deported to their deaths.

Some readers may be wondering whether all this really happened. Perhaps they feel, like those who in the early 1940s first greeted with disbelief the reports of mass murder, that tales so nightmarish must be exaggerations, that nothing so horrible could really be true. The fact is that few events in human history have been so exhaustively documented or fully researched. Hundreds, perhaps thousands, of books and articles have been published on the subject, and the painstaking task of studying the Holocaust goes on at the YIVO Institute for Jewish Research, in New York City; at the Yad Vashem Martyrs' and Heroes' Memorial Authority and at the Central Archives for the History of the Jewish People, both in Jerusalem; at the Centre de Documentation Juive Contemporaine, in Paris; and at numerous other archives and research institutes in Israel, Europe, and the United States. And those who directed and perpetrated the atrocities are still being discovered. The most sensational case was that of Adolf Eichmann (1906–1962), the Nazi official who supervised the Final Solution. Found by Israeli agents in Argentina in 1960, he was brought to Israel, where he was tried and executed for crimes against humanity in general and the Jewish people in particular. As recently as 1983, Klaus Barbie, the Nazi "butcher of Lyons," was extradited from Bolivia (where he had been living since 1951) to France for trial.

THE HOLOCAUST AND THE GENTILE WORLD

A Western thinker has written, "Those who do not remember the past are doomed to repeat it." The question is whether memory is enough to avoid repetition. Here the Jewish experience has its own particularity. No other family of the human race has ever been such a constant target for hatred, violence, and defamation. Yet in the larger historic perspective, the Jewish anguish is a metaphor for the entire human condition.

A group of Jews, including a small boy, being removed from the Warsaw Ghetto by armed German soldiers in 1943. It was the Warsaw Ghetto that had put up the first armed Jewish resistance to the Nazi tyranny. This picture, regarded as one of the classic photographs of World War II, was introduced as evidence at the War Crimes trials that were held at Nürnberg in 1945.

What is it that the Holocaust teaches the human race as a whole? It teaches, first of all, that any attempt to classify people by race or creed or color into superior and inferior beings is bound to end in doom and disaster for them all. The modern international concern, such as it is, for human rights and fundamental freedoms, for decolonization and equal status in society, is largely a traumatic response to the disaster of the Holocaust.

The Holocaust also teaches us that suffering does not automatically generate solidarity. There is always the cry: "Well, it hasn't happened to *me*." This predicament was poignantly stated by the great Protestant theologian Martin Niemöller, himself a victim of the Nazis. He said, "When the Nazis went after the Jews, I was not a Jew, so I did not react. When they persecuted the Catholics, I was not a Catholic, so I did not move. When they went after the workers, I was not a worker, so I did not stand up. When they went after the Protestant clergy, I moved, I reacted, I stood up, but by then it was too late."

A third lesson of the Holocaust is that we should not put blind trust in scientific rationalism. The Germany of the 1930s was rich in scientific and technological achievement, but in the absence of an enlarging moral and human dimension, science and technology can be put to the service of systematic slaughter, not of human welfare.

Survival is one of the mysterious lessons of this tragic era. There are islands of escape and alleviation even in the most traumatic conditions of siege. If old doors were closing —with devastating impact—new doors were about to open, with equally unprecedented effect. The toll exacted by the Holocaust was so vast, and the response of the Allied powers to the refugees' plight so inadequate, that we tend to overlook the hundreds of thousands of refugees who did escape Nazi Germany, largely through the efforts of international Jewish organizations. One group alone, Youth Aliyah, rescued more than 10,000 children from certain death in Europe and resettled them in Palestine. Of approximately 811,000 Jewish refugees absorbed by various states between 1933 and 1943, 190,000 went to America, 120,000 to Palestine, and 65,000 to England. Most of the brightest lights of Jewish intellectual life did make their escape—Einstein and Schoenberg (and countless other musicians) to the United States, Freud to England, the eminent philosopher Martin Buber (1878–1965) to Jerusalem. Unhappily, what this diaspora of the intellectuals did not include was the Jewish masses of Eastern Europe, who lacked the money and the connections to escape, or who were not yet aware of the enormity of the peril they faced.

Nor can we fail to note the thousands of Jews who were saved from extermination by "righteous Gentiles," those who at the risk of their own lives acted out of a common bond of compassionate humanity. Distinguished among these was the Swedish diplomat Raoul Wallenberg (b. 1912), through whose good offices hundreds, perhaps thousands, of Hungarian Jews were saved; what happened to him after he presented himself to Soviet occupying forces in Budapest is one of the great unresolved mysteries of World War II. Special mention should also be made of the Danish underground, which in 1943 smuggled some 7,000 Jews out of Nazi-occupied Denmark to safety in Sweden. Danish, Dutch, and Polish resistance groups have all been honored, along with some 600 individuals, by the State of Israel at Yad Vashem, the Martyrs' and Heroes' Memorial, as among the "high-minded righteous who risked their lives to save Jews."

The most positive force to rise from the ashes of the Holocaust was the "new Jew"— the Jew who would no longer passively accept his fate, the Jew who would fight to survive, who would trade blow for blow with his oppressors. Within Eastern Europe the

Dit is een foto, zoals
ik me zou wensen,
altijd zo te zijn.
Dan had ik nog wel
een kans om naar
Holywood te komen.
Anne Frank.
10 Oct. 1942

Anne Frank, whose famous Diary portrayed a young girl's feelings while living in hiding in Nazi-occupied Amsterdam during World War II. The inscription, in her own writing: "This is a photo as I would wish myself to look all the time. Then I would maybe have a chance to come to Hollywood. Anne Frank, 10 Oct. 1942."

outstanding example of this new Jewish attitude was the Warsaw Ghetto uprising, although it must be said that this heroic insurrection—mounted by Jews who, hearing of the fate that awaited them at Treblinka, refused to collaborate any longer in their own extermination—was of greater symbolic than practical import, since no more than a few dozen Germans were killed in the fighting. There were, in fact, sporadic uprisings and acts of sabotage in many of the death camps, including Auschwitz, and Jews played valuable roles in whatever partisan resistance groups were willing to accept them.

The place where the "new Jew" was most clearly emerging was in Palestine. Here the Jewish population had grown from 78,000 in 1900 to 475,000 in 1939; the Jewish share of the total had increased from 12 percent to 33 percent—a proportion that would have risen still higher had not the British government, responding to Arab pressures, imposed through its "White Paper" of 1939 strict quotas on further Jewish immigration and an absolute ban on land sales to Jews. In the meantime, under the mandate, the *yishuv* was rapidly developing its basic cultural, educational, and welfare institutions, and although immigrants of European origin

dominated the *yishuv*'s political life, a new generation of native-born Israelis, or *sabras*, was beginning to make its presence felt. Since 1920 there had been an underground defense force, the Haganah. Now these Jews in arms, the first Jewish fighting force in the Holy Land in more than 1,800 years, faced a threefold struggle: to protect Jewish settlements against Arab assaults; to fight with the Allies at Britain's side; and to frustrate Britain's policy for Palestine, which was antagonistic to Jewish interests, and defy the authority of the British colonial regime in preparation for independence in a Jewish homeland.

Palestinian Jewry was now asserting its claim to one of the central positions in the Jewish historic process. In the two decades between the World Wars, Zionism had nei-ther squandered its opportunities nor fully used them. By 1945 the National Home had a Jewish population of about 600,000. Its economic and technological levels were spectacular by Middle Eastern standards, but well below the European average. Nevertheless, it was a source of pride to the Jewish people and for the world a fascinating and original spectacle. Here and only here Jews faced history in their own authentic image. They were not a marginal gloss on other societies. The national attributes were all reflected on a miniature scale but in growing completeness. The salient feature of this society was its Hebrew character. The ancient language, expanded and renewed, was not only the vernacular and mother tongue of a newborn Jewish generation; it was also the vehicle of an impressive literary movement. More than

FAR LEFT: *U.S. Infantry reinforcements debarking from landing craft off the Allied beachhead on the Normandy coast a week after D-Day, June 6, 1944;* LEFT: *a mushroom cloud, now the dreaded symbol of the Atomic Age, here in a test explosion in the Pacific; and the "unbelievable" devastation wrought on Hiroshima, Japan, when the first atomic bomb was dropped, August 6, 1945.*

anything else, it gave individual form and color to the nascent community. It was also a link with a universally revered past. In order to be itself, a Jewish national society had to be different from everything else. The driving force was a quest for identity. An intense solidarity inspired its life and conduct. Its ideals and priorities were collective, not individual. What mattered was a man's service to the growing nation, not his prowess in self-advancement. Palestine Jewry had a Utopian outlook and was gripped by a profoundly moral preoccupation. Life was earnest, austere, responsible, resolute, effervescent, somewhat irrational, and, to strangers, a little ponderous and self-conscious. Every first tree, road, street, settlement, school, library, orchestra, university, was ecstatically celebrated. The Jews lived, at last, with the unique taste of national creativity. . . .

For above its other achievements was the *yishuv*'s talent for autonomy. The ties with the British administration remained formal and tenuous, and the *yishuv* had no prospect of any intimate commingling with the Arab environment. It had built a wall around itself for protection against external hostility and internal corrosion. It was very nearly a national state in miniature. It largely administered its own agriculture, industry, education, and social welfare. It commanded its own labor organization. Defense and foreign policy are usually the last prerogatives that a community attains in the pursuit of its sovereignty. But even here the *yishuv* was be-coming increasingly independent. A citizen army was under its control, and its leading representatives, Weizmann, Ben-Gurion, and Moshe Sharett, were accepted and admired in the international diplomatic community as representatives of an entity that was a state in all but name. When its opportunity came a few years after the war, it was well advanced along its destined journey.

CONCLUSION

This chapter ends with one of the most revolutionary events in Jewish history. Israel's flag first went up on May 14, 1948, the day when David Ben-Gurion proclaimed the nation's independence. A year later, it had become the fifty-ninth flag in the United Nations. The world, which had witnessed the birth and death of many nations, now for the only time beheld a resurrection. Israel had resumed its place in political history.

We must remember that for most of 2,000 years, Jewish history had consisted very largely of what Jews suffered, endured, resisted, overcame, not of what Jews themselves fashioned, decided, and resolved. The keynote had been passivity. Now, at last, Jewish decisions were able to levy taxes, create institutions, move armies, and open the gates of freedom to hundreds of thousands of kinsmen, far and near. It was a moment that would linger and shine in the national memory forever, a moment of truth that would at last move Israel to its ultimate generations.

Two women who lived through three years at Auschwitz meet after thirty-five years at a reunion of 5,000 Holocaust survivors in Israel in 1981. Tattooed on their arms are their concentration camp numbers, records as alive and as indelible as their memories of the horrors they endured.

Jerusalem Landscape, a canvas painted in 1928 by Israel Paldi (1892–1979), who was born in the Ukraine and emigrated to Palestine in 1909.

T HE JEWS as a people have been part of the great currents of world history for 3,000 years. Their view of human destiny is long and penetrating. Having struggled arduously to preserve their existence and identity, they are not likely to accept submergence or to disappear. Yet marks of interrogation still hover over their future.

Eighty percent of the Jews alive today live in three countries—the United States, Israel, and the Soviet Union. In the early 1970s, Soviet Jewry, with powerful international aid, breached the wall of enforced isolation around them, and more than 150,000 migrated to Israel and North America. Nothing comparable has ever been achieved by any other body of Soviet citizens. But with the replacement of détente by tension and cold war, the Soviets have shown less interest in burnishing their own image for Western governments and peoples, and their incentive for flexibility in their attitude toward Soviet Jews has waned. Will the Jews in the Soviet Union continue to battle for cultural freedom and the hope of exit, or will they accept their condition as best they can?

There is a dilemma for American Jewry as well. Much of the resilience that marks the Jewish talent for separate identity has blossomed as a response to external challenge. Some historians even doubt that any group can long maintain its cohesion without the spur of danger. The challenge for American Jewry is whether it can survive when no one is attempting to prevent its survival. In this paradox much depends on the use that American Jews make of the pluralism of American society. Will they use it the easy way—to abandon their separate identity? Or

12· Israel and World Jewry: The Modern Age

The golden Dome of the Rock, which was built by Muslims on the site where they believe Muhammad ascended to heaven and where the Temple of Solomon may have stood, fittingly symbolizes the rich religious heritage of Jerusalem, now a united city under the State of Israel.

will they build a distinctive civilization within the broad scope of American experience?

It might seem that Israel's choice is the easiest of all. One of the aims of Zionism was to make Jews in their homeland more confident of their identity than Jews elsewhere had ever been. Citizens of a sovereign nation do not usually awaken every morning and ask themselves who exactly they are. On the surface it seems that Israel has solved the problem of Jewish identity. There is sovereignty, statehood, land beneath the foot, and the na-

tion's flag flying reassuringly above. But can Israel really assure its vocation on the basis of national autarchy without the sustaining force of worldwide Jewish solidarity? A predominant part of the material and intellectual resources of the Jewish people still lies outside Israel. Can Israel develop the sort of magnetism that will bring a greater proportion of the total Jewish strength within its own gates? The paradox of the future is that Israel's most intricate and sensitive relationship may come to be not with the Arab world or the international community but with the Jews—that is, in a deeper sense, with its own self.

Whatever may happen, the Jews carry with them a unique asset—a vivid consciousness of their past. In the words of the Western theologian Kierkegaard, "life must be lived forward but can only be understood

The young and (by his own testimony) not very successful farmer standing in the front row center is David Ben-Gurion, shown in a photograph taken at the Rishon le-Zion settlement in 1906. Ben-Gurion became the first prime minister of independent Israel more than four decades later.

backward." When all is said and done and written, the greatest wonder is that the Jews are still here. Battered by every tempest, afflicted by every ordeal, sometimes appearing to be crushed by the weight of a tragic destiny—here they still are, always resilient, never defeated, a people whose future may be as long as its past.

ISRAEL: THE FIRST FOUR DECADES

Few events in human history have seemed so startlingly improbable as the rebirth of Israel. On a patch of land no more than 200 miles (320 km) long and 100 miles (160 km) wide at its broadest point, a people now numbering only a few million out of all the world's billions has, 3,000 years after the Kingdom of David, nineteen centuries after the devastation of Jerusalem by Rome, reestablished its home in the land where it was born and from which it was largely separated for thousands of years. This was achieved against every calculation of chance. The land was barren, despoiled of its ancient fertility, the people dispersed and enfeebled by the recent Holocaust, its national aims resisted with fierce obduracy by the Arab world and cruelly frustrated by British antagonism. This was the lowest point in the modern history of the Jewish people, when many must have wondered if an end had come to its time on history's stage. How could it summon the energies and hope necessary for its own recovery? Yet within a few years of its darkest days, the Jewish people would see its flag planted in the family of nations from which it had been absent for so many tragic epochs. Warm waves of pride would flow in every home across the world in which the traditions of the Jewish people were cherished. Never was this people stronger than in its moment of weakness, never more hopeful than in its moment of despair.

Ben-Gurion in his library at Sedeh Boker, a kibbutz in the heart of the Negev Desert.

Little of this could have been foreseen when the curtain went up after World War I on a European continent saturated with Jewish blood. During the years of World War II, Jews had confidently believed that the defeat of the Nazis and their collaborators would herald a new era of fulfillment. They had placed their hopes in Churchill and Roosevelt, who had promised Chaim Weizmann to protect the interests of the afflicted Jewish people when victory was won. Neither of them had supported the repressive policy whereby the British government of Neville Chamberlain had decided in 1939 to restrict the development of the Jewish National Home by cruel limitation of the right of Jews to immigrate to Palestine and to purchase land in the greater part of the country. This terrible blow to Jewish hopes had coincided with the intensification of Nazi persecution in Germany. The world would soon come to be divided between lands in which Jews could not live and lands to which they could

מולדת

חרות

During the 1940s, Menachem Begin (b. 1913) directed the Irgun Zvai Leumi, which used violent tactics to fight the British. After nearly three decades as an opposition leader in the Knesset, Begin served as Israel's prime minister, 1977–1983.

not go. Even the United States and Britain were closing their doors to refugees, and conferences on the "refugee problem" held in Evian, France, and Bermuda ended in almost total futility. The aim of Britain and France was not to resist Hitlerism but to "appease" the Nazi regime by acceding to some of its aggressive claims. When the Western powers betrayed Czechoslovakia in 1938 by handing it over to Hitler's "mercy," Chaim Weizmann predicted that the same thing would happen to the Jews. He uttered this gloomy prophecy to Jan Masaryk, the foreign

minister of Czechoslovakia and son of the lib-
erator-president Thomas Masaryk, who had
gone to London to stimulate British resistance to Nazi aggression. The world in which
the Jews and other small peoples had gained
recognition of their national rights in the
aftermath of World War I was dying fast.

The anti-Zionist policy of the British government in the late 1930s was expressed in
the White Paper of 1939, which was a black
document for the Jews. David Ben-Gurion,
the leader of the Labor Zionist movement,
spoke in militant response for the Jews of
Palestine:

It is in the darkest hour of Jewish history that
the British government proposes to deprive
the Jews of their last hope, and to close the
road back to their homeland. It is a cruel
blow; doubly cruel because it comes from the
government of a great nation that has extended a helping hand to Jews and whose
position in the world rests upon foundations
of moral authority and good faith. This blow
will not subdue the Jewish people. The historic bond between the people and the land
of Israel will not be broken. The Jews will
never accept the closing against them of the
gates of Palestine, nor let their national home
be turned into a ghetto. Jewish pioneers,
who in the past three generations have
shown their strength in the upbuilding of a
derelict country, will from now on display
the same strength in defending Jewish immigration, the Jewish hope and Jewish freedom.

But Palestine Jewry was heavily outnumbered by the Arabs and could not match the
power of the British administration with its
huge garrison force. Worse, it found itself
ambivalent toward this adversary. Britain
had been the ally of the Jews against Hitlerism once the war had erupted in September
1939; but in Palestine, Britain was the oppressive ruler who had to be resisted.

The idea of a "Jewish revolt" had been lost
to history since the days of Bar Kokhba: Dias-

*Chaim Weizmann, long the leader and chief
spokesman of the Zionist movement, and Israel's
first president until his death in 1952.*

pora life allowed no such idea. All that Jews
could do was to protest, bemoan, and seek
protectors. But the uprising of the Jews of
Palestine from the late 1930s onward was national in character, and its method and mood
belonged to the anticolonialism that was to
become more widespread and familiar after
the war. A Jewish self-defense movement
called Hashomer had accompanied the struggle for survival of the early pioneers. The
Labor Zionist movement had discovered that
if the pioneers were to be pacifists, their life
in the land of Israel would be very brief. Out
of the Hashomer had sprung the Haganah
organization of self-defense. This was a secret organization about which everybody, including the British authorities, knew all the
"secrets." It embraced the entire manhood of
Palestine Jewry, was firmly under the authority of the Labor party leaders, and would
become the central source out of which the

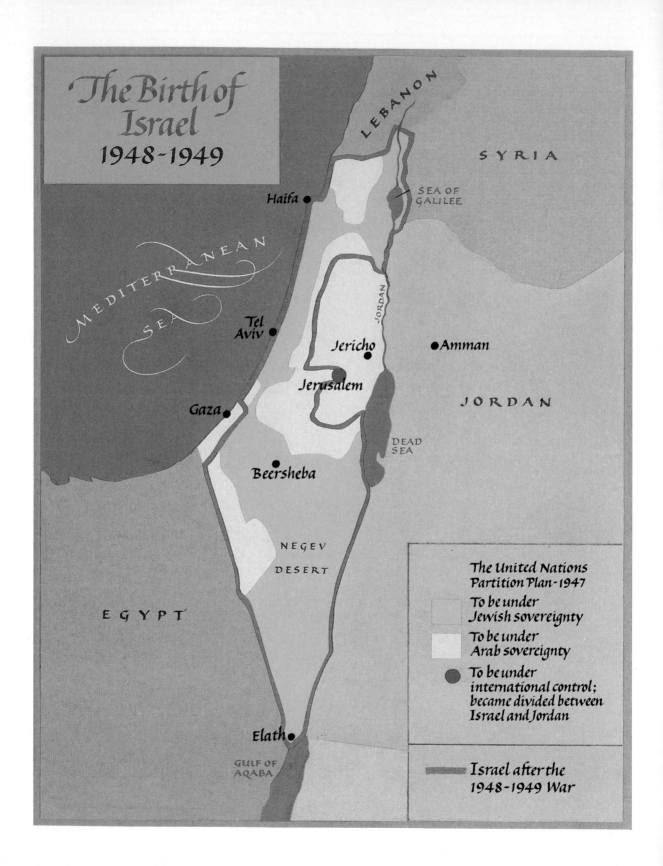

The Birth of
Israel
1948-1949

LEBANON

SYRIA

Haifa ●

SEA OF
GALILEE

MEDITERRANEAN
SEA

Tel
Aviv ●

JORDAN

Jericho ●

● Amman

Jerusalem

Gaza ●

JORDAN

DEAD
SEA

Beersheba ●

NEGEV

DESERT

EGYPT

The United Nations
Partition Plan-1947

To be under
Jewish sovereignty

To be under
Arab sovereignty

● To be under
international control;
became divided between
Israel and Jordan

Elath ●

GULF OF
AQABA

Israel after the
1948-1949 War

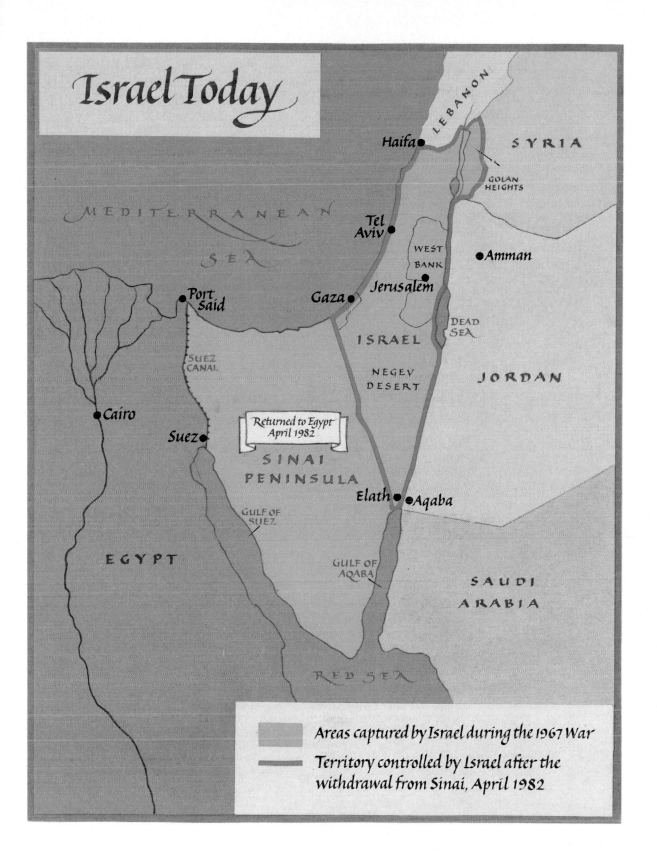

Israel Today

MEDITERRANEAN SEA

LEBANON

SYRIA

Haifa

GOLAN HEIGHTS

Tel Aviv

WEST BANK

Amman

Jerusalem

Gaza

DEAD SEA

ISRAEL

JORDAN

NEGEV DESERT

Port Said

SUEZ CANAL

Returned to Egypt April 1982

Cairo

Suez

SINAI PENINSULA

Elath

Aqaba

GULF OF SUEZ

EGYPT

GULF OF AQABA

SAUDI ARABIA

RED SEA

Areas captured by Israel during the 1967 War

Territory controlled by Israel after the withdrawal from Sinai, April 1982

Israeli Defense Forces would grow when statehood was proclaimed in 1948. The War of Independence would be fought by 50,000 members of the Labor Haganah, 2,000 members of Menachem Begin's Irgun Zvai Leumi (National Military Organization), and a few hundred members of the Israel Freedom Fighters (Lechi), known to the British as the Stern Gang. But the Irgun's technique consisted mainly of individual assaults and guerrilla-type raids. The dramatic nature of its exploits, such as the blowing up of the King David Hotel in Jerusalem—with great loss of civilian life, Arab, Jewish, and British—made headlines out of all proportion to the marginal benefits achieved.

Although Arab hostility to the Zionist program had been anticipated, the need to engage the British government in armed conflict came as an unpleasant surprise. When the war ended, Churchill had been defeated and Roosevelt had died. The British Labour party had promised a lavish fulfillment of Zionist aims when in opposition, but having attained office and come face to face with British interests in the Arab world, it proceeded to an astonishingly severe and callous repression of Palestine Jewry. The Labour Foreign Secretary, Ernest Bevin, warned the Jewish victims of the Nazi Holocaust "not to push to the head of the line" in seeking relief for their plight. He summoned them to "take part in the reconstruction of Europe"—the continent that had been their slaughterhouse and torture chamber. He taunted President Harry S Truman, who had urged the immediate admission of 100,000 Jews to Palestine, with wanting to "avoid letting them into New York." When a refugee ship crowded with fugitives from the death camps reached Haifa harbor, Bevin had the British troops turn hoses on them and ordered them sent back to Germany. The brutal vulgarity of these measures seemed foreign to British traditions and to the special style of the British Labour movement, but Bevin was

clearly being impelled by an intense rancor beyond anything that his country's interests demanded. A UN commission that was working in Israel when the deportation to Germany was enacted reached the conclusion that if the gallows and the policeman's club were the only way in which British rule could be perpetuated, it would be better not to perpetuate it at all.

In these conditions of depression sometimes verging on despair, the Jewish leaders and populations in free countries embarked on a diplomatic enterprise without parallel in Jewish history. The aim was to secure an international judgment in favor of Jewish statehood once the British mandate came to an end. The opportunity presented itself when the British government, harassed by the drain on its resources and weight on its conscience arising from what Winston Churchill called "a squalid war," submitted the future of Palestine to the judgment of the United Nations General Assembly. One of the most moving and dramatic chapters in modern Jewish history was now enacted on the international scene. In April 1947, the Soviet Union, represented by its UN delegate Andrei Gromyko, shocked the Arabs and exhilarated the Jews by supporting the idea of a Jewish state in a part of Palestine. And on November 29, 1947, the UN General Assembly voted by 33 against 13, with 11 abstentions, for the establishment of a Jewish state in a partitioned Palestine, side by side with an Arab state and linked by an economic union that would ensure a large measure of integration and accessibility. This astonishing change in Jewish fortunes elicited a violent response from the Arab states, which sent their armies into Palestine to overthrow the nascent Jewish state by force. Although afflicted by heavy loss—more than 6,000 dead of a population of 650,000—the Jews of Palestine held their ground and proclaimed their statehood in Tel Aviv on May 14, 1948.

It was a moment of climax in the Jewish

David Ben-Gurion reads the proclamation of independence, May 14, 1948

The Zionist movement fought the British closed-door policy in Palestine not only with arms but with diplomatic pressure. This photograph, taken in 1945, shows former U.S. servicemen picketing the office of the British consul in Chicago.

Jubilant at the passage of the partition plan that will make a Jewish state a reality, Jews in Tel Aviv carry a British soldier on their shoulders in celebration.

In this scene, typical of Israel in 1948, a tractor driver bears a rifle on his shoulder as he works to reclaim the soil and defend his new homeland simultaneously. What is less typical is his agricultural settlement—a kibbutz named Buchenwald, for the infamous German concentration camp which ninety of the settlement's members survived.

story. Much of Jewish history had consisted of what Jews had suffered, endured, resisted, and overcome, but not of what Jews themselves resolved and accomplished. Now, for the first time, Jewish decisions would be able to raise armies, to levy taxes, to open gates to kinsmen, and to build a coherent national society. It was a moment that would linger and shine in the Jewish memory, a moment of truth that would move all Israel to its ultimate generations.

Nearly nineteen centuries had passed between the loss of Israel's independence in 70 C.E. and its restoration on the night of May 14, 1948. The emotion of the world on the morning of this renewal was partly clouded by the tensions of the war. But it was also enlarged by vistas of memory. Nothing in history was comparable to the resurgence of a people in a land from which so many centuries had kept it apart. The bond between the people and the distant land, long preserved in dreams and prayers, was now becoming a part of the world's tangible reality. A world that had seen the birth and death of many nations now, for the only time, beheld

a resurrection. Hundreds of thousands in Israel and millions across the world went to sleep that night with a sense of being larger and prouder than they had been at dawn. But amid the popular joy, there was still a sense that nothing was yet fully secure. Before the sounds of Jewish exhilaration had died away, the Arab armies were on the move. Many in the world believed that Israel had scored a short-term triumph. It was now holding the joy of birth and the fear of death within a single taste.

The first two decades after independence would bring war, hostility and siege. But within the siege there would be a great eruption of creativity. A million Jews from dozens of lands would join the 650,000 Israelis who had laid the foundations of the state. They would bring with them a great diversity of skills, devotions, experiences, and talents. Hundreds of cooperative villages and collective farms would spread a green carpet over the expanding landscape. New cities, schools, universities—above all, thousands of homes—would give Israeli society a new breadth and a new solidity.

By land, air, and sea, Jewish refugees from Europe, North Africa, and the Middle East—hundreds of thousands of them—flooded into Israel. These immigrants are coming from Cyprus, where the British detained more than 50,000 Jewish refugees between 1946 and 1948.

The mark of imperfection is written on all human achievement, and it is inscribed on Israel's as well. Not every goal was achieved, not every standard fulfilled. But in the broad perspective of history, Israelis at the end of two decades could face mankind in a posture of confidence. They could say: "We have not disappointed all your hopes. We have renewed our nation's pride. We have given the Jewish people a new sense of its collective creativity. We have given beauty and life to some of mankind's most cherished but most neglected landscapes. We have vindicated democracy as the highest expression of man's social personality. We have made some communication to the world of dynamism, intellectual progress, social originality, and recuperative power. Above all, we

Because housing was insufficient to meet the immigrants' needs, temporary "tent cities" (maabarot) sprang up throughout the nation. Within a decade the tents had been replaced by permanent dwellings.

Gamal Abdel Nasser, president of Egypt during the 1956 and 1967 conflicts with Israel.

If Israeli public life during the 1950s was dominated by the figure of Ben-Gurion, the 1960s brought new leaders to the forefront. ABOVE: *Golda Meir (1898–1978), prime minister from 1969 to 1974.*

Levi Eshkol (1895–1969), finance minister under David Ben-Gurion and then prime minister from 1963 until his death.

Moshe Dayan (1915–1981), foreign minister under Menachem Begin but best known as a military man who fought against the British, ran operations against Egypt during the Sinai war of 1956. As minister of defense in 1967, Dayan became a popular hero of the Six-Day War.

have fulfilled our human vocation; we have brought hundreds of thousands of our kinsmen from the depths of peril and despair into the emergence of a new life and a new hope. This is a great and noble adventure." Those two decades would live on and on, deep in the mind and heart of the nation, as long as any memory of the past endured.

There was much in which the Israeli of the mid-1960s could take justifiable pride. First and foremost, the new nation, freed from the restrictions of British mandatory rule, had thrown open its doors to all Jews who wished to return to their ancestral homeland. And the immigrants came—101,819 from Independence Day to the end of 1948, 239,076 in 1949, 169,405 in 1950, 173,901 in 1951, and another 550,000 during the next fifteen years. Between 1950 and 1970, the nation's Jewish population more than doubled, from about 1,203,000 to 2,582,000. Immigration was not the sole source of this increase; during the

Israeli Foreign Minister Abba Eban makes a case for Israel before the UN Security Council during the Six-Day War. RIGHT: a group of Israeli soldiers, having conquered the Jordanian half of Jerusalem, gaze in wonderment at the Western (Wailing) Wall, the last surviving stones of what had been Herod's Temple.

same period, the proportion of native-born Israelis increased from 26.3 percent to 45.8 percent. A source of special pride was the rescue of Jews not only from the displaced persons' camps in Europe but also from ancient but now threatened communities throughout the Middle East and North Africa. An estimated 121,500 Iraqi Jews were resettled in Israel through Operation Ezra and Nehemiah, and some 45,200 Yemenite Jews were rescued through Operation Magic Carpet. Tens of thousands of Jews also brought their distinctive skills and traditions from Iran, Egypt, Libya, Tunisia, and Morocco. The "tent cities" that sprang up in the early 1950s were a positive sign that the great ingathering had taken vast dimensions; within a decade the elimination of the tents and their replacement by permanent buildings would complete the saga. The absorption of this great immigrant flood in the first

years of independence must rank as one of the most resourceful and dynamic enterprises undertaken by Jews since the beginning of their history. So too must the verdict be drawn on the hundreds of new townships and villages, farms and factories, that spread themselves with remarkable speed across the land. A new social and human reality had entered history, and its creative energies, so long pent up, would erupt in an exuberant burst of pride.

There was one large cloud that brooded over these successes; it was the lack of any affirmative relationship with the neighboring Arab world. There was more fighting than negotiation in the first two decades, and Israel always emerged victorious. Yet along with victory came the consciousness that Israel was still marked by vulnerability. In 1956 its armies broke out of siege to strike at the armies of the Egyptian leader Gamal Abdel

Nasser, who had tightened his blockade of Israel-bound shipping in the Suez Canal and the Strait of Tiran. A graver peril was the fact that Egypt had been lavishly equipped by the Soviet Union with armaments of a higher technical quality than had been made available to Israel by its friends. The Israeli action was synchronized with an assault on the Suez Canal by the armies of Britain and France, whose position in the Mediterranean was being threatened by Nasser's defiance. This alliance was less popular than an isolated and single Israeli action would have been, for Israel's predicament was coming to bear on world opinion, while the Anglo-French action struck no idealistic chords anywhere. As a result of arrangements obtained by Israel in return for a withdrawal from Sinai, the Strait of Tiran remained open for eleven years, after which it was successfully closed for a brief time in May 1967; and for those eleven years Israel's southern regions were free from assault from Gaza, where a United Nations force had replaced the Egyptian army. There followed Israel's most dynamic decade, in which a pipeline from Eilat brought oil from Iran to the Israeli Mediterranean coast, the national water carrier distributed water from the north to the parched Negev, Israel forged strong links with scores of countries in the awakening continents of Africa and Asia, and tens of thousands of Jews reached Israel from Europe and North Africa.

It was probably the very spectacle of Israel's consolidation that inspired Nasser with an ambition to seek a showdown with Israel before it was too late. There was a hint of "now or never." But the assault, while sending some initial reactions of fear into a beleaguered Israel, came to an inglorious end. In six days Israel passed from a sensation of being menaced with destruction by a fierce and united Arab world, to the reality of total military supremacy and political triumph. Israel now held 26,500 square miles of territory

previously in Arab hands—in the Golan Heights, in Sinai, in the Gaza Strip, and in Judea and Samaria on the West Bank of the Jordan. A few weeks later it would become evident that on this occasion the Arabs, even with Soviet support, would not be able to recover their losses by diplomatic pressure without offering peace.

Nineteen sixty-seven was Israel's unforgettable summer. After six days of fighting, Israel's population centers were separated from hostile armies by a belt of territory three times as great as Israel had been before. Israel had withstood a heavy diplomatic assault. Its network of international relations reached into all the continents of the world. The Jewish diaspora, which had been shocked by what seemed to be the prospect of Israel's annihilation, increased its solidarity and support. In the territories newly brought under Israeli administration, there was a deep-seated conflict but also a surprisingly large area of day-to-day tranquility. There was discomfort in Israel about the idea of ruling a foreign people. But in the policy and doctrine of Israel, this was regarded as a temporary paradox that would somehow be resolved in the context of peace.

At first sight, there was every reason for ease in Zion. But the very sensation of greater security encouraged Israelis to turn their eyes inward on themselves. *To be or not to be* was not the question. How to be and how not to be—*that* was the question. It related not to the fact of existence but to the nature and quality of society. There was now a tendency for the Israelis to ask themselves searching questions, many of which would reverberate across the ensuing decades. How should Israel seek to reconcile its security with its wish not to dominate another nation? How should Israel close the gaps that seemed to threaten the national cohesion: the gap between the settled population and immigrants, the gap between immigrants from Western countries and immigrants from Oriental lands, the gap between the new opulent classes and those who dwelt in slums? And there was also the generation gap: the gap between the founding fathers and the new, rising generation that had not known the trauma of the Holocaust or the exultation of Israel's struggle for independence.

As if these matters were not sufficient cause for concern, the 1970s and 1980s brought vexing new questions. To what extent were the goals of a consumer society compatible with Israel's economic and military position and its military needs? Could the tactic of trading land for peace, employed with Sinai and Egypt in the late 1970s, be applied to other lands captured in the 1967 war? By what steps not yet taken could Israel come to terms with Palestinian aspirations, which were bound to affect the Arabs living as full citizens of Israel as well as those living within or outside the borders of the administered territories? There was also unease over the matter of American influence, both the intellectual and financial power of American Jewry and the great leverage of the United States government, which between 1946 and 1984 provided Israel with more than $10 billion in economic development assistance and nearly $16 billion in official military loans and grants. At what point did a true partnership of two great democracies become an unhealthy dependence of the weaker nation on the stronger? New questions—and divisions—were raised by the invasion of Lebanon in the summer of 1982. Had Israel, schooled in war after war to look to the military as its instrument of national survival, come to rely on armed force not as a last resort but as too ready a substitute for diplomatic effort?

The outside world looked with respect upon this new Israeli self-appraisal. It was not regarded as a sign of weakness or decline. On the contrary, it was accepted as a sign of greater maturity. Sometimes, in the pain of bereavement or in the toll of constant stress, Israelis would ask themselves what had been gained by all their sacrifice and resistance. And then the answer came back loud and strong: "What have we gained? Everything that we would have lost without it—life, home, honor, purpose, and the special destiny that our fathers have conserved and that this generation has been able to renew." Israelis could say with qualified pride that they had not betrayed their triple trust: to safeguard the interests of the Jewish people, to guarantee its legacy, to ensure its future.

YOM KIPPUR 1973 AND THEREAFTER

The 1967 war had ensured Israel's survival, but it had not accorded Israel the gift of peace. The question was whether the Arab states would succeed in restoring their former territorial situation without a peace settlement or whether Israel would be able to trade territory for peace and thus escape the somber destiny of continual war. The Arab world was to make one further effort to achieve its aims by war. When Egyptian armies fell upon Israeli forces in Sinai with a deadly surprise effect on the Day of Atonement in 1973, while Syrian columns advanced against Israeli positions in the Golan Heights, Israel's self-confidence was suddenly deflated. The first days of the war witnessed dangerous losses of Israeli tanks and aircraft; there were apocalyptic visions of defeat, followed by a spectacular recovery that brought Israeli forces within 62 miles (100 km) of Cairo and 25 miles (40 km) of Damascus.

It was the traumatic effect that the war had on Egypt and on Israel alike that led to the breakthrough toward peace. After a series of disengagement agreements skillfully negotiated by Secretary of State Henry Kissinger of the United States, President Anwar Sadat of Egypt made an audacious journey to Jerusalem in November 1977, where he announced to an astonished world that his country was abandoning the doctrine of Israel's illegitimacy and would give Israel peace in return for Sinai and a promise of eventual peace for the Palestinians. President Jimmy Carter of the United States assiduously followed up with a mediatory effort at Camp David, Maryland, which culminated in the signature of a peace treaty in March 1979 by Israeli Prime Minister Menachem Begin and President Sadat. It was a momentous event in Israel's history. For the first time there was recognition by an Arab state of Israel's place in the Middle East; and the Arab state concerned was the largest one of all, with a population nearly equal to the combined populations of all the other Arab nations. Peace with Arab neighbors had always been the second Zionist dream, second only to the attainment of independence itself. A combination of obduracy and compromise over the years had brought this vision within view. It remained true that without a settlement with the Palestinian people this victory would not be complete, but a massive assault had been made on the alienation that had separated the two peoples who had written so many central chapters of Middle Eastern history.

It would not be easy to complete what Egypt and Israel had begun. The legitimate aim of Israel in the tragic and costly war in Lebanon three years after the peace treaty was to secure Israel's northern regions against the threat of bombardment by PLO mortars and artillery. But 580 Israeli lives were lost in the process—a greater cost than PLO terrorism had inflicted on Israelis in all the decades of independence. The "cure" had evidently been more lethal than the disease. Moreover, Syrian influence became greater than before Israel's intervention. Lebanese anarchy was more intense, Western prestige more eroded, and terrorism in and

from Lebanon no less rampant than before. For the first time Israel had fought a war that most Israelis came to regard as an unsuccessful enterprise. This crisis provoked Prime Minister Begin's resignation and, in 1984, a new election. Yet Israelis had shown resilience in adversity before, and the reflective mood that gripped the country was the strongest guarantee that it would find a fruitful outlet for its considerable energies once again.

Beyond the aftermath of war, Israel faced its most acute dilemma in the continuing rule over 1.3 million Arabs in the territories taken in the 1967 war. Control of these territories would add to Israel's strategic depth. But control of the inhabitants, who had all the attributes of a separate, national entity totally alienated from Israel's flag and legacy, would make Israel different from what it had always aspired to be. It would be a society held together by physical power rather than by voluntary and consensual allegiance. For this very reason, our story ends with the issue still in suspense. While there are those who aspire to perpetuate Israeli control of the heavily populated Arab areas, at least as many would probably welcome a compromise under which Israel's boundaries would be improved to some extent while the heavily populated Arab areas would be free to pursue an Arab destiny in association with Jordan, thus solving the Palestine question in a noncoercive atmosphere. Yet the fact remains that Israel is one of the few countries in the world with a mark of interrogation poised over its dimensions, configuration, and human composition.

The best hope is that the principles that enabled a breakthrough to peace with Egypt will assert themselves in a wider context. Men and nations sometimes behave wisely once they have exhausted the other alternatives. In the Middle East outside the Egyptian-Israeli realtionship, almost every alternative has been tried: wars, sieges,

Egyptian President Anwar al-Sadat, United States President Jimmy Carter, and Israeli Prime Minister Menachem Begin clasp hands at the White House in 1979 following the signing of an Israeli-Egyptian peace treaty.

Yasir Arafat, chairman of the PLO.

blockades, cease-fires, armistices, terrorism, oil embargoes, Great Power pressures, UN resolutions. Peace is the only thing that has not been tried. The road seems open for the adventure of peace.

THE CULTURAL CHALLENGE

After forty years of statehood the contours of Israel's culture are still subject to versatility, paradox, and change. On the one hand, Israel represents the rational, progressivist, modernizing element in Middle Eastern life. There is an intense devotion to scientific rationalism which has had encouraging technological results. It is no usual thing to find a small state in Western Asia exporting air-craft engines, advanced electronic apparatus, and sophisticated chemical products across the world. But Israel is no Esperantist nation writing its history on a clean slate. It is, both in its own consciousness and in that of the world, the lineal descendant of Biblical Israel, using the Hebrew language as the bridge between the old inheritance and the new potentiality. Archaeology is a popular passion among young Israelis. Such discoveries as the Dead Sea Scrolls excited an immense popular emotion. Israel is the story of a people searching restlessly for its own roots, the only people whose continuous historical memory embraces the entire cultural experience of mankind—from Biblical prophecy to atomic science, from the dim roots of man's past to the shining possibilities of his future. The large sweep and variety of Israeli culture contrast with the country's physical smallness. It is a nation small in geography but very large in history.

THE DIASPORA TODAY

By 1982 the Jewish population of the State of Israel was 3,373,200—probably about 25 percent of the world's Jewish population. This means, simply, that more than three decades after the rebirth of the Jewish homeland as a national entity, three out of every four Jews remain in the diaspora. This is not a new phenomenon: probably the overwhelming majority of Jews chose to remain in diaspora after the Babylonian exile, and the phenomenon is also familiar from Roman times. For most Jews outside Israel, the decision to remain in diaspora represents a positive choice. Nearly 6 million Jews live today in the United States or Canada; most of them surely have the means to emigrate to Israel, yet they choose to remain in the land of their birth. There are between 1.7 and 2.7 million Jews living today in the Soviet Union; the economic and political disadvantages of classifying oneself as a Jew have caused the Soviet census to undercount, some demographers believe. Plainly these Soviet Jews, harassed, persecuted, denied the right to build synagogues and print Jewish books, cannot lead fully Jewish lives, and they are not allowed to emigrate except under strictly controlled conditions. The experience of the past decade suggests, however, that of those who do emigrate, 75 percent settle in lands other than Israel, with the United States overwhelmingly the destination of choice.

It is possible to find the same self-examination among American Jews that one finds in Israel. For all the splendid temples and well-equipped Jewish centers, how deep is the American Jew's commitment to Judaism? Have American Jews moved so far into the mainstream of American life that they have lost their essential Jewishness? Is American Jewry static or declining, having lost its dynamism to the self-centered imperatives of career pressures, late marriages, zero population growth, and intermarriage? And what of the undercurrents of anti-Semitism: is the sense of security in diaspora merely self-delusion?

It is possible, if one looks hard enough, to find negative assessments of the American Jewish experience. Here, for example, is a jeremiad published in 1963 by Rabbi Arthur Hertzberg (b. 1921), who, having surveyed the evidence of intermarriage, assimilation, and the declining birthrate, found only negative portents:

The sociological problem is, however, not the most important. The essential crisis is the crisis of faith. . . . As ways of belief our contemporary sects have failed, without exception, to produce either an answer that compels the perplexed to believe or a source of emotional power that touches their hearts. . . .

Will there be Jewish survival? On the basis of present trends . . . the answer must be in the negative. History, sociology, and the emptiness of contemporary Jewish religion all point in the same unhappy direction. . . .

Such a pessimistic argument is difficult to refute on rational lines. It is surprising that Jews, mindful of how rapidly the successful Jewish sojourn in Germany was terminated, should be mistrustful of the comfort and luxury that America offers. Despite such anxieties, the facts—and my personal experience and conviction—lead me to an optimistic conclusion. In the United States, as nowhere else in Jewish history, varieties of Jewish worship, from the ultra-Orthodox to the ultra-experimental, coexist and enrich each other. In the United States, as nowhere else in world history, women have come to play a prominent role not only in Jewish life but also in Jewish worship as ordained rabbis in the Reform and, most recently, the Conservative movement. Recent decades have witnessed a Jewish secretary of state, Henry Kissinger (b. 1923); a Jewish ambassador to the United Nations, Arthur Goldberg (b. 1908); Jewish Supreme Court justices, senators, and congressmen; and a seemingly endless array of Jewish scientists, novelists, musicians, popular entertainers, and professionals in all fields. Generous contributions to self-help groups and Zionist organizations give the lie to any thought that American Jewry has forgotten its wider obligations. During the 1983 fiscal year, the United Jewish Appeal collected $326.5 million for Israel, $39.7 million for the American Jewish Joint Distribution Committee, and more than $200 million for local Jewish welfare activities, primarily as aid for the Jewish poor. The Jewish National Fund, supported largely by American Jewry, has planted more than 200 million trees in the State of Israel; its annual budget of more than $160 million is spent on 400 different projects within the Jewish homeland, and the land-reclamation techniques pioneered by the JNF have been applied in more than fifty countries of Africa, Asia, and Central and South America. Another multinational program to which American Jewry has contributed heavily is the Organization for Rehabilitation through Training, which operates educational and training programs for 78,000 enrollees in Israel and 34,000 students in fifteen other countries—Argentina, Brazil, Chile, Colombia, France, India, Italy, Mexico, Morocco, Paraguay, Peru, the United Kingdom, the United States, Uruguay, and Venezuela.

Some 15–20 percent of world Jewry live in lands outside Israel, the Soviet Union, and the North American mainland. Because of the Holocaust, the Eastern European diaspora is only a small fraction of its former dimensions; growing Arab-Jewish hostility and the availability of *aliyah* to Israel have similarly reduced the importance of Jewish centers in North Africa and the Arab Middle East. The existence of a few other large Jewish communities—notably those of Iran (32,000 in 1980) and Ethiopia (the Falashas, also numbering 32,000)—has been endangered by unfavorable political conditions.

After the United States and the Soviet Union, the largest of the diaspora communities are France, with an estimated 535,000 Jews in 1980; the United Kingdom, 390,000; Canada, 308,000; Argentina, 242,000; Brazil,

110,000; and South Africa, 108,000. The Jews of Argentina and France have endured outbreaks of anti-Semitism in recent years, and the Jews of South Africa face the awkward challenge of making more humane the racial policies of a government with which the State of Israel has close economic and political ties. For the most part, however, the outlook for diaspora Jewry outside the Soviet Union has rarely seemed so bright, the more so because of the presence of a homeland in Israel and the protective umbrella of American Jewish interest.

THE JEWISH MYSTERY

What is the Jewish mystery all about? It is about a small people with a large experience. This experience extends over a huge expanse of time and space—across 4,000 years and throughout the continents of the world.

We have seen how more than 3,000 years ago at Sinai, where the Israelites, fleeing from Egyptian slavery, stood in awe at the foot of the mountain and received a message of Divine unity, of moral choice and ethical duty, of retribution and compassion. Then came the embattled years of the Jewish kingdoms, during which the prophets expanded the Law of Moses into a universal vision of justice and peace. And then came the dispersion.

From this point onward, there are two impulses at work. There is a longing of Jews to live within their own context, their own land, their own tongue, their own faith, their own particularity, and ultimately to renew the conditions of their original independence. This theme came to fulfillment and expression in Israel's rebirth. But for most of history and in most places, the Jews have not been content to be as the ancient prophet described them, a people that dwells alone and is not reckoned among the nations. On the contrary, they have been a people that has

The old and new cities of Jerusalem, which were united during the 1967 Mideast War. Israel affirmed the entire city, encompassing Arab East Jerusalem, as its captial in 1980. BELOW: *Tel Aviv, a bustling modern metropolis on the Mediterranean and Israel's second most populous city.*

What is an Israeli? Occidental and Oriental, Jew and Arab, urbanite and kibbutznik—these are only a few of Israel's many identities as a nation small in size but large in history and culture. BELOW: *an Arab woman near the Damascus Gate inside the Walled City of Jerusalem.*

Touching the Torah with the prayer shawl as it is carried past in a synagogue in Moscow.

insisted on sending the repercussions of its history far and wide, into the ocean of universal culture. Thus, there is virtually no civilization that does not have a Jewish component, just as there is no Jewish civilization that does not bear the mark of another culture.

When all is said and written and recorded, this is a history unending and unsolved. Questions can be asked, but they can never be fully answered. They come down to us across the centuries in four circles of mystery.

First, there is the mystery of preservation. How did this people manage to preserve its identity in dispersion and exile, without a territorial base or political institutions, in conditions under which no other people has ever survived?

Second, there is the mystery of resonance. Why do so few people have so large a voice, so that whatever men do and think and say to this very day has been profoundly affected by the Jewish experience? Religion, philosophy, law, drama, science, art, political systems, social institutions, moral ideas—these have all been profoundly agitated by the currents of the Jewish mind.

Third, there is the mystery of suffering, a mystery that passes all understanding and defies all parallel. And finally, there is the mystery of renewal, the ability to take a language, land, and people separated for centuries and bring them back together again in a new birth of independent life.

As we come now to the end of the twentieth century, the Jewish future is uncharted; there are no certainties ahead. But a people that takes its past into its future with such intensity of recollection, such poignancy of affliction, and such creative vitality will not easily renounce its hope of planting its seed in future civilizations and taking its share of the common harvest from their midst. And so, after thousands of years, the Jews stand as they have so often stood, small, dispersed, vulnerable, but still inspired by a large and spacious ambition, still hoping to see great visions and to dream great dreams, the people with a voice whose echoes never die.

Reading from the Torah, a formative force in the education of the Jewish young.

INDEX

Page numbers in *italics* refer to illustrations.

ILLUSTRATION CREDITS

The author and Summit Books gratefully acknowledge the following for their permission to reproduce the illustrations on the pages listed below:

* Photographers who shot production stills for the TV series: Will Apelt, Rudy Cohen, Avram Karpik, Felip Lopez, Tsaki Ostrowsky, Norman Potter, Don Purdue, Ilan Rosenberg, Michael Rosenfeld, Marc Siegel, Therese Steiner.

ABOUT THE AUTHOR

STATESMAN, DIPLOMAT, SCHOLAR, AND WRITER, ABBA EBAN is presently a member of the Knesset, Israel's parliament, to which he was first elected in 1959. Between 1959 and 1974 he served successively as Minister without Portfolio in the Israeli cabinet, Minister of Education and Culture, Deputy Prime Minister, and Minister of Foreign Affairs. In May 1948, after having participated in the diplomatic effort to secure creation of the State of Israel, Mr. Eban was appointed Israel's ambassador to the United Nations, serving from 1950 to 1959 a dual role as ambassador to the United States and the United Nations.

Educated at Queen's College at Cambridge University, where he distinguished himself for academic excellence, Mr. Eban was a research fellow and lecturer at Pembroke College for Persian Studies at Cambridge. From 1959 to 1966 he served as President of the Weizmann Institute in Israel. He is the author of many books, including *My People, My County*, and his *Autobiography*.